Most of us can recall th
though few of us can re
which will interest othe
succeeded admirably i

The scene is the town of Hadleigh and the time 1914 to 1919, when the author became ten years old. In those days Hadleigh was a self-contained town of about 4,000 inhabitants where everyone knew each other intimately, where the Squire and the Rector held sway and where the quiet routine of village and country life went on as it had done for centuries past.

As a keen-eyed little boy the author observed and noted every facet of the countryman's day and tells of the happy hours he spent on a large farm, watching the year's work throughout the seasons, the ploughing, threshing, the mating of animals and countless other agricultural activities. He also depicts the many fascinating characters who peopled the district, the prim, the proud and the profligate.

Although these memories concern a small Suffolk village, it is a scene which was typical of any part of England and can be read with enjoyment and nostalgia throughout the country.

Other titles published by Barbara Hopkinson Books

SUFFOLK IN COLOUR - Barbara Hopkinson
46 full colour illustrations with accompanying text.

THE SUFFOLK WE LIVE IN - Paul Fincham
A clear, concise and beautifully illustrated outline of the county's long life and varied fortunes.

SUFFOLK TALES - H. Mills West
A collection of short stories of days gone by.

EAST ANGLIAN TALES - H. Mills West
28 short stories of rural life fifty or so years ago.

MARDLES FROM SUFFOLK - Ernest R. Cooper
A taste of East Anglian humour

GHOSTS OF EAST ANGLIA - H. Mills West
22 ghost stories old and new.

A SUFFOLK CHILDHOOD

SIMON DEWES

A Suffolk Childhood

Decorations by
J. S. GOODALL

BARBARA HOPKINSON BOOKS

First published by
Hutchinson Publishing Group Ltd in 1959

Barbara Hopkinson Books
Kingston Road
Woodbridge
Suffolk
Tel: 039 43 2099

All rights reserved. No part of this publication may be reproduced, stored in a retrieval system or be transmitted in any form or by any means, electronic, mechanical, photo-copying, recording or otherwise, without the prior written permission of the publisher.

ISBN 0 9507963 7 9

This edition published by
Barbara Hopkinson Books
in 1985.

Printed in England by
Galliard (Printers) Ltd
Great Yarmouth, Norfolk

Contents

1	An East Anglian Family	9
2	The 'Hadleigh Express'	11
3	The Air-Raid	24
4	The Rectory	30
5	The Market	50
6	Dummy	62
7	Peyton Hall	73
8	The River	108
9	Church	148
10	Great Aunt Mary	169
11	Hintlesham	188
12	The Outing	197
13	The Bells	212

To ·
the Proud Memory of my Father
JOHN MURIEL
of Hadleigh

Born St. Swithin's Day, 1859
Died St. Luke's Day, 1946

1. An East Anglian Family

ALTHOUGH my own memories, which I have assembled here, cover only the years 1915-19, the reader will find that, from time to time, events from a more distant past intrude themselves.

Many of these happenings were told me by my father, to whose memory this book is dedicated. And he, in his turn, had them from his father, who came to live in Hadleigh in 1854. Thus our family connection with this little town covers only just over a hundred years. But we are proud indeed to be able to trace, in unbroken descent, our lineage, as East Anglians, to my sixteen times great-grandfather who, nearly seven hundred years ago, was mayor of Lynn in Norfolk. For all that time the family has lived in Norfolk and Suffolk and the Isle of Ely, never making any great splash, but serving Church and State in whatever station it found itself.

My sister and I are the last of the family to live in East Anglia and it has seemed to me fitting, while memory serves, to make this small chronicle of the world of my childhood (not fifty years ago) that has disappeared for ever; for, like Anthony Trollope, with his beloved Barsetshire, I know every acre and every street and alley and I know every house in this little town and the sweet, sluggish river and the great barns where the harvests of my childhood were garnered and the old red brick bridge and the 'new' iron bridge and the little hills that surround us on all sides so that we in Suffolk know it as 'Hadleigh in the Hole'.

Many of the people here written about are still living, but they will find here nothing set down in malice but all in a deep gratitude that I was allowed to spend my childhood among them.

2. The 'Hadleigh Express'

IF, as a child, I had travelled to Hadleigh from London, I should have been able to come all the way by train, for there was a passenger service operated in those days which we thought very convenient, though the speed-kings of today would despise it entirely.

Indeed, my first considerable railway journey, at the age of six or seven, started from Hadleigh Station, 'a neat brick and tiled edifice', in the words of White's *Suffolk*, which was one of the termini of the Eastern Union Railway. Sixty or seventy years before my journey, in the days of the real railway enthusiasm, when Mr. Tomline was building his own branch line from Ipswich to Felixstowe (which has not yet been closed), there had been plans for the line which ended at Hadleigh to be continued through Lavenham and Long Melford to Bury St. Edmunds. For various reasons this plan was dropped and the 'neat brick and tiled edifice' at the top of one of the hills leading out of Hadleigh was as far as the Eastern Union Railway ever penetrated.

The reason why, in the second or third year of the first war against Germany, we took this journey, was the war itself, for on the flat pasture land two or three miles out of the town on the road to Ipswich, one of the first aerodromes had been built. In addition to that, Hadleigh itself was the headquarters of the Fifth Suffolks and, in Holbecks Park, many hundreds of the Royal Horse Artillery were under canvas, with their guns—all oiled and shining—drawn up under the oak and elm and chestnut trees and their horses, hundreds of them, tethered in their lines. Our own stables at home were occupied by the officers' chargers, while three or four private soldiers were billeted in the servants' quarters and two or sometimes three officers had taken possession of our day nursery.

It was all very exciting and I spent many hours helping (as I supposed) to muck out the stables, though I imagine I got in everyone's way. But already horses had become, as they have remained, a passion with me and I remembered the peculiar thrill I got when, out for walks with our nursemaid, we would meet a column of four or five hundred horses (that were so soon to be slaughtered in the unimaginable horror of Flanders) and I could, as they trotted past us, pick out those horses that were stabled with us.

But all this war-like activity in Hadleigh—the Suffolks, the Gunners, and the Flying Corps—had not gone unnoticed in Germany as we were soon to learn, in spite of the dreadful persecution that people suspected of German antecedents suffered. Mr. Richter, who kept a small sweet shop and had done so for some forty years, consulted my father and changed his name to Riches, but, for a long time, his shop was boycotted and the pennies and half-pennies which could buy so much in those days were taken to Mr. Berry or Mrs. Kettle until, in his turn, Mr. Berry became suspected of German sympathies (all he had ever actually done was express the mildest criticism of British conduct over the Boer War) and my mother bade my brother and sister to transfer our custom to Mrs. Kettle.

This was indeed a blow, for Mr. Berry, a jolly, fat little man, who rode the only bicycle I have ever known that could also be described as jolly and fat (it had a jolly fat basket on the front of it and in this basket rode a jolly fat pug!) had a soul above niggling over half and quarter ounces. Good Mr. Berry bothered not about trifles, but tipped the large glass jar upside down while an avalanche of aniseed balls poured into the paper bag until it was almost bursting, when he would announce, 'There, that will be enough', and took our pennies.

The 'Hadleigh Express'

This kind of glorious abandon never happened in Mrs. Kettle's shop, which had none of the rather blowsy full-blownness of Mr. Berry's.

There were other differences. The door of Mr. Berry's shop was never, so far as I know, closed. One *raced* in from the street. One laughed and joked and was given a pear drop or other delectable treat, before the business of the purchase was started. There were jokes. There was hearty laughter. There was the pug to pat and roll on its broad little back ... and one, at the age of five or six or whatever it was, was addressed with a punctiliousness—that might for all I knew or cared be Teutonic—as 'Sir' or 'Master Jack'. Under this treatment one felt a little man and not as one did in Mrs. Kettle's a little worm. And I do not think that because I liked being called 'Sir' or 'Master Jack' I was really a SNOB. While, of course, it *is* nice to be treated with courtesy, it is even nicer for a child to be treated as an individual and just as, in adult life, one will return again and again to a restaurant where the waiters remember your name and your preferences (though the food may not be so good as in other places where one is subjected to a kind of anonymity), so, as a child, I would, had my mother not forbidden it, have continued to rush in at the open front door of Mr. Berry's.

No open front door at Mrs. Kettle's! No such thing at all. The door was always tightly closed and it was one of those doors that had a kind of knob in it which had a very stiff spring in the wood behind it. You had to push this horrible door very hard before the spring would budge and, when it did budge, you literally tumbled into the shop after it. As though the noise of your sudden intrusion had not been enough to warn Mrs. Kettle that she had a customer, somewhere above you a bell went off with a terrifying clang so that, no matter how frequently you went to this shop, the bell always gave you a shock and Mrs. Kettle's first words never altered. With a flat unwelcoming intonation, she would remark, 'I should have thought a boy from a *good* home would have learned to shut doors behind him'.

You shut the door. But, by this time, all the joy of making your purchase had dissipated, so that, dumbly and probably rudely, you pointed with a grubby finger at whatever first came into view and then, with bitter thoughts, watched Mrs. Kettle weighing out—oh, so carefully—or counting—oh, so slowly—the exact quantity or number to which you were entitled.

There was another thing too.

At the rear of the shop there had once been a door leading into a small sitting-room, but that door had, years before I was born, been taken away, and in its place had been hung a really fearful bead curtain. This bead curtain—of red and yellow and purple and green and gold and crimson and blue—stretched from the lintel of the door to the floor itself and it stretched right *across* the doorway. Unlike curtains made of material, it had no centre parting or opening, for the very good reason that whoever wanted to come through this monstrous decoration just pushed at any part he or she liked and the beads fell away with a melancholy tinkle and there was Mrs. Kettle, all twelve stone of her, in her rubber soled and heeled shoes like some fearsome octopus ready to take you in her tentacles.

That curtain was not nice, because, even as children, we knew that the only reason it was a bead curtain and not a cloth one was on account of its transparency. As though the dreadful door after whose opening you *tumbled* into the shop were not enough; as though the beastly bell clattering above you were not enough, Mrs. Kettle had to have a curtain which she could see through, so that she could *spy* on you.

And that spying of Mrs. Kettle (not, I am sure on reflection, that Mrs. Kettle did spy, she just wanted to know what was going on) leads me back to my first considerable railway journey.

Although Mr. Richter was now Mr. Riches, although Mr. Berry had only criticised the British conduct of the war in South Africa and although an unfortunate man of definite German descent (but so far as was ever proved complete loyalty to Britain) had been whisked off from Hintlesham and incarcerated in Norwich Gaol, the Kaiser had heard of the military and Flying Corps concentrations at Hadleigh and we had two or three air-raids. (Strangely enough in the 1939 war Hadleigh was again one of the first places to have bombs dropped on it, so it may well be that the German General Staff thought the same concentration of troops still lingered there after a quarter of a century!) These air-raids were, to us, great fun and my father, who was Medical Officer at the aerodrome, continually took us

The 'Hadleigh Express'

to the 'bomb craters' where we paddled about picking up bits of exploded bomb and trading them for toffee or other sensible things with children whose fathers were not of such curious turns of mind.

Eventually, my father himself brought home one day a really splendid bit of bomb, weighing three or four pounds. It was part of the outer casing, with intensely sharp jagged edges. For years it lay on the pantry window sill, getting dustier and dustier, for none of the maids would touch it—the nasty thing—until one day I took it down to exhibit it proudly to some visitors. Sure enough, the maids had been right not to touch it, for I scratched myself on it and blood poisoning set in and I was jolly lucky not to lose my arm. After that, my mother considerately gave this piece of bomb to Mrs. Letts of Semer Lodge, who had a formidable collection of war relics, all neatly labelled, but she also had the good sense to keep them in locked glass cases.

The immediate result of the air-raids, so far as we were concerned, was evacuation. Hadleigh, with its soldiers and air-raids and bombing, was no longer considered safe for us: and as my Uncle Charles knew of a house that was to be let cheaply for the duration of the war, my mother, my brother and sister, my aunts Flo and Kathleen and I went to, of all places, Margate.

Presently you will hear what happened when we got there.

But, first, I must tell you, for this kind of thing can never happen again, of our journey.

After all the packing, which was considerable, for, although the house was furnished, we had to take plate and linen and blankets, which was customary in those days, two cabs were ordered from Mr. Makin, who was the jobmaster, with premises just beyond the Iron Bridge.

In these cabs we proceeded to the station.

And here what a greeting we had and what a send-off! For Mr. Hurd, the stationmaster, came in person to direct the unloading by his porters and escorted my mother to the booking office where the clerk, Mr. Powell Spooner, already had our tickets prepared, for who was there in Hadleigh who did not know of this momentous journey?

So now, armed with the tickets, with the luggage all neatly labelled, we were on the platform.

It was here that there was a division of labour, for Mr. Hurd escorted my mother and my aunts to a reserved carriage (which was only a piece of delightful courtesy on his part as, so far as I remember, there were no other passengers) while Mr. Thorpe, the guard, superintended the stowing away of the trunks and suitcases and gladstone bags and hat boxes in his van.

I watched all this with the greatest interest and excitement, feeling, indeed, as though I were the man of the party and must see everything in its place, for my brother and sister had joined the grown-ups in the reserved carriage: and it was on this day, when so many momentous things were happening to us, that I first met Mr. Thorpe, the guard, who was, in years to come (as six times a year I travelled to or from school) to become such a friend.

Today, however, I was seeing Mr. Thorpe for the first time as it were in full fig, in the full regalia that less than half a century ago was worn by the guard on even such a potty little train as the 'Hadleigh Express'. He was a fairly tall man—or so he seemed to me, at that age—and subsequent recollection does not contradict me—with a full and very ginger moustache. His cap had, I think, even more gold braid on it than had the cap of Mr. Hurd, the stationmaster, and he wore a full-length double-breasted frock-coat with brass buttons. His whistle was suspended from his neck by a chain, and not once during all the time that he and the porters were shifting our luggage, did I see his green flag other than tucked deftly under his left armpit.

This, as I say, was the first time I had seen Mr. Thorpe in full fig, but I had known him under other and equally happy circumstances ever since I had become a very junior member (probably the most junior member ever!) of the Hadleigh Fur and Feather Society, for Mr. Thorpe was a prime fancier of Belgian Hares and he also kept pigeons.

Today, however, as Mr. Hurd came towards the guard's van to see that all was well and to advise me to join the rest of the family in the reserved carriage, Mr. Thorpe appeared in a suddenly new and most unexpected light, for, without consulting me as to my wishes, he made the astonishing suggestion to the stationmaster that I might like to travel as far as the junction at Bentley on the engine. My ears fairly buzzed. My head swam. And I am afraid it was not till I *was* actually on the engine that

The 'Hadleigh Express'

I remembered how Mr. Hurd had gloomily shaken his head, which I had at first taken for a refusal of any such hare-brained scheme, but which later appeared to be only his way of saying that I might as well go that day, because, what with the war and one thing and another, there probably would not even be any engines in the future.

Anyway, he gave his consent and, reluctantly, my mother gave her consent and I was lifted up into the cab of the engine and delivered into the care of the driver and his fireman.

Now, all this may not, after two world wars and the atom bomb, appear to the children of today as very exciting, but it must be remembered that, at the time of which I am writing, it was the dream wish of nearly every little boy to be an engine driver. The magic of the railways which our grandfathers had seen supercede the glory and romance of the stage-coaches was at its zenith and even today the glory has not fully departed, for many schools have railway clubs and suburban stations are daily besieged by armies of small boys who have come 'engine spotting'.

But for me there was to be no substitute like a railway club, no second-best like train-spotting. This was the real, the authentic thing, and as I stood on the footplate beside the enormously fat driver, whose name I cannot now remember, I am obliged to state, looking back down the long years of memory, that this pride was not untinged with a most pleasurable satisfaction that I—and I alone—was on the footplate, while my brother and sister were safely locked up in the reserved first-class carriage.

These pleasant ruminations were, however, interrupted by the fat driver lifting me out of his way and seating me on a kind of little bench at the side of the cab that, in other circumstances, he would have occupied himself. On either side of this bench, looking up and down the line, there was a little window. Through these, the driver told me, he was able to see if the signals were with him or against him.

And, as I was contemplating this, I was aware that a heavy feeling of responsibility and impending decision rested on everyone and that Mr. Hurd, the stationmaster, Mr. Thorpe, the guard, and the fat driver had each produced a great turnip of a watch and that each—Mr. Hurd and Mr. Thorpe on the platform, the driver in his cab—was looking intently at his watch and then at each other as I had seen the starters of races at the Elementary School sports look at each other before they dropped their handkerchiefs and shouted 'Go'.

It was, indeed, rather like that, though, instead of a white handkerchief, Mr. Thorpe had a green flag which he had now taken from under his armpit and held furled, ready to wave it aloft when the three watches simultaneously reached zero hour.

I watched all this from my narrow little seat in the cab with breathless excitement while the little engine gave the most satisfactory 'puff-puff-puff' from its tall, narrow chimney and the fireman fidgeted about as though he were impatient to be shovelling his coal, and Mr. Hurd, whose duties were now over, and who must hand over the train with its precious cargo to driver and guard, ostentatiously put away his great watch: and Mr. Thorpe, still holding *his* watch in one hand, raised his green flag aloft as though about to shout 'Go', while, at this, the driver put away *his* watch and moved to the extraordinarily complicated pattern of knobs and wires and buttons on the board in front of him.

We were, it seemed, about to be 'off'.

From my narrow bench I saw Mr. Thorpe finally dispose of his watch: I saw his green flag raised and about to be dropped; I saw him put his whistle to his mouth: and I saw, at the very moment that he did this, Powell Spooner, the booking clerk, come galloping on the platform and heard his wild cry of 'Hold on! Hold hard! There's a passenger coming up the hill'.

It is, at this distance of time, pleasant to look back on that little scene, for there was no hesitation on Mr. Thorpe's part. There was none of the attitude of dictatorship which the guards of today so frequently display. Quite deliberately and most amiably Mr. Thorpe removed his silver whistle from his mouth, popped his little green flag under his arm, shouted to the driver, 'You'll have to hold on a minute, boy', and to Mr. Spooner, 'That's all right. Tell 'em there's no need to hurt themselves hurrying up the hill', and then, in the company of Mr. Hurd, disappeared from the platform to greet the late arrival.

It was only I, sitting on my narrow bench, whose face must have expressed disappointment at this stupid delay. And the fat, splendid, wonderful driver must, indeed, have spotted that look of disappointment, for his next remark was, indeed, memorable.

The 'Hadleigh Express'

'There,' he said, 'that's a bit of luck for you. Now we'll be able'—and he patted the engine as he said it—'now we'll be able to show you a bit of speed, making up time.'

. . . . .

But, at last, we were off. The green flag was dropped. The whistle blew. An enormous belch of feathery grey smoke was spurted out of the tall narrow chimney. The driver pulled a most inadequate looking piece of string, so that the engine gave a deafening shriek and we were off! Looking forward, I could see the straight single line of track that ran the eight miles to Bentley Junction. Looking back, already a part of the past, I could see in the valley the tapering spire of Hadleigh Church, the broad straight thread that was the High Street and the winding narrow thread that was the sleepy River Brett.

The engine gave another prolonged whistle and the driver told me he always did that when he passed the top of Cranworth Road, to let his wife know he had got away safely. And, looking out, sure enough, I saw what looked like a white flag being waved in reply.

We trundled on. We travelled over the bridge which crossed Hook Lane and under which, on our walks, we children would stop and shout the most fearsome war-cries for the delight of hearing the terrifying echo. The fireman opened his firebox and a blast of hot air was in our faces. With tremendous urgency, as though he feared the train might stop at any moment, he shovelled on coal and, when he had finished and shut the door again, the driver did odd things with his knobs and buttons, the train slowed down and finally stopped and I saw that a level-crossing gate was closed against us. How long, I wondered, would we have to wait? And I was impatient at even this little delay, when the driver had promised me we would have 'a bit of speed'.

The delay was not much, for the fireman pushed past me, dropped out of the cab, walked up the line and opened the gates. When he returned to us, the engine moved sedately forward until, when Mr. Thorpe's van was past the gates, it stopped again and, looking out of my rear window, I saw Mr. Thorpe—frock-coat and all—descending from his van and go back to close the gates. He returned to his van; he waved his little green flag and, in that way, with these courteous gestures between driver and fireman and guard, we came, at last, to Raydon Wood Station where we stopped and hung about for what, I remember, seemed to me an unconscionable time, for passengers who did not appear.

It was between Raydon Wood and Capel that we did 'the bit of speed', for here there were between two and three miles without any level-crossings and here it was that the fat, angelic driver announced he would 'let her go'.

He did. The little engine seemed to take the bit between her teeth. She shuddered. She hiccuped and then, by God, she bolted and the dear, fat driver lifted me from my seat, yelled in my ear, 'Take a hold of that' and thrust the piece of string that hung on what one would—in a car—call the dashboard, into my hand.

I took a hold on it. The engine's whistle screamed and shrieked away. 'That'll let 'em know we're coming', said the driver and, when I would have let go of the string, he yelled, 'You hold on to it, sonny. We don't want no one in our road the rate we are going.'

So I held on to the string and the whistle continued to blow and the little train bucketed along as though it were a mad thing, until I was told to let go of the string and the noise stopped and the knobs and buttons were pressed and twisted and we came to rest, sedately, as though we had never had 'a bit of speed' at all, at Capel Station.

Memory has left nothing of what happened at Capel or, indeed, on the rest of that journey, as though 'the bit of speed' and the prolonged agonising whistle had been enough to absorb in one day: but I do remember our arrival at Bentley Junction, where we had to cross over the line and pick up the London train which had, four or five minutes earlier, left Ipswich.

We were escorted by the entire personnel of the 'Hadleigh Express', now reinforced by the stationmaster and the porters at Bentley. I do not remember there being any other passengers waiting to catch the London train. There may have been, but if there were, they must have been forced to manage their luggage themselves, for the Bentley porters avidly seized on our mountains of luggage, while Mr. Thorpe took my brother and sister in tow and the driver and fireman lifted me out of the cab and

The 'Hadleigh Express'

followed the others up the platform to cross to the other side. And here another memorable thing happened.

At the end of the platform there was a bridge built with—at the foot of it—notices announcing—for I could read even then—that it was dangerous for passengers to cross the line except by the footbridge. My mother, my aunts, my brother and sister, all law-abiding people, who preceded us, did exactly as they were told and I would have done the same thing had not the driver and fireman stopped me, remarking that we did not want to climb all them stairs, and, with a fine disregard for their personal safety and my own, without once looking up or down the line to see if some monstrous creature of steam and steel was descending on us, calmly *walked* across the down and up lines of the main London to Norwich track: and, just as calmly, they expected me to follow them.

I did. But I was far from calm. Fearfully, I looked up and down the shining steel rails. Had I have understood them, I would have looked at the signals. And my fear was increased by the fact that, in each direction, either towards London or towards Norwich, the line curved away, so that one could not see more than perhaps two hundred yards in either direction. Remembering the frantic career of the 'Hadleigh Express', I knew—oh, I knew for a certainty—that, should a train appear round either of those bends, it would be on me before I could reach safety. And, just as certainly, I knew that, in my terrified rush for sanctuary, I should trip over one of the rails and my wretched body be cut in two just as had been the body of one of my maternal uncles who had had both legs cut off by a train in America. (This fearful story had been told us in answer to one of our repeated queries as to why we never saw my mother's brothers. The story was perfectly true, but I never did see this uncle, whose name was, I believe, Herbert, and, up to the time of my own fearful crossing of the permanent way at Bentley, I had always had a rather patronising picture in my mind of Uncle Herbert sitting calmly with his legs across the track, and waiting, with an infinitude of patience, for a train to come and chop them off. He must, I had long since decided, be an odd kind of man. But on this day, I knew, for the first time, that he was not an odd kind of man at all. I knew it had all been a dreadful accident and I knew, too, that it was just the kind of accident that was—in a very few minutes—going to happen to me.)

The whole trouble was, of course, that, by the time these fears assailed me, I was at least a quarter way across the lines. If I turned back and followed the law-abiding family up all those steps, I was as likely to be mown down by a train as if I went on.

So on I must go. And I can remember today, with sweat pouring out of me, grimly following those two broad and unconcerned backs of the driver and fireman until, miraculously, we reached the other platform and safety.

We were, of course, there long before the others who had gone up those steps on one side and had come down those steps on the other. And, in those few moments that elapsed before the rest of the family appeared, all the nightmare terror evaporated. And a certain disgusting jauntiness must have taken possession of me as, when my mother and her party finally arrived on the platform, rather out of breath after all their climbing and descending, my mother exclaimed with surprise:

'How on earth did you get here so quickly?'

And I answered, with a nonchalance and airiness that, two or three minutes before, I had been far from feeling, 'Oh, we just crossed the lines'.

'You mean you *walked* across the lines?'

'Yes,' I said, jaunty as ever, and added, lying, at any rate on my part, 'we knew there weren't any trains coming.'

And, with that, the matter was ended, for round the curve of the line from Ipswich came the London train (that might so easily have cut off my legs) and our army of retainers sprang into immediate action, rushing this way and that way up and down the platform until they had found us a carriage that was, so far, empty, and while we were being hustled in and the Bentley porters were telling my mother in what part of the train the luggage was and my mother was dishing out silver coins to everyone except the driver and fireman of the 'Hadleigh Express' (which seemed to me very unjust), the London train began slowly to move out of the station and I suddenly realised that, with its moving out of Bentley Station, all our individualities had gone; were, with the grinding wheels, being swept away from us, and we were becoming just another anonymous lot of passengers in a cold, unfriendly train that could not, I was sure, be a match in speed for the 'Hadleigh Express'.

. . . . .

We travelled from Liverpool Street to London Bridge in two horse-drawn growlers and the wretched horses might have come out of Mr. Makin's stable at Hadleigh, so thin they were: but I remember nothing else of that first journey across London. And I remember nothing of the journey to Margate or of our arrival at the little house that my Uncle Charles had found for us: for I suppose that all the excitements in the early part of the day had left my mind quite unreceptive of other excitements, so that that first night I must have slept soundly.

Before we had been there many more days we were none of us sleeping at all.

3. The Air-Raid

THE house was opposite the Bowling Green, so that, unless the Bowling Green has been moved, I could find it again today, but I can remember nothing about its interior except that the enormous bed in which I slept was so high off the floor that the landlord had provided a box-like contraption (which contained our linen when not in use) made in the form of three steps up which one ascended when going to bed.

This was exciting: and I have never seen a similar piece of furniture.

My bedroom also had a balcony with a wrought iron balustrade, on which I could sit and watch the bowls players: and a balcony was also a new thing to me, giving one the idea of being suspended in space, so that one clutched at the balustrade rather nervously: but, as I say, these are only two features of the house which memory recalls.

There were still, however, donkeys on the beach: and my mother and aunts were always willing to pay for our donkey rides, which none of us wanted, for the donkeys were so small and so underfed, with their poor, tired heads hanging down to their knees and their large wistful eyes full of an eternal sadness as they stood, day after tragic day, in the full blaze of the sun on the beach, with no shade, no grass, no water.

The Air-Raid

That was bad enough—what was infinitely worse—and a thing which none of the grown-ups seemed to notice at all—was that all the donkeys' little rumps were quite raw where the donkey drivers goaded them with sharp pointed sticks to hurry them along the sands with their lumpish burdens. No one seemed to care about the donkeys' behinds, nor about their sad, wistful eyes, nor about the lack of water and shade and grass.

The only other interesting thing at Margate where, we understood, we were to spend the rest of the war, was the spy.

For, of course, there was a spy—a far more satisfactory spy than any we imagined we had at Hadleigh—who spent all his days—and, for all we knew, his nights—looking out to sea through an enormous telescope which was mounted on a tripod in his front garden. He lived in the house next door to us: and soon my mother and he were on visiting terms and she was allowed to look out to sea through the telescope.

We warned her of the danger she was running. We pointed out that he *must* be a spy with a telescope like that. But my mother, trusting woman, replied that, if he *was* a spy, he would not have the telescope in the garden for everyone to see. We, however, knew better than that. Clearly, we told her, he exhibited the telescope so blatantly simply to put people off the scent.

She laughed and would not be persuaded.

So here we were in this ghastly place, Margate, away from the fields and the hedges and the ditches and the woods that we loved; away from our dogs and our cats and our rabbits and guinea-pigs and pigeons; away from the sleepy river and the church clock that chimed at every quarter and the church bells that were not silenced in that war, and the horse-drawn mail cart coming every night at eight o'clock to the Post Office opposite our house to collect the letters and take them on to Ipswich, where they were sorted, and those for distant places then caught the train to London to be delivered by eight o'clock next morning.

Yes, here we were in exile from all these things, condemned to look at the beastly English Channel, when, at one stroke, the most satisfactory thing that could be imagined happened and we all scuttled back to the bliss and comfort and warmth and friendship of our own sort.

For there was an air-raid! Just as there had been air-raids on

Hadleigh, so now there were raids on the South Coast—raids all over England—and it was decided that, if we were going to be raided, we might as well be raided in our own home and among our own people.

Telegrams were sent backwards and forwards. Arrangements were made. The lease was disposed of: and, in fact, nothing could have happened more opportunely for us than this raid on Margate.

But, first, I must try to give you some idea of this raid as I remember it: and my memory is not so much of the actual mechanics of the raid, which must, I suppose, by modern standards, have been negligible anyway, as of my own utter and devastating terror: a terror that I felt not at all in London during the blitz of the Second World War, when I was armed with a conviction that, though thousands fell at my right hand and thousands at my left hand, it would not touch me. There can be no rationalist explanation of this, nor, indeed, any spiritual one, for I had no belief that God was looking after my goings out and my comings in, save, in the sense, that He always looks after them. I certainly had no faith that He was keeping a particular eye on me that I might be spared. I just knew it would not happen.

But it was a very different story forty or more years ago at Margate.

We had gone to bed in the usual way: and, after I had climbed up the ladder to my great bed and my mother had kissed me goodnight and the door had been shut and she had gone downstairs to join the other grown-ups, I had—as I did every night—got out of bed again and gone on to the balcony to watch the bowls players on the green opposite until the light faded and the old gentlemen (and they were really old gentlemen in those days, for all the young men were away at the war) trooped into the pavilion to wipe and polish their woods before putting them away. Only then, when the green was quite deserted and the midsummer night descended on us, did I climb back to bed where I must have fallen asleep straight away.

Sometime later I was woken by either my mother or one of my aunts, who whispered urgently that there was an air-raid and I was to come downstairs at once. Still half asleep, I was hauled out of bed, stuffed into my dressing-gown, had slippers rammed on my feet and, understanding little, was hurried

The Air-Raid

downstairs to the dining-room, where my brother and sister, younger than myself, were already sitting, side by side, on the couch. Their eyes sparkled. They looked immensely excited and only then, I think, did I become aware of the rattle of machine-guns which were, I was told years afterwards, all that we had in the way of anti-aircraft weapons.

At about this stage, when I first became conscious of the racket going on outside and conscious of the twins' excitement, I also became aware that my mother had left us and that my aunts Flo and Kathleen were in charge.

Where, I wanted to know, had my mother gone?

She was in the garden next door, one of the aunts told me, looking at the zeppelin through the telescope that belonged to the spy. And, so that we should not be disappointed, this aunt suggested, with the very kindest of intentions, that, although we could not all go to look through the spy's telescope, we might like to go out on our front lawn where we could get a good view of the zeppelin.

The twins were madly excited. Both the aunts seemed to think it was—like seeing Naples and dying—a chance not, on any account, to be missed. I honestly cannot remember what my first reactions were: but I do know that we all trooped out on the lawn where the rattle of the machine-guns was louder than ever and we could, over the fence separating our lawn from that of the spy next door, see my mother, in the moonlight, looking through the telescope.

The night was bright with moon and stars, but disturbed and broken by the noise of the guns, the excited shouting of the people from all the houses up and down the road, and now, suddenly lit up more brilliantly by the criss-cross pattern of searchlights, diligently cutting the sky up into sections, in their quest for what was to be the prey of the guns.

And then, as though by magic, all the searchlights seemed to meet and fuse on a cigar-shaped thing of a beautiful silver colour that was, without any sound, so far as one could tell, gracefully and beautifully coming in from the sea.

'There it is!' everyone screamed, hands waving, fingers pointing. 'There it is!'

And the heavens were rent with the appalling noise of the guns and rent too by the violent and hateful shouting of the people, just as, years later, I have heard the voices of people—kindly, humane people—scream with vicious glee as an exhausted otter hauls herself on to the bank of the stream with the hounds after her, to tear her living flesh in pieces—'There she is!' they have screamed—'There she is!'

So now, 'Look,' my aunts told me—'Look, there is the zeppelin.'

And I looked and saw a thing of beauty sailing in serenely to the thunder of the guns and the hateful shouting of the neighbours and my excited brother and sister jumping up and down and I was terribly, desperately afraid.

I began to cry. I held on to one of the aunts' hands. I needed comfort to sustain me, someone to help me, because, I knew, as sure as I knew anything, that we were all going to be killed. The zeppelin would drop its bombs—just like the bombs that had been dropped at Hadleigh—and we should all be killed, the whole lot of us, and never see home again.

I wept noisily. The zeppelin, still in the blaze of the searchlights, swept in from the sea. The guns blazed and blazed again: and all the people in the road were a-tiptoe with expectancy, with a pleasurable anticipation just like the kindly people at a later otter hunt were filled with pleasurable anticipation for the death of the otter. The zeppelin, they shouted cheerfully to one another, would be shot down.

But I was the only person who knew that, whether the zeppelin was shot down or not, we should all be killed first.

There was a terrific explosion, an explosion a hundred times louder than those of the little machine-guns.

'She's dropped a bomb', someone said.

And I cried and cried and cried.

'We had better go in', said the aunts. So in we went and the twins took up their position on the couch again while I lay in a chair with my face in a cushion, racked with sobs, and consumed with terror.

'Look at the twins', the aunts said. 'Look at the twins. They're not afraid.'

But I did not want to look at the lumpish, doltish twins. Looking at the twins was not going to help me, was not going to save any of us . . . nothing could save us and I cried and cried and cried, until at last, from a long way away, cutting through

The Air-Raid

the sound of the guns, which had now—though I could not appreciate that yet—become less, I heard someone say, 'I never knew you were such a coward—the twins aren't afraid'.

A coward. A coward. A coward, my spirit whispered. But that night, if they had thought, by such reproach, they were going to shame me, they must have been disappointed, for I continued to howl and to shake with terror and to know—oh, for certain, I knew it—that I should be killed. That, please note, that *I* should be killed. The others no longer mattered. I cared not at all if the twins and the aunts and my telescopic-devoted mother were killed. Death, to them, could not be the thing of terror it was to me, for they were not cowards. Only I, the coward, was afraid of death . . . the vast dreadful unknown with Kate pulling the glass-sided hearse in which my coffin was carried and the starved Rufus and the other starved horses pulling the cabs in which travelled the mourners, the ones who, because they were not cowards, had not been killed.

A long time afterwards, when the beautiful midsummer night had given place to the sun rising in the east and the guns had stopped their chatter and the people in the road had all gone back into their houses to make pots of tea and speculate about what damage had been done and how many lives had been lost, and the zeppelin had, I suppose, flown silently away out to sea again, I, little and frightened and branded a coward, lay again in the great bed with the steps leading up to it, watching the light of the morning grow brighter through the drawn curtains as the sun rose higher and higher.

And presently, when it was quarter light and there were noises in the road outside of milk bottles being dumped on doorsteps and newspaper boys whistling, as they delivered the papers, I crept out of bed and knelt on the floor against the strange contraption that formed the steps. I remembered one of the prayers that already I had learned by heart—the third collect for Evensong—and, in the morning sunlight on that summer day in Margate, I prayed, 'Lighten our darkness, we beseech thee, O Lord, and, by thy great mercy, defend us from all the dangers of this night, for the love of thy only son, Jesus Christ'.

And thus comforted, I climbed back into bed and I must, at last, have slept.

4. The Rectory

UNTIL, at the age of ten, I went to my prep. school at Frinton—in those days a remarkably exclusive place—I never left Suffolk again, for which, to this day—when I am back in the beloved county—I am very grateful, for, in the next four years, I was allowed to enjoy and to suffer things which might, had I lived in a larger world, have had the very sharpness of the ecstasy blunted and the pain of the wounds anæsthetised.

My father was a doctor, who was greatly beloved by his patients, most of whom were very poor people, for he had been born in Hadleigh where his father had been a doctor before him, so that, as children, we were always moving in and out of other people's houses with a perfect naturalness and an unconscious adaptability: and, as a child of less than ten, I was as at ease and as happy in the company of old Sir William Hyde Parker or of Larkin, his butler: in the company of Dean Carter or of Cheek, his gardener: in that of Teddy Norford, the market-gardener or old Charlie Cousins or Tinter Cutting, who had a little donkey and came from Semer, selling swedes, or Mr. Emeney, the rent collector and second-hand bookseller, or of the labourers—Dick and Ginn and Spot Oxford and Fons—at Mr. Waller's farm at Peyton Hall.

Yet, surely, among these people—each of whom now be-

The Rectory

longs to a vanished world—there was no more lovable and remarkable character than Edward Aldous Lane, the Rector of Whatfield, which is a little village, just three miles from Hadleigh, with a plaster-built church dedicated to St. Margaret of Antioch who, you will remember, was once swallowed by an alligator. At the time that the alligator swallowed her, St. Margaret was carrying a wooden cross and, finding herself suddenly and most unpleasantly incarcerated in the alligator's stomach, she had the faith to tap the inside wall which imprisoned her with her cross, whereupon the alligator promptly spewed St. Margaret back into the world. There are only seventeen churches in England dedicated to St. Margaret of Antioch and two of them—the other one being at Shottisham—are in Suffolk.

Mr. Lane, who was the Rector during my childhood, was, I believe, one of my father's patients. He was married, but childless: yet his house, in the years that I knew him, was filled with children, for Lane, with a heart big enough to encompass the whole world had, when the German armies overran Belgium, hurried to London where he let the right people know that he had a large rectory which, save for himself, his wife and his adopted son, was empty and needed inhabitants: that he had acres of glebe which he farmed, in a rather haphazard way himself, and that he kept ponies for children to ride, goats to provide them with milk, chickens and ducks to produce eggs, and fine pigs for meat.

So the house was soon filled with little Belgian children and they were joined by Italian children and then, as though to show that all people were equal in the sight of God and the Rector of Whatfield, various German grown-ups, who would otherwise have been interned, came to join the refugees. These were wanted, Lane said, to teach the children, as he, with his parish to look after and his glebe to farm, had not the time to do it.

At this time Lane was about fifty years old. So far as I can remember he was of rather less than medium height, of a somewhat stocky figure, accentuated, perhaps, by the fact that he usually wore black leather gaiters or buskins, which all the farmers wore, but, unlike the farmers, whose jackets and trousers might be of grey or brown or some tweedy mixture,

Lane's jacket and trousers were invariably black—a funereal black without even the compromise of a 'clerical grey'. The complexion of his face was absolutely dead white (it never bronzed at all, though he was out in all weathers) with a pair of very startling dark eyes and a full, untidy black beard. His voice was stentorian: so that, although a bell hung on the roof of Whatfield Rectory which could be pulled by a rope in the hall downstairs to summon us to meals, Lane's shouts were even more effective and could be heard from one end of the village to the other.

It was in Whatfield Church, therefore, that I heard, for the first time, real community singing. On Sundays the little church (which had and still has pegs for the worshippers to hang their hats and coats on, 'just like in a tea-shop', as one of the foreign children said) was packed with all the people in the village who did not belong to the Salvation Army, which was also a flourishing institution in Whatfield. The farmers were there, the farm labourers were there, the tradespeople were there. There were no gentry in Whatfield or, I have no doubt, they would have been there. Miss Martin, the schoolmistress, sat at the tiny harmonium. The choir, a dozen boys and perhaps eight men, emerged from the belfry, which acted as vestry, and the end of the procession was brought up by Lane himself, transfigured by his surplice and black and white Cambridge hood from the parson-farmer of week-days.

Unlike Hadleigh Church, where the order of Morning Prayer was followed exactly, here the service started with a hymn (as is quite customary nowadays). It was always a hymn that was familiar to the congregation, one that they had sung from childhood—'O God, our help in ages past'—'New every morning is the Love'—'Through the night of doubt and sorrow' —so that few of them had to look at the words in their hymn books, but, watching the Rector, sang with the full strength of their lungs.

Now, there is no doubt that Lane himself was a musical man. I have been told that, in his Cambridge days, his voice was much in demand: but fourteen years as Rector of Whatfield had wrought havoc with it. He sang with gusto and fervour. He bellowed. He—and all the congregation—made a joyful noise unto the Lord, until the sweat fell off us and, surreptitiously, as we recited the General Confession, handkerchiefs were got out and a general mopping-up process began.

The Venite, the Psalms, the Te Deum, each of the great canticles was thundered forth with the same enthusiasm, the like of which I have never heard again, for here there was no question of a choir 'leading' the congregation, with its self-conscious and self-important choir practices week after week. Here everyone sang to the glory of God and, I must add, to the great satisfaction of Mr. Lane.

Sometimes he read the lessons, but more often old Sam Clark, the Sexton and Rectory gardener, whose face was encircled with a halo of white whiskers and whose complete lack of teeth made the pronunciation of some words difficult, read, with a beautiful reverence, the first lesson, so that today I can, through the years, hear his old Suffolk voice as he implored, 'Comfort ye, Comfort ye, my people', or read us the story of Daniel in the lions' den: and Abraham sacrificing his son, Isaac: and Balaam smiting his ass: and Moses looking from a high mountain upon the Promised Land, the land flowing with milk and honey, which he was not to enter.

And the second lesson—the lesson from the New Testament of our Lord and Saviour—was, nearly always, so completely a Christian was Mr. Lane, read by one of the Germans, who, but for him, would have been interned, whose relations were, so we were told, crucifying Belgian babies and whose descendants a quarter of a century hence were to be the engineers of Dachau and Buchenwald and Belsen, the manufacturers of the crematorium ovens, the mass exterminations of the Jews, the loathed and feared of all civilisation.

Maybe, had those things happened in the 1914 war, Lane would not have let Germans read the lessons: but, from what I remember of him, I doubt if it would have made any difference, for his heart was large enough to contain all suffering humanity, all the lost and sinful and hopeless and those in darkness and in the shadow of death.

And I can hear again now the foreign accent of the bearded doctor as he read the last words of the Epistle of St. John, 'Little children, love one another'.

In London and other large towns, at the outbreak of war, German shops had closed at once and had been lucky in some places if their windows were not broken: for the hate against Germany (at home, I mean; fighting soldiers rarely hate their enemies) was much greater than ever it was in the 1939 war: but in primitive Whatfield, with its population made up of farmers and their labourers, who had never been farther than Ipswich, of Belgian boys and girls and Serbians and Italians, whose frontiers were lost in the maelstrom of war, it was safe for a German to read the words of St. John, 'Little children, love one another'.

And the force, the spirit that made this possible, was the driving force of love and understanding that poured out of Lane, as the living breath of God.

One day in the street at Whatfield I learned a lesson. I must have been seven or eight, I suppose—I was staying at the Rectory, as I did for three or four months every year—a fact which must, in some measure, account for the lack of intimacy that there has always been between my family and myself: this and that my brother and sister are twins, with that peculiar 'oneness' which is one of the particularities of twinhood.

The street at Whatfield is a drab, depressing affair, for Suffolk is singular in that boasting such places of beauty as Kersey and Chelsworth and Earl Soham and Grundisburgh, it also has, almost next door to them, such depressing streets as that of Whatfield. There are a few thatched cottages, but, in most cases, the thatch is rotten and mildewed. There are a few pre-1914 war 'Council houses'. There is an ancient metal water tower and a number of red-brick villas. In fact, the whole place is a shocking hotch-potch: though, since those days, new Council houses have been built towards the Rectory and these are, at any rate, fairly innocuous to look at.

But at the time of which I am writing, very few of these cottages—even the Council houses—had a baking oven. In most of them cooking was done over an open stove, though a few of the more progressive residents had small and very smelly oil stoves. So the custom was for those who had no ovens, but wanted a roast bit of meat for their week-end dinner, to make some arrangement with a neighbour whose house was better equipped, that they would have their hot dinner on Saturday if the neighbour would cook it in her oven, which would leave the oven free for its rightful owner on Sunday. You will note that

The Rectory

even in those houses which did possess ovens, the oven was so small that it would not take two joints at once.

I was standing in the street, opposite the Five Horse Nails Inn, talking to Phil from the Rectory when out of one of the newer houses a small boy came, walking with great circumspection and bearing before him a baking tin with the week-end joint on it, which he was carrying to some good neighbour to be cooked.

This was such an ordinary sight that it occasioned no comment from either Phil or myself as we watched this child, of about our own age, carefully carrying his burden up the garden path. There were a number of labourers standing about in the street at the time, so it must have been a Saturday morning, when they stopped work at midday and met in the 'Horse Nails' for a game of dominoes and a drink before dinner which, for most of them, on Saturdays and Sundays was at two o'clock. On the other days of the week it was at noon.

I remember one of the men leaning his bicycle against the privet hedge and going forward to open the little wicket gate for the boy to come through with his burden. And I remember the boy, for an instant, taking his eyes off the load he carried to look up at the man, smiling his thanks.

In that instant it happened. Before anyone could stop it: indeed, before anyone was aware of his presence a white dog that had, a minute before, been lying apparently asleep at the side of the road, leapt up and, sending the boy sprawling, had the lump of meat in his mouth and was racing, hell for leather, for some quiet place where he could enjoy it.

The boy burst into tears. Some of the men raced madly after the dog. I laughed. I—from the security of my home with its four meals a day and meat every day—burst out laughing at the white dog racing down the street with the family joint in its mouth, at the labourers running clumsily and, quite clearly, without a chance of success after it, at the little boy, still holding his now empty tin, howling his eyes out.

I laughed. It was funny. My own feelings were all on the side of the dog. The little boy crying by the side of the road was comic. Fancy crying over a bit of old meat! And the lumbering farm labourers were still trundling down the road after the dog.

Someone spoke to me. I have never known his name.

Indeed, if I ever saw him again, I must *wilfully* have *refused* to see him, for the shame that was in me.

'That's not funny for them', he said soberly. 'That's not funny at all. That means that little old boy and his family won't have no more meat till this day week.'

I did not understand. I was not to be blamed for not understanding, for, in my home, had an accident happened to a joint of meat, one of the maids would have been sent to the butcher's to buy another one. This kind of deprivation could never have happened to us, though we considered ourselves far from well-off.

But to have no more meat till next Saturday . . . It did not make sense. I remember I mumbled something about them getting some more and I remember the man who had spoken to me becoming very angry, the first time in my life that a person like that had ever been angry with me.

'Get some more!' he shouted at me. 'Where the hell's the money coming from? It's all right for you. Your dad can always buy meat. Where's his ma to get the money to buy any more meat? They'll go without, that's what they'll do.'

I ran away.

I could not bear the man shouting at me. I was frightened of him. I thought he would strike me: and I still could not see what I had done wrong: because the naughty dog racing down the road with the joint in his mouth *had* been funny. But not, it became clear to me, to the little boy who had *lost his dinner*.

Very gradually, very gradually indeed, it became clear to me that the boy and the boy's family had really and truly lost their dinner—not for one day, but for the better part of a week: for, although, naturally, I did not know the economics of the thing at that time, I did find out not very much later that a labourer's wages were around eighteen shillings to twenty-four shillings a week: and that a bit of meat such as the dog had stolen had cost about five shillings, something between one-third and one-fifth of the weekly income.

All of this, of course, with its full implications, was ahead of me; but that night, lying in bed at the Rectory, I thought of the meatless family, and how awful it must be to go without meat. But more than that, more deeply than that, I was so ashamed of myself, bitterly ashamed that I should have laughed at the little boy's distress.

The Rectory

I wish I could tell you that I went to Lane in the morning and asked him to send the family a joint to make up for that they had lost. But I did not do that. I did nothing when I got home to Hadleigh. I did nothing at all, except hide myself at the Rectory, not going up the street again in case I met the man who had abused me, in case I met the little boy who had lost his dinner—not one dinner, but all his meat dinners for a whole week.

I was afraid to see him and afraid to see the man: and, in quite another way, afraid to ask Lane or my own parents to give them some more meat. I think that fear came from my dreadful shyness, from being afraid—a fear which I have never lost—of making myself conspicuous: a fear which persists to this day, so that when I have, from time to time, been asked to read the lessons in my parish church or in a school chapel, if I have, with terror engulfing me, done so, I have been ill, literally ill, for days afterwards. It is a very cowardly thing this being afraid to make a fool of yourself in public. But it is a more frightening kind of cowardice than the terror I felt in the air-raid at Margate.

But, after that day when the boy lost his meat in the street at Whatfield, I have never laughed at other people's distresses, however incomprehensible they may have seemed to me at the time, because I learned then, with the man's angry shouting in my ear, that every one of us has his own little world to live in and that, in each particular world, there are things which, once lost, can never be replaced, like the little boy's dinner that the dog ran away with.

And sometimes, even now, I wonder where, when the little dog had escaped from the lumbering labourers, under what hedge, at the bottom of what ditch, behind what tombstone, he lay down and ate his magnificent feast. And I hope, I do hope, that when, fat and sleek and sleepy and replete, he ambled back to his home, he did not get beaten.

. . . . .

Whatfield Rectory was heaven. The low white house was completely surrounded by a moat with two wooden foot bridges over it (one of which was not particularly safe as there were various boards in it which had rotted away) and two gravelled carriage drives, that had been built by one of Lane's predecessors. One of these drives led to the front door which, with the drawing-room on one side and the dining-room on the other, faced due north: and the other on to a plantation of cedar trees, planted some sixty or seventy years earlier. They were beautiful trees and I suppose they are still standing, though it is many years since I was there. Under them we had picnics, with Lane's goats tethered near us and the foxhound puppies that he 'walked' treading in the sandwiches and the jam, and the turkey cocks gobbling at us and the conversation going on in French and Flemish and Italian and broken English, and the great black beard of Lane waggling backwards and forwards all the time as he tried—usually, I think, successfully—to have a share in each conversation that was going on.

Hidden behind the cedar trees was a remarkable flint-built summer-house which had been put up by a former Rector named—I believe—Rackham. It was a most extraordinary building with the door at least eight feet high, and some of the village people, who remembered Mr. Rackham, told us he built it that way because he was more than seven feet tall himself. We all believed them: but whether it was true I cannot say.

There never was such a place for animals.

As though having the house full of children of almost every European nationality were not enough, Lane and his gentle wife were surrounded by four-footed creatures.

It was here that I first learned to ride, beginning with a series of broad-backed Shetland ponies and graduating up to Brownie, a Welsh cob of uncertain temperament. There were great tithe barns, where Lane kept pigs, doing all the work himself: and here there was also housed a herd of goats, which supplied all the milk for the household. This was my introduction to those most charming and profitable animals: so that when, thirty years later, I started a herd myself, things which I thought had long been forgotten returned to memory.

Lane's goats were a very mixed lot, for, at that time, goat breeding had not become the specialised thing that it is today with the British Goat Society publishing a Herd Book, with sections devoted to Anglo-Nubian, Saanan, Toggenburg and Alpine goats. His were what we would now call scrub goats, giving two to four pints a day each, which is a long way from the eight to ten gallons a day that the wonderful Malpas Melba has given. But we loved them, except the billy goat. He was black. He had long and dangerous horns. He was very savage at certain seasons of the year. He stank abominably. But, oddly enough, in spite of his savageness, I do not remember being frightened of him.

The little refugee children, who, for Lane's sake, tried hard not to hate the Germans who had killed their parents and burned their homes, whispered to each other that the billy goat was a German. That was the very worst thing they could say about him!

There were hundreds of chickens, all—except some chickens with furry legs like Shire horses, which were kept separately—allowed to wander where they liked, laying indiscriminately in the hedges and ditches, so that it was nothing to come across great clutches of a couple of dozen eggs in a haystack. But what eggs they were! Not like the dreadful anaemic things that come from the tortured creatures kept in batteries today. These eggs had deep brown shells and their yolks were more gold than the guinea that hung on my father's watch-chain. On the moat there were Indian Runner ducks for egg production: and, in one of the orchards, feeding on grass, a flock of cackling geese and another of Aylesbury ducks for the table.

One of the most exciting events of the year was 'taking the honey' from the bees: for there were a dozen hives in the orchard: and, at the right time, the Rector of Whatfield, with veil and gloves and a thing like a balloon to puff the bees to sleep, came and collected the combs and we had honey for breakfast and honey for tea and took honey home to my parents at Hadleigh.

As I mentioned before, apart from his own dogs, which were Airedales, Lane managed 'to walk' a couple of puppies for the Essex and Suffolk Hunt. I can only remember the names of one couple which were Hamlet and Harlot. I knew all about Hamlet, of course, but I did not know who Harlot was. When I asked, it appeared nobody else knew either, so I thought it was a silly name to give a puppy.

Maybe it was. I shall never know.

And, on top of all this—yes, I mean literally on top—up in the attics, Lane had built a great aviary where he bred Norwich canaries. There were hundreds of them, so that their singing floated down the attic stairs into the house as though it were the singing of the cherubim and of the angels above.

They were, indeed, happy days that I spent at Whatfield Rectory in the years of the first war: and now figures appear out of the past that I have not thought of these forty years. There was Mr. Mowles, the carrier, who went daily to Hadleigh. He could not go any further, because his old white horse always carried its head at the level of its knees, and, if it trotted, it was bound to fall over, so Hadleigh was as far as Mr. Mowles, with his great black beard blowing about his face, could travel: but here he made contact with the Hadleigh carriers—Benny Beeston and David Sadler—who each had pair-horse vans and travelled to Ipswich every day except Wednesday, taking orders from the Hadleigh housewives early in the morning and delivering those orders the same evening. Mr. Beeston and Mr. Sadler had small squares of white cardboard printed with the single letters B or S on them. If you put the appropriate card in your window in the morning, Mr. Beeston or Mr. Sadler would spot it and call on you. There was fat Mr. Nunn of Barrards Hall, who drove a fast chocolate coloured cob and wore, on week-days, the kind of square black hat that Sir Winston Churchill used to wear: and, on Sundays, a black topper. For some reason which I have never fathomed Mr. Nunn and Mr. Lane were not on good terms, so at the Rectory we saw little of Mr. Nunn. There was Miss Martin, the schoolmistress, who came for musical evenings to the Rectory, when Mr. Stephenson, the blind organist at Hadleigh (who, happily, is still with us), would walk over—no one guiding him—and join us. On one occasion Mr. Stephenson was sitting in a rocking chair in the drawing-room with at least three refugee children on his lap, swinging gently backwards and forwards, backwards and forwards . . .

'Faster! Faster!' cried the children.

And faster they went until there was a resounding crack and the chair broke in half and scattered the lot of them, Mr. Stephenson at the bottom, on the floor. For a moment everyone was terribly alarmed. The children screamed. The German doctor rushed across the room. Lane's stentorian voice yelled for silence . . . and in that silence, we heard Mr. Stephenson's deep laugh and knew that no one was hurt.

The Rectory

The bathroom at Whatfield Rectory deserves to be mentioned, because it was the only bathroom I have ever come across that was in the front hall! Lane himself had put it in. He had a pump in the backus to pump the water from the moat to the top of the house. Regularly, before breakfast, he pumped the tanks full and that was the only time of the day you could not approach him, for he counted every stroke of the pump and, at breakfast, he would announce before we had Family Prayers, that he had done three hundred or four hundred strokes. I remember we were never sure whether to look our admiration at his tremendous strength or our shame at having used so much water in our baths.

Now, to many people, putting a bath in the front hall would seem a very eccentric thing to do. To Lane it seemed the most natural thing in the world. When he first went to Whatfield Rectory there was no bathroom at all. Mr. and Mrs. Lane, Phil, and their maid had their baths in hip-baths in their bedrooms: and, by the time Lane realised that, with his house full of children, hip-baths would no longer suffice, there was not a square inch of space anywhere to put a fixed bath except in the hall. So a corner of the hall was measured off and a partition of plywood was erected and there, behind the partition, in the company of the bicycles which were also kept there, we had the baths that were made possible by the Rector's herculean pumping before breakfast.

I imagine, however, it has gone now.

But the halcyon days had to come to an end: and, in this case, instead of just petering out as so many of the things of childhood do, they went out with a tragic and terrible suddenness, leaving such desolation behind as only those who knew the great-hearted man could have imagined.

I was not staying at the Rectory when the fire broke out. I was at home and my father, who had been out on his rounds all the morning, came back at luncheon time with the news. It was decided that he and I would go to Whatfield Rectory as soon as the meal was over.

. . . . .

Memory tells me that when I was a child there were many more fires in the country than there are today. But, in this, I may be quite mistaken, because, in our adult concerns, a fire, particularly a stack fire, where there is no loss of life, affects us very little. The whole thing nowadays is arranged so mechanically, so scientifically, so anonymously. But, in my childhood, it was a very different matter!

There was no National Fire Service then. The firemen, with their magnificent brass helmets, their hatchets, their red fire-engine which was hand-pumped, were all volunteers. They were The Fire Brigade: and, in our local festivals, they had a very honoured place in the processions.

Mr. Kettle, whose wife, you will remember, kept one of our sweet shops, was the captain and, in spite of his deafness, was most efficient. When Fred Foster came back from the war, he succeeded Mr. Kettle. Mr. Willis from the Guildhall was a fireman. So was Mr. Prike. And Mr. Double. And Jake Sutcliffe. And many others whose names I cannot remember.

I cannot be quite sure about the actual drill of getting ready to go to a fire: but, in those days without telephones, the message was usually brought by someone on a bicycle to Mr. Kettle or to the police station. The homes of some of the firemen were on a kind of alarm system which either the police or Mr. Kettle could sound and, when that happened, they tumbled out of bed, dressed in their uniforms, and bicycled or ran like hell past our house to the fire station. By that time, someone had raced up to Benny Beeston's in The Long Bessels and commandeered his two horses that had already that day done the twenty-mile journey to Ipswich and back.

Benny was dressed as quickly as the firemen, and flinging himself bare-back on one horse and leading the other came galloping full pelt down George Street, up High Street and through the Market Place to the fire station. In no time the horses were harnessed; the men were on the engine, hanging on wherever they could; the oil lamps—that were the only illumination—were lit, the bell started its infernal ringing and the horses began that mad gallop to the fire.

That was what happened at night.

The fire of the farm buildings at Whatfield Rectory broke out in the morning and was not discovered until sometime after breakfast. And a fire breaking out during the day had to be dealt with in quite a different way by the Hadleigh Fire

The Rectory

Brigade. In the first place, although the news generally reached Mr. Kettle sooner than it would have done at night, the gathering of the firemen was much more difficult; for, at night, they could mostly be relied on to be at home in bed. During the day they were scattered all over the place. Mr. Willis was a postman and might be anywhere on his rounds, so that, in actual practice, he could usually be counted out altogether: and most of the others worked on farms in the neighbourhood. Everyone knew the farms on which they worked and Mr. Harris, the schoolmaster, was most co-operative in sending his boys to warn them that they were needed: but, having got to the farm, the boy then had to find on what field the fireman was ploughing or harrowing or muck-spreading: and, when he had finally run him to earth, the fireman must stable his own horses first before he set off for home to get into his uniform.

There was, too, the difficulty of the horses. Any time after ten in the morning Benny Beeston and David Sadler were away to Ipswich and their horses were not available. Makins, the jobmaster at the Iron Bridge, of whom you have heard, had horses of a sort, but you will already have realised that these poor devils were quite unable to pull the heavy fire-engine. Sometimes Mike Emeney at the 'King's Head', who did all the station goods work, was able to help: but more often than not the police commandeered a couple of horses that were actually in the town. They might be waiting at Mr. Hazell's to be shod or they might be standing outside Mr. Kersey's, the harness-maker's, having some repairs done or they might be pulling a load of corn to one of the mills to be ground. Wherever they were available they were taken and everyone knew it was for the good of the community. This difficulty of getting horses had other drawbacks, for some of the horses thus borrowed were farm horses whose normal pace was a steady walk of four miles an hour. Being thrashed into a gallop was an unmerciful and risky business and Mr. Cottis of Frog Hall lost a beautiful five-year-old gelding that way which broke a blood vessel and fell down dead halfway up George Street, pulling the other horse down with it and the fire-engine with the firemen piling on top of it.

So, you see, the fire brigade which normally set out to the scene of a fire in the daytime was a very makeshift affair: often being made up of one horse of fifteen hands, another a hand and a half shorter and with only six men on the engine. The others got there however they could and as quickly as they could.

And this was more or less what happened on the day that the farm buildings at Whatfield Rectory went up in flames. The fire was discovered late, when it was well alight. There was delay in getting the engine to the scene, and there was precious little water in the moat when the brigade arrived.

My father and I did not get to the Rectory until the afternoon, and by that time the fire was practically over. Two rows of men—six or eight on each side—were still vigorously pumping a little water and a lot of mud out of the moat and the firemen were playing their hoses on the still smouldering timbers and the soaked thatch. The two horses, who had been forced into service, were on the Rectory lawn eating the roses, and the whole village and a good many from neighbouring villages were standing about giving advice, asking questions and debating how on earth it could have started.

Sometimes a fireman would throw a chicken out of the smouldering ashes. The chicken had been roasted alive and now, with no feathers at all, it lay on the lawn with dozens of its fellows. The pigs had all been burned to death before Lane could get them out. Fortunately, the ponies had been out at grass and the goats had been milked at their usual time and tethered away from the barns under the cedars. For all that, when the fire did break out and the smell of it reached these creatures, they were first puzzled and then terrified. Some of them managed to tear up the sticks to which they had been tethered and, their stables being the only safe place they remembered, tried to rush back into the middle of the flames. They were chased away and stood, crying piteously, on the side of the road . . . all except the billy goat who, being more securely tethered to a stouter post than his wives, could not tear it out of the ground: and, in his agony, raced round and round in circles, all the time making his chain shorter and shorter and shorter, until his throat was jammed right up against the post and there he was slowly and agonisingly strangled. Lane did not find him till late that evening, for, seeing the other nanny goats being rounded up by the village children, everyone assumed that the billy had got away as well.

The Rectory

We were very sorry that we had ever called him a German.

It was, as my father and Mr. Lane and myself, stood on the lawn on the edge of the moat, with the villagers still pumping mud and slush on to the ruins, a scene of utter desolation. The great tithe barn, that had stood for four hundred years, was completely gutted. The fire had spread to the stables, the goat houses, the pig-styes, and, had the wind been in another quarter, would have spread to the house as well! Nothing, except the ponies and the nanny goats, was saved.

And I remember as we stood there, Lane trying to assure himself as he looked at the dead pigs and chickens lying about, that it could not have been he who had started the fire.

'I remember,' he cried, 'I only had one cigarette when I got up this morning' (he smoked Woodbines, which were, I think, twopence for ten), 'and I said to myself I'll keep that to smoke in the lavatory after breakfast.'

He kept saying it. He kept trying to convince himself that he had not been responsible, almost as though, by so convincing himself, he could bring those dead beasts and birds back to life and build up again the great barns and farm buildings.

'I only had one cigarette,' he said again and again. 'I kept it to smoke in the lavatory.'

Presently, as there was nothing we could do there, we went into the house where gentle Mrs. Lane, who had always seemed so overwhelmed by her husband's tremendous personality, was pouring out endless cups of tea from a great copper urn. The refugee children were running backwards and forwards with the cups to the firemen. One of the Germans had bicycled to the pub and brought back several milk churns of beer, for water must continue to be pumped on the still smouldering timbers in case a wind got up that fanned them into flames again. They continued to pump water and mud on to the ruins for the next two days, when, at last, they deemed it safe to leave the place.

And that was the end of my happy childhood days at Whatfield Rectory: for the great barns were never rebuilt, and, one by one, the remaining animals—except the ponies—were disposed of. It was as though, with this frightful destruction of his barns and his yard, Lane had no more heart to go on. The chickens with the feathered legs were sold for a song in Hadleigh Market, for no one wanted that breed of chicken, seeing they were very poor layers and the days of the supremacy of Rhode Islands and Light Sussex were coming in. The goats were killed and eaten. The ducks disappeared, but I do not know where they went. All that remained were the ponies and Nell, the Airedale. Even the canaries in the attics were sold to a bird fancier—Mr. Sergeant—in High Street, Ipswich.

But more than it being the end of a certain phase in my life, the burning down of the buildings at Whatfield was the end of a certain way of life in Suffolk rectories.

For years before the fire the parson who farmed his own glebe had been dying out. He had become an anachronism. The great Rectory at Semer (that, too, has since been burned to the ground) had been sold to a school and Mr. Donkin, the Rector, lived in a small house, 'not a gentleman's house at all', in the village. Mr. Scratchley at Elmsett, who suffered from eczema and carried a green-lined parasol, let his glebe go wild, though he kept up tradition by retaining his carriage and coachman. When Mr. Thompson at Layham died, the last herd of Red Polls from Layham Rectory was driven off to Hadleigh Market. The death of Mr. Eld at Polstead saw not only the disposal at Christies of his incomparable collection of snuff-boxes, but the dispersal of his flock of Suffolk sheep and Essex pigs. Mr. Anstruther Wilkinson of Hintlesham disappeared from the scene and with him went his cattle. A new type of parson—that was to last for less than a quarter of a century—took over from the parsons who had been priest and farmer. Parson Eld of Polstead was succeeded by Archdeacon Buckley, a notable scholar. Mr. Donkin's small living at Semer was amalgamated with another. Mr. Anstruther Wilkinson gave place to Mr. Goffe at Hintlesham who, in his way—for he was, I believe, the son of a Lincolnshire blacksmith, who had been sent to Lichfield Theological College by the squire and married the squire's daughter—was, of all the new clergy, perhaps nearer to his flock than any of the others. For he, too, had followed the plough. He, too, could tell the points of a horse: and, perhaps, most important of all, he had served under Bishop King of Lincoln, and seemed to have caught some of the reflection of that saint's radiancy which, from that dour rectory at Hintlesham, he, in his turn, passed on to his parishioners, the Greens and the Welhams, the Routs and the Kinseys, the Turners and Moyes.

The Rectory

And soon at Whatfield, where Lane had kept his flock in such boisterous fashion, there was to be the greatest change of all, for Lane was succeeded by that great scholar, J. H. Burn, who spent his whole life in his study, only emerging on Sundays to preach twice to a packed church, for, not only had Mr. Burn great scholarship, but he had utter simplicity and his sermons were the Bible stories, told again and told so beautifully, to a people which had been reared on them and which, after the holocaust of war, came back to them as a thirsty hart to clear streams.

I was in Mr. Botwright's shop when I heard the end of the story.

There were two Mr. Botwrights, Fred and Tom: and Fred had cut my hair the very first time it ever was cut, when I howled the place down. But, apart from the strained relations which always continued between us in the barber's chair, Mr. Botwright was a great friend of mine, for he was, I think, secretary of the Hadleigh Fur and Feather Society and, as I, in my amateurish way, was a great breeder of Dutch rabbits (the mother and father of which I bought from Mr. Norford in Angel Square, which has now been pulled down and a new lot of houses put up in its place, called Garden City) we had much in common! And on many mornings before my lessons started at ten o'clock, I would go and sit in Botwright's shop, just to listen to the conversation and, when there was not a customer for a few minutes, be taken through to the back to see his canaries and his pigeons.

At this time of the day, Botwright's shop did little haircutting, for quite a number of the professional men of Hadleigh still went there to be shaved. The two whom I remember as regular everyday customers were Mr. Alfred Newman, the Solicitor, and Mr. Gall, the Manager of the Bank which had only fairly recently changed its name from Gurney's to Barclay's. Mr. Gall was a very big man, who stood up very straight, his shoulders kept back, his stomach thrust forward in an alarming way: with a little Schipperke at his heels. During the early part of the war Mr. Gall was much criticised for keeping what was regarded as a German dog, but he stuck to his guns (and his dog) and, eventually, they both went into retirement at Woodbridge where each lived to a great age.

Mr. Bobby Cook and Mr. Christy, our two grocers, also occasionally were shaved at Botwright's: but I do not remember my father ever being shaved by anyone but himself until he was past eighty-six. He then, occasionally, but only occasionally, let someone else do the job for him.

The great thing about Fred Botwright, to my mind, was that he spoke to me on equal terms. He did not regard me as a child. He told me his opinion of other things besides rabbits and expected to hear my opinions as well. In his company, though I was shy with most other people, I willingly gave them.

But, on this particular morning of which I write now, I heard the name Lane mentioned when I entered the shop: and then, as the four of them, barbers and customers, saw me in the mirrors before them, they dried up completely—so completely and so self-consciously that, although I was itching with curiosity to know what it was all about, I asked no questions. My curiosity was not unnatural, for, for some months, I had not been to Whatfield Rectory (from which the children had all gone now) and Lane had not been to visit us. But, in the 'busy-ness' of a child's life, the absence of Lane was only brought to my upper consciousness by his name being mentioned and, as it were, quickly suppressed, in Botwright's shop while the lather was being slapped on Mr. Alfred Newman.

When I went home I asked my mother where Mr. Lane was and why we had not seen him. She said quite simply and, without preparing me in any way for what—even to a child who had, for the time being, forgotten him—was bound to be a shock, 'Mr. Lane is dead. Your father and I are going to his funeral this afternoon.'

And that, so far as she was concerned, finished that.

It was only later that I learned, bit by bit, here a little and there a little, from the maids and from my friend, Fred Emeney (of whom more anon) that Mr. Lane had had what in those days was called a breakdown—the word 'nervous' had not yet been attached to it—that he had been in a London nursing home and that, one morning, he had, without any fuss or ado, walked out quite calmly and made an end of his mortal self.

I remember my parents coming back from the funeral: and I remember particularly how they remarked that Mr. Nunn, Lane's old enemy, had been the only one present who had worn a top hat. They seemed to think this was unnecessary ostentation. I liked then and I like now to think it was the special mark of Mr. Nunn's regard and esteem for his old enemy.

What agony Lane must have suffered before he decided he could bear nothing further and that, although he was committing a mortal sin, his Redeemer was the only person who could understand, only those of us who have been perilously near the same thing can have any conception. And we, by the mere fact of our being still alive, can know not a quarter of the suffering.

But for so many—and those, 'our worthiest and our best' —there does come a time when the frailty of our human flesh can no longer bear the endless suffering of day and the eternal agony of the night watches.

The small boy who heard his name in Botwright's shop knew nothing of this, except that the world was no longer such a place of sunshine and that there would no longer be that pale-faced man with the great black beard bawling the psalms and the hymns, out of tune and out of time, to Miss Martin's feverish playing on the harmonium.

But, very often, in the years that were to come, when I had a bicycle, I would go to the churchyard at Whatfield and stand, for a little, by the grey granite cross they had raised over his grave. There was some comfort in that and some comfort in entering the misty, little white-washed church and kneeling again where I had knelt so many Sundays in the past when that great heart had lived among us.

For his example of love and his tenderness to all young things and his joy in living, while he was with us, I can never be sufficiently grateful.

5. The Market

MONDAY was Market Day at Hadleigh. There is still a market held every Monday at Hadleigh, but it is a poor substitute for the grand business it was in my childhood. Now there are a few sheep, cattle and pigs. There are—when fowl pest is not prevalent—a few chickens, a few tame rabbits and a heterogeneous collection of stuff known as 'Dead Stock'; an old dressing-table, half an old washstand, for the marble top has long since been taken by some housewife to be used to make pastry on; rolls of wire netting, skilfully tied together so that the novices (if there are such) cannot see the holes that must have been especially made to let rabbits through; and rolls and rolls of depressing linoleum.

But market days forty years ago! That was a different story altogether. Early in the morning the market men were at work, making pens for the pigs and sheep of movable Suffolk hurdles, trundling into position the wheeled hutches (each one numbered) that would soon be filled with chickens and ducks and rabbits. All this started soon after seven o'clock. By eight o'clock the first consignments of livestock could be seen coming 'on the hoof' to be numbered and penned. They came thus early—the selling did not actually start until about midday—so that the men who drove them, sometimes as much as five miles, could

The Market

get back to their work on the farms. In those days there was no such thing as a guaranteed price. Very rarely was a reserve price put on an animal. You bred and reared the sheep and the pigs and the cattle and took the best price you could get.

Hadleigh market has been continuously held for over six hundred years. That is certain. It may be much more ancient than that, but the records are lost. The actual market place is almost dead in the middle of the town, a square off the High Street, opposite the beautiful White Lion Hotel which has an enclosed galleried courtyard—all the bedroom doors opening directly on to the gallery. When I was a child a wistaria of great age and incredible beauty grew in the courtyard, its branches spreading and climbing all round the gallery. Progress, however, killed the wistaria. After old Miss Spooner retired, the 'White Lion' came into the possession of a Brewery who modernised the place. The courtyard had gimcrack little tables dotted about here and there. The little 'snug', that would hold no more than eight or a dozen, had a sliding glass door put on it. Privacy was gone for ever. Central heating was installed. The fools put one of the radiators over the roots of the ancient wistaria—it was dead in a year.

Progress . . .

The Market Place had a few private houses at its north side, where Miss Cross and Mrs. Woods lived and Mr. Charles Grimwade and his son, Mr. Harold, had their offices, for they were solicitors. Opposite these houses was The Lawns, a large house where Mrs. Archer, a widow, lived alone with her maid, Ellen. Mrs. Archer had been a widow for many years when I was a child. Like Queen Victoria she had put on widow's weeds on the death of her husband. Until her own death, many years later, she never wore anything else. She was the only person I can remember who kept to this ancient custom which, everywhere else, had died out.

Years before I was born The Lawns had been the home of a solicitor and his wife named Ffennell. The house had a large garden, surrounded by a high brick wall and overcrowded with evergreen trees and bushes. The house also had a basement with the usual 'area', and there was a little space underneath the dining- and drawing-room windows where a person could conceal himself without being seen and hear all that was said in either of those rooms.

Mr. Ffennell had a partner and neither Mr. nor Mrs. Ffennell could get on with the partner's wife. The two men worked together amicably enough, but Mrs. Oldman, as I will call her, was never asked to the Ffennells' house nor did the Ffennells accept any of Mrs. Oldman's invitations. On one occasion the Ffennells gave a grand dinner party. All the élite of Hadleigh—except the Oldmans—were invited and accepted the invitations. The great gates of The Lawns, opening on to Duke Street, were thrown open and the carriages deposited the guests at the front door.

There was much laughter and happy conversation. But I am afraid some very unkind things were said about poor Mrs. Oldman. People shook their heads and said she was quite impossible. They said how sorry they were for her husband. What a dreadful life he must have. It was, indeed, wonderful, they said, that Mrs. Oldman had never been prosecuted for libel. But the day would come . . . never fear that . . . it was bound to come.

To all this Mrs. Oldman, who, naturally, had heard of the dinner party to which her husband's partner's wife had not invited her, listened attentively. For she too was, in a sense, present, though not actually in the room. Before the carriages began to arrive, Mrs. Oldman had—discreetly clothed in black—slipped in through the side door that led on to the Market Place. Taking good care not to be seen from the house, she had managed to get down into the area and there standing, first, beneath the drawing-room window and, later, beneath the dining-room, she heard all the dreadful things that were said about her.

But she had not been unprepared for this. She had, indeed, expected it: and, for weeks before the dinner, had been collecting fabulous stories about the Ffennells and their guests.

On the night of the dinner, it was warm and the great windows of the dining-room which looked over the area were open at the bottom. Presently, as sometimes happens in a room full of people, there was a silence at the dinner table. Then, like Venus rising from the waves, Mrs. Oldman rose from the area, propelled herself, hot and dusty, through the open window and

The Market

confronting the astonished company, reeled off all the most intimate secrets of the Ffennells' lives.

Everyone was speechless with astonishment and fascinated horror as the list of hitherto unmentionable things was recited. ('Finest show I was ever at in my life', Major Gales told my father.)

Then Mr. Ffennell, his face set white, turned to his butler. 'Show that woman out!' he commanded.

Poor Mrs. Oldman was escorted to the door and let out into the Market Place. The dinner proceeded. It was, of course, agreed by everyone that the less said about it the better. The woman was mad, no doubt about that. Poor Mr. Oldman, they said. Not a word of truth in any of those awful allegations.

The partnership between Mr. Ffennell and Mr. Oldman was dissolved. Everyone expected that Mr. Oldman would take his naughty wife away from the town where she had caused so much trouble.

But things did not work out that way at all, for Mr. Oldman did not budge. It was the Ffennells who left Hadleigh never to return.

As people said—especially the people who had been at the classic denunciation—it made you think.

Years later, when I was a small boy, during the 1914 war, I used to go to tea with Mrs. Oldman. We never had tea, but lots of rich fruit cake and port wine. Mrs. Oldman swigged away at her port and told me wonderful things about our neighbours in Hadleigh. Inexperienced and excited, I ran home and repeated these monstrous fables to my parents.

But, in the end, these revelations got really too much for my parents, who forbade me to visit Mrs. Oldman again. I thought this was very unjust.

But the ban stood. There was no more rich fruit cake and port with Mrs. Oldman.

Nearly opposite The Lawns was—and is—the Corn Exchange, a large building of Peterborough brick, built about a hundred years ago, where, on Monday afternoons, after the livestock had been auctioned, the farmers with grain to sell gathered.

Every farmer of any standing had a little portable 'desk', very like the desks which copying clerks used to work at in the offices of old-fashioned solicitors. These 'desks' were too high to sit at: but the farmer stood behind his own 'desk', which had his name painted on it.

Unlike the market outside there was very little noise in the Corn Exchange. Everything was a bit hushed and reverent as the millers went from desk to desk, watching the farmers run the golden grain through their fingers, for, by these little samples, whole granaries would be sold. After the farmers had trickled the grain from their hands on to the desks, so that, if the sun was shining, it caught the rays, the millers might, if they were interested, pick a sample up and rub it in their hands, testing it for its hardness—soft grain was no good to anyone. There was little talk and a bargain was rarely concluded at the first desk. The millers moved slowly along the line from one end of the room to the other, looking, pressing, almost listening.

A special corner was reserved for the farmers who had barley to sell. Here the maltsters and the brewers congregated. Barley was always a sure market—though it had to be of the best—while sometimes the farmers with corn or oats only had to take their samples home and try another day: at Ipswich on Tuesday or Bury St. Edmunds on Wednesday or Colchester on Saturday.

You heard people say so and so was a 'bad farmer' when he was out most days of the week at markets. They did not mean he was lazy and perpetually having rather jolly jaunts, so much as that the stuff he had to sell was pretty poor.

Looking back it is hard to believe that, so few years ago, there were so many millers in such a tiny area. But there were, literally, dozens of them in addition to the farmers who, having themselves mills, ground all their own horse and cattle and pig fodder. Down Tinker's Lane at Hadleigh was Mr. Alderton's mill and close to that were Mr. Wilson's maltings, outside which we children used to stand fairly revelling in the lovely smell of the grain as it fermented. There was another mill (Mr. Cocksedge's, I think) at the other end of the town by the Iron Bridge. And there was Mr. Mason at Layham and another Mr. Mason at Kersey, and a very large mill, owned by Mr. Ladbrook, at Elmsett. The millers all seemed very prosperous, which embittered the farmers who said they (the farmers) did all the work and ran all the risk. In a measure I suppose this was true.

But the millers worked very hard indeed, and when I was told, by someone who professed to know, that Mr. Alderton was worth £100,000, my immediate reaction was why a man with so much money looked so worried and always had his clothes covered in flour. It never occurred to me that, if Mr. Alderton was rich, he worked as hard as any of his men.

Beyond the quiet hum and murmur of the Corn Exchange stood the great bulk of the Town Hall that, built of red brick and with the Hadleigh Coat of Arms (a Paschal Lamb standing on three wool sacks) carved on its south front, had been 'erected by public subscription' in the middle of the nineteenth century. But, by the time I was a child, the great days of the Town Hall were already over. Only two or three times a year was it really filled to overflowing, as when the Operatic Society gave its annual performance of some Gilbert and Sullivan opera and, on the final night, when bouquets and boxes of chocolates were presented to the players, there was much bitterness because this one had got more than that one.

Indeed, it was frequently alleged that some of the ladies, fearful that they would be less regarded than others in the cast, ordered flowers and various other gifts in fictitious names to be handed up after the last curtain.

'Of course,' the crabbed ones said, 'she bought them herself. I knew it for a fact.'

Worse than the competition as to who should have the most tributes after *Iolanthe* or *The Mikado* or *Patience* were the fearful hints and warnings that were given about what went on behind the scenes. And I remember one particularly rewarding evening when one of the gentlemen players appeared to take his curtain with a lovely splodge of lipstick all over his face, making him look rather like a clown.

The tongues rattled all night that time!

But, in its great days, the Town Hall had been the scene of lavish subscription dances and bazaars that were, with suitable illustrations, reported in the *London Illustrated News*: and the Market Place had been crammed with carriages and, before the town was lit with gas, with link boys guiding ladies and gentlemen to their equipages.

When I was very small the 'old Town Hall', dating from the fifteenth century, was still being used as a 'Stay Factory'. This was in the days of whalebone corsets, and in this little room anything from fifty to a hundred girls worked from eight to one and two to six—or longer if they had a rush order. There were no half days. The room in which they worked was all plastered over and very inadequately ventilated. When we walked by as children, we could hear the hum and rattle of the sewing machines that the women used for hemming and other refinements.

But presently whalebone corsets went out in the early 'twenties and my father, who was Chairman of the Urban District Council, persuaded the Council not to re-let the old Town Hall again. It should, he said, be used for Council meetings. So the place was stripped and in the large room beautiful oak beams were uncovered, while the panelling, which had been plastered over in the Council Chamber, was exposed and the place came back to the purpose for which it had been built.

Right at the end of the Market Place is the oldest public-house in Hadleigh, 'The Ram'. 'The Ram' is—or was—a Free House, belonging to the Grand Feoffement, who let it to the market trustees who, latterly, I believe, have sub-let it to a Brewer, so that it probably is not a Free House any longer.

When I was a child, it was very dark and gloomy and kept by an old man, named Mr. Wix, whose face was rather like the colour of the belly of a frog. Mr. Wix must, I think, have suffered from some kind of trouble with his feet, for I rarely remember seeing him move from the chair he occupied at a round table in the back parlour. On this round table he had a bottle of port and a glass, which, throughout the day, he replenished. His regular customers helped themselves from the shelves or from the wood and put the money down on the round table by Mr. Wix's port bottle. If they wanted any change they took it from the pile by the port bottle and, if there wasn't enough, they took the difference out of the price of the next drink they had.

I don't think the system can have worked very well, for Mr. Wix retired from 'The Ram' and ended up in the Row Almshouses. But that may have been on account of his feet.

My father gave me my first drink in 'The Ram'. I was about nine or ten and we were watching my mother playing her part in one of the Gilbert and Sullivan operas at the Town Hall.

The Market

Mercifully for my father and for many other gentlemen sitting on those utterly crippling hard chairs crammed together with no room to stretch out your legs, there were two fairly long intervals. All the men slipped out—some to 'The Lion', some to 'The Ram'.

My father muttered, 'Are you coming out?' and, without waiting for an answer, nipped down the gangway and down the stairs. I followed.

When we got to 'The Ram', he ordered himself a large whisky and asked me what I would have. I had seen the word BASS on a notice outside, so I said, 'Bass, please', and drank it.

It was disgusting, but I pegged away until I had finished it and then spent a most uncomfortable second act until I could get to the lavatory.

Normally, as I say, 'The Ram' was so quiet that Mr. Wix could sit all day at his round table with his bottle of port: but market-days were quite different. Then the pubs opened at six in the morning and stayed open all day till ten or eleven at night. All the farmers came to market in dog-carts and gigs, so that there would be thirty or forty horses stabled at 'The Lion', another dozen or so at 'The Ram', twenty more at 'The King's Head'; and 'The Wheatsheaf', 'The George', and 'The Shoulder of Mutton' all had their quota.

Trade was tremendously brisk and every bargain was sealed with a drink. After the bank closed Mr. Gall carried on his business in the 'snug' at 'The Lion' until Jim, the ostler, had the last pony harnessed, the last farmer with the reins in his hands, and the last hoof beats echoed down the High Street, leaving Hadleigh to its peace and somnolence until the next Market Day.

. . . . .

The livestock market was a very different thing from the corn market. Where, in the Corn Exchange, all was hushed, almost as though the farmers and millers were at some mystic rite, in the open market all was noise and uproar. The lowing of the frightened cattle, the terrified screaming of the pigs as they were carried by ears and tail from float to pen, the plaintive bleating of the sheep made the market a place of tragedy, for, for every one of these creatures, there was but a common end.

After the agonising terror of the market where, to my childish eyes, everyone seemed to be armed with a great stick and everyone used it, where no one spoke softly, but all shouted and swore, using coarse jests, there could be but one end to each of these creatures.

After the sale, when the auctioneer's stick had banged on the side of a pen clinching a bargain, perhaps not this day, but certainly not many days hence, each of the animals would be driven up one of those ghastly yards which were still situated right in the middle of the town, hemmed in by the houses on either side, to the small shed at the far end from whence the smell of blood never departed. And then, indeed, when they got that smell in their nostrils, a mad fear possessed the animals, so, not infrequently, one would charge, heedless of sticks and stones, past his drovers, out into the High Street, there to be pursued by every man and child in the place until at last it was recaptured and brought back, beaten unmercifully all the way, to the place of torture and torment.

As time goes it is not so very long ago that there was a law that no cattle could be killed for meat until it had been first baited. That law was soon rescinded: but at the time of which I write there were no such things as humane killers. Cattle were supposed to be stunned with a pole-axe which, crashing through the skull, made a small aperture into the brain. As the creature fell on its knees, the slaughterman rushed forward and poked a bamboo stick through the hole into the brain. Thus, slowly and revoltingly, they died. Calves were slowly and painfully bled to death to give veal its distinctive white colour. Pigs and sheep had their throats cut in full consciousness—and all this was done in the smell of blood and corruption lingering from previous butchery.

It was bad enough when the butcher was skilled. It was infinitely worse when, sometimes drunk, he bungled the whole thing, so that a heifer once charged down the High Street with one of its eyes knocked clean out where the butcher had landed his pole-axe instead of on the head.

Cruelty was ingrained. Perhaps it still is. But today there are more R.S.P.C.A. inspectors and the police are more watchful and, in some markets, no one but bona fide drovers are permitted.

The Market

I remember, as it were yesterday, a pig—a great unwieldy sow—with a broken hind-leg in Hadleigh market. The leg was broken up by the hip, so that this poor creature, with what must have been excruciating agony, propelled itself along on its two front legs, dragging the broken hind-quarter after it. And no one cared. Not only did no one care, but drovers and foul children, armed with great sticks, mercilessly beat this suffering beast as, bearing its leg that was surely a cross, it somehow reached the pen where, under the sweltering sun, it was to lie, without water, until evening when another road to Calvary must start. And then, just as the pig had at last got itself almost into the pen and there was only the trailing broken limb to be dragged a few more inches, one of the drovers, impatient to be on to another job, lifted his great hob-nailed boot and kicked, with all his strength, the broken limb.

There was such a scream as I hope never to hear again. And, following the scream, there was foul, coarse laughter from all those standing round: laughter at this awful suffering.

Terrified, shaking with fear, I ran away from the market, unable any more to see all this cruelty, feeling in myself, I believed, some of the pain the pig was enduring, and horribly, bitterly ashamed of myself because I had done nothing, had not rushed at the brutal drover and kicked him, though, indeed, my kicks would have been puny and achieved very little.

But, weeping, in the sweet-smelling hay in the loft of the stable, I promised myself—never, I think, believing that I would be able to keep the promise—that, if I saw such a thing again, I would *do* something.

And it was not very long before I had the opportunity and kept my promise to myself.

In Calais Street* there lived a wretched little man who made a worse than wretched living selling coal, here a hundredweight and there a hundredweight. The price of coal wavered between fifteen shillings and one pound a ton, so it may be seen

---

* A much loved Rector of Hadleigh, Rowland Taylor, was burned as a martyr on Aldham Common in the reign of Mary Tudor. The people of Hadleigh, wishing to perpetuate their loathing of Queen Mary, named this street Calais Street as a perpetual memory that it was in her reign England had lost that last French possession.

that he had to sell many hundredweight before he could make any kind of a living.

This man bought a broken-down old horse, well over twenty years of age, which should have gone to the kennels, but its owner preferred to take the extra pound that the coalman offered him. The old horse was nothing but skin and bone and, as the coalman did not want to waste time going to the yard at the station to get his coal more often than necessary, he regularly overloaded it and cruelly beat it with a thick knotted woven whip as it staggered along under its burden.

On the day of which I write I had come out of our house in Church Street with our dogs and was going into the High Street, when I saw the coalman coming towards me past Aldridge's, the chemist's; his horse, his ribs all sticking out and his great hip-bone raw where he had caught it against his ill-fitting harness coming down Station Hill, was struggling under his burden. The horse's master was trudging beside him and then, as I came towards him, the man seemed to lose all control of himself and shouting at the horse, began to lash him round his genitals. For an instant, the poor beast pushed forward into his collar, but, while he did that, I, with the dogs' leads in my hand, had rushed at the little coalman and was thrashing him across his face with the metal ends. I was only a small child and, although the metal clasps drew blood on the man's cheeks, I do not think I can have hurt him much.

Anyway, if I had, he had no time to pay attention to me, for that last straining against the collar had broken the heart of the old horse and he lay down in the road and died.

I felt very proud of having avenged the pig in the market. But, later on, I heard—from whom I do not remember—that the loss of his horse had been the end of the man's business as a coal dealer, for he could not scrape enough money together to buy another horse and, after a spell of pushing a handcart round with a hundredweight or so on it, he gave up and went to the workhouse, where he stayed till he died.

Quite illogically, I blamed myself for the failure of the man's business, though he had beaten his horse round the genitals first and it was the final feeble spurt, in answer to that, that the horse had made which had killed it.

But, at that age, all the world seemed too full of suffering to be borne: Lane and the pig and the heifer running up the High Street with its eye knocked out and the coalman's horse and the coalman himself, all, in a different degree, had suffered; and that Sunday in church this was made very clear to me when it was read that 'the whole creation groaneth and travaileth together'.

6. Dummy

AND then there was Dummy.

Whatever may be our opinions on society today—whether we rejoice that we have come so far on the road of progress or whether we look back with nostalgia to the good old days—I think that it would be impossible for one such as Dummy to endure again all the horrors that he endured in my childhood. I have read in many books how, in old days, the village idiot, of which nearly every village possessed an example, was always treated with affection and a certain amount of local pride. I have no way of discovering the truth about this.

Perhaps, in some villages, the simple-minded were cared for: as, so we are told, in the Edinburgh of the time of Burke and Hare and Dr. Knox, Daft Jamie was cared for, so that, when he was no longer seen in his usual haunts in the city, there was a hue and cry raised and Dr. Knox, it is reported, took good care to dissect his corpse before it could be traced to his possession.

Be that as it may, Hadleigh was certainly not a city like Edinburgh and just as certainly it was not a tiny village where nearly every household would be bound with ties of kinship with its neighbours. In my childhood Hadleigh had about four thousand inhabitants (it has just over half that now). There were three flourishing factories, a maltings, two mills, at least four boot and shoe makers, three tailors, two visiting dentists, and practically every single commodity that an ordinary household wanted could be bought in the town itself.

It was almost self-supporting. In the same way that its material needs were catered for, so were its spiritual needs, for, in addition to the Parish Church (which had a chapel of ease at Hadleigh Hamlet and a chapel at 'The Row' for the benefit of the people who lived in the almshouses), there was a Congregational Church, a Baptist Church, a Primitive Methodist Church and a tremendously vigorous Salvation Army. Later on, a Roman Catholic Church was built as well.

With all these churches, each with a full-time priest or minister to serve them, you would have thought that the place would have been united. But not at all: for, although only very roughly, the worshippers at each place of religion could be grouped according to 'class' and money. East Anglia has always been a breeding place for dissent and innumerable reasons have been given for this, from the dissenters' own claims that they are the spiritual heirs of the men of Cromwell's armies, to their enemies counterclaim that they are dissenters because it is less expensive than being Church of England.

Of course, both these claims are rubbish: but it is not my purpose here to try to present any rational explanation of this vigorous and persistent non-conformity. The fact remains that, in my childhood, *all* the professional people and *all* the gentry went to Church. Each family had its own pew that had been used by generation after generation and woe betide the stranger who inadvertently sat in a pew that was the 'property' of a regular. Nearly all the *prosperous* tradespeople (and I use that word 'prosperous' advisedly) went to the Congregational Chapel, along with a number of farmers and millers from outlying villages. It was noteworthy too that the farmers and millers who attended the Congregational Chapel were, mostly, in some degree or other, related to each other. The Cooks, the Aldertons, the several families of Partridges had all some degree of kinship and were able to live a closely-knit clannish life of their own, hardly ever marrying out of their own circle; and, by degrees, acquiring more and more acres and becoming more and more prosperous.

Below the Congregationalists (and again I use the word 'below' advisedly) were the cottage dwellers who chose to worship at the Primitive Methodist or the Baptist Chapels. These people were very definitely of the working class. Their ministers were men of working class origin, who were almost entirely dependent on the gifts of their congregations for their livelihood, whereas Mr. Cowe at the Congregational Chapel was certainly a step up the social scale, being a graduate of some university and coming from a lower middle class home. One of my greatest friends, as a small boy, was Mr. Debnam, the Baptist Minister. He must have been well over eighty, but, when I went away to my prep. school, he took the trouble to write to me regularly, although writing was, to him, a fearful undertaking. Brought up to the plough somewhere in the Stowmarket neighbourhood, Mr. Debnam was entirely self-taught, for there had never been any money to send him to school and, born in either the 'thirties or 'forties of the nineteenth century, he had not the benefit of compulsory education. Nevertheless, when I knew him, at the end of his long life, living in his little cottage on the road to Gallows Hill, his shelves were filled with books and he could—and did—tell me stories of the great Spurgeon, who had converted him, and how, in the rougher villages round Stowmarket and Needham Market, travelling preachers, like himself, were frequently stoned. He had had his share of tragedy, for his first two wives had both died within a few years of marriage. His third wife, who was related to Aggiss, the butcher at Hadleigh, also predeceased him.

Till he was more than eighty Mr. Debnam ministered both at the Baptist Church in George Street and, mounted on his tricycle, a massive and tremendously unwieldly contraption, would pedal away to Hadleigh Hamlet where he had another congregation. He believed firmly in eternal damnation and hell fire: but, just as firmly, he believed in the loving kindness of Our Lord who could understand and forgive all things: and though, from some of his more sombre utterances, you might have guessed Mr. Debnam would be a gloomy man that was not the case at all. He was gay and almost carefree and very young at heart. Sometimes I went to tea with him and the third Mrs. Debnam. Unlike Church of England people who always addressed God either kneeling or standing, Mr. Debnam, before

Dummy

the start of any meal, firmly established himself seated at the head of the table. When his wife and guest were also seated, he, as it were, put his shoulder to the wheel, and embarked on the longest grace (it was always extempore and varied each time) that I have ever heard. But, as soon as the 'Amen' had been said and I opened my eyes, such an array of scones and rusks and brown bread and white bread and ice cake and plum cake and chocolate cake and, for good measure, ham or boiled eggs, met my gaze as to make the grace well worth while.

How I stuffed, while the old Baptist, his talk interspersed with verses from the Bible, as, we are told, was that of the Puritans, reminisced about his congregation.

There was yet another religious body in Hadleigh, which was extremely alive and vigorous. This was the Salvation Army, which had local off-shoots at Raydon and Whatfield. Today the Salvation Army has its own Citadel where the services are held. In my childhood, in all weathers, they met on the corner of George Street and High Street. Here, every Saturday night and every Sunday afternoon a drum-head service was held with the band playing fit to burst itself, the girls banging their tambourines, the little children, already in uniform, singing their heads off and, finally, the Captain giving an impassioned address. The trouble was that he shouted so loudly and spoke so fast that his words all ran into each other and I could not understand what he said.

Only in very wet or snowy weather did the Army forsake the street corner when it borrowed the Drill Hall from the Territorials and had its meeting there.

But, with the exception of the Salters, who kept a prosperous hardware shop and one of the Mr. Willises, who was a tailor, the other soldiers in the Army all came from the poorest quarters of the town. (Mr. Willis, I recall, practised assiduously on the clarinet. Unfortunately, he had always been tone deaf and, as he grew older, he became stone-deaf. His neighbours suffered abominably!) So poor were most of the members of the Army that many of them wore their uniforms on all occasions except when they were at work in the fields: and this was pointedly brought home to me when, years later, an old rascal whom I knew in East Suffolk was telling me how, as a young man, he had seduced one of the Army's lassies in the

Brickfields. 'And that's a fact,' he added appreciatively, 'she kept her bonnet on all the time.'

You would have thought that, with all this variety of religions, so that almost every household in the parish subscribed to one of these creeds and attended one of the Churches or chapels I have mentioned, that the Christian virtues of kindness and compassion would have flourished.

But such was not the case, for Hadleigh, in my childhood, was the most cruel place I have ever known. It may have been no worse than other places, but it was very cruel indeed and to stop this wanton cruelty seemed to be the business of nobody. The police took no notice. The upper and middle classes turned a blind eye and, anyway, it was no concern of theirs.

Today men like Mr. Makin, with his starved hirelings, men who took a pig to market with a broken leg, men who overworked horses and cruelly beat them, would, undoubtedly, be prosecuted and fined or imprisoned. Then no action was taken at all. Unwanted puppies were chucked in the river, without the benefit of a stone tied round their necks, and the place was swarming with unwanted cats and kittens.

The humans, who were different from the other humans, also suffered, but in an even greater degree: and that brings me back to Dummy.

Dummy was a man of, I suppose, thirty to forty, when I was a child of about eight or nine. He had been a deaf-mute from birth. He lived at the top of Angel Street with his widowed mother in a tiny little cottage that was, I remember, scrupulously clean, for Dummy worked hard at home, digging the garden and scrubbing the floors and fetching the water from the pump that was a little higher up the street.

He was all right at home, but nobody could keep Dummy at home all the time. He was young. He was strong. He could not read or write, but he could stand on street corners and watch the world go by and, in his dim brain, he must, I think, have been able to appreciate things like the swallows who gathered on the telephone wires before their migration and the excitement of market-days when he could see movement all around him and he must have been able to enjoy the warmth of the sun. He was short and stocky and had a full reddish brown beard and his face was a mass of scars, for, in those days, all our roads were of untarred granite or gravel and it was the easiest thing in the world for Dummy's tormentors to pick up a stone at their feet and hurl it at that bearded figure that stood motionless on the corner.

No sooner, of course, had one stone been thrown than all the other louts in the area began to pelt them at this wretched creature who, as the granite and stones cut into his unprotected flesh, uttered the most horrible and heart-rending shrieks and wails which were all that his wretched vocal organs could produce.

This it was for which his tormentors had waited. No sooner did the dreadful sounds start than the hail of stones and pieces of granite grew stronger and faster, until Dummy's face was streaming with blood and his beard was clotted with it, and, still making those animal sounds, he fled, as though he were, indeed, some hunted animal, and hid in any backyard he could find.

For years this had been the best fun to be had in Hadleigh. The louts from Cook's factory, where mats were made, initiated the children from Mr. Harris's Church of England School and Mr. Ringer's Council School into this filthy sport and, time and again, my father was sent for to bandage and get grit out of wounds and generally patch up. But, apart from this, my father did absolutely nothing and I have never been able to understand his attitude.

He was a just and good man. I do not think he had a great deal of imagination: or, if he heeded it in his youth, he had rigorously schooled it out of himself when he was young. He had himself suffered both physically and emotionally, but, as I remember him (he was fifty when I was born and I was thirty-eight when he died), he never showed any emotion at all. Somehow, he had managed to cut all emotion out of his life, so that neither physical hurt nor emotional disturbance could affect him: and, in the same way, he seemed to think these things should not hurt other people.

To me, as a child, the sight of Dummy, blood streaming from his wounds, those unearthly sounds coming from his wretched mouth, was such a shock and horror that it has remained with me all through life, so that, for years, I would awake in the middle of the night, screaming as though the louts of Hadleigh were pursuing me.

But, so far as I could see, to the rest of the people of Hadleigh, Dummy might have been just a piece of stage property: to be used when necessary, a pleasant accessory to come across on an idle afternoon. The police did nothing. The Church did nothing. My father did nothing. Only each generation of louts taught what would become the next generation of louts to carry on with the sport.

After I had gone away to school, Dummy's mother died and the Guardians, as they were known in those days, decided that Dummy could not go on living by himself. They sent him away. I do not know where they sent him for at about this time Semer Workhouse—'the bugger and spike' in Suffolk language—was closed (which was a great deprivation to the not inconsiderable number of 'casuals' in those days, for now there was no workhouse between Sudbury on one side and Ipswich or Tattingstone on the other): and, anyway, what with his persecution, by now, Dummy had been driven quite mad and went away like an animal afraid that it is going to be killed. A person, not a deaf-mute, could have been sent to the Suffolk County Lunatic Asylum where the inmates were all locked up day and night and many of them still chained to their fixed beds. If Dummy went there, he would, no doubt, have provided sport for some of his fellow patients.

It *is* possible the Guardians got him into a home for deaf-mutes, for he could use the old deaf and dumb sign language. I hope they did.

But I hope that he is now dead and his troubles are over and he has peace at last.

. . . . .

There was at this time in Hadleigh another person who should have been certified; and it was one of the most monstrous things that her brother was able for years to prevent this happening.

Miss Norford, 'Tippy' Norford as she was called, was a woman with a little property and a certain amount of money. Her brother, Teddy, one of the shortest, roundest men I have ever known, was a prosperous market-gardener, who kept some good horses and owned a good deal of slum property. Teddy had been a notable drunkard in his earlier days, but, after he had had DTs once or twice, he surprisingly 'took the pledge' and, even more surprisingly, kept it. He died in rather squalid circumstances for, having got gangrene in one of his legs, he was so frightened of an amputation, that he refused to have an operation and died in frightful agony. It was Teddy who persuaded everyone not to have Tippy certified, because he had heard that the estates of lunatics were vested in the Board of Control and, as Teddy said, 'Once those b——s get hold of it, where are you?'

So he hung on, watching his sister (though, from a distance, for he never went near her) getting madder and madder, hoping against hope that she would die before he did and he would get his hands on her property. I cannot actually remember which one died first, but the Board of Control did, in the end, get hold of Tippy's estate: though, by the time that happened, I doubt very much if there was a great deal left for her heirs.

Miss Norford owned a nice block of property in the High Street. This consisted of Sun Court, a very beautiful Tudor House which the Misses Byers ('the Church Mice') rented from her and where they conducted a school which all the children of all the professional men and most of the rich farmers attended. Sun Court is now a private house, scheduled as a place of historic interest and visited regularly by archaeologists from all over the world. Miss Norford also owned a large shop, where Mr. Churchyard, who had a fearful squint, carried on a draper's business and, sandwiched in between the two, a nice little house with a large bow window where Miss Norford lived herself.

Miss Norford suffered from what we should today call a 'persecution' complex, and, as the years went on, this got worse and worse until, for reasons which I will give later, all but strangers in the town, who knew no better, walked on the pavement on the opposite side of the road.

The mania took what, to many people, must sound a reasonable turn, for Miss Norford came to the conclusion that Rates were unjust and should not be paid and that the demands which came to her at regular six-monthly intervals were imposed specially to persecute her.

So she refused to pay her rates. But, unlike many people who don't want to pay rates, but, realising they must, take the passive line of paying them at the last possible moment, Miss Norford, carrying—for some inscrutable reason—a broomstick and followed by her little Pomeranian dog, marched to the corner of Church Street (where the obelisk stands which says London LXIV miles) and made an impassioned speech to a crowd of delighted children who, when she had finished, followed her all the way home, making cat-calls and throwing stones at the wretched little dog.

To her disappointment, the speech appears to have made little impression and, in due course, she was served with a summons. Her answer to this was to slap the process server's face and stick the summons in her front window for all the world to see. When she had done this she sat down at her harmonium and played 'Rule Britannia' over and over and over again with great stress on the 'Britons never shall be slaves' part of it.

The display of the summons in the window and the continuous noise of the harmonium had the desired effect. Quite a considerable little crowd gathered outside the bow window and, when she considered she had a large enough audience for her purpose, Miss Norford opened her front door and told them that she would address them from her bedroom window.

Expectation ran high as the audience waited for her address.

Presently she threw up her bedroom window and began, in what at first seemed quite a rational way, to expound her reasons for not paying rates. The audience listened for a bit and began to grow restless. Miss Norford, evidently sensing that they were no longer with her, changed her tactics and screamed out an order that they should all look at Mr. Churchyard's shop, for she was responsible for the rates on this establishment which, it will be remembered, was her property as well.

Obediently, the audience looked at Mr. Churchyard's shop.

Then, like a flash, while all eyes were turned in the direction she had bidden them, Miss Norford whipped out her overflowing chamber-pot and emptied the lot on them. With a scream of delight, she slammed down the window and retreated to the back premises. But, oddly enough—so I have been told—everyone was very good humoured about the whole episode, saying, with understanding winks and nods, that 'it was only old Tippy' and went off home to get into dry clothes.

That was the beginning of Miss Norford's private war. The

local Council was as patient as it could be, but, in the end, an order for distraint was given and, one by one, at regular intervals of six months, the bailiffs came and removed bits of furniture which were sold in the market place to settle the rate demands.

It was all very sad, and, had her brother or some friend ever helped her, I am sure the thing could have been straightened out. As it was, the old lady came to see herself more and more as a martyr. Her perambulations with her broomstick and her Pomeranian became more regular and more militant and then a day came when, receiving her rents from Mr. Churchyard and the Misses Byers, she noticed that the amounts were not as big as previously. She made enquiries and found that, to protect themselves, her tenants were paying their own rates and deducting the appropriate amount from the rent.

This time Miss Norford brought her heavy artillery into action. She issued summonses against her tenants for rent due (oddly enough, she saw nothing inconsistent in this, though she repudiated all summonses served on herself). The County Court Judge decided against her and, being responsible for the costs of these unsuccessful actions, which she refused to pay, further distraints were levied. Mr. Churchyard gave her notice and moved into another shop. The poor Misses Byers were unable to find other premises suitable for use as a school and continued to pay both rent and rates. Perhaps this unsatisfactory state of affairs might have continued indefinitely had not Miss Norford overstepped what even the most liberal-minded regarded as the bounds of fair play.

Like all ancient houses Sun Court and Miss Norford's own house had been built in a haphazard, not to say happy-go-lucky way, so that, though most of the walls were very thick and solid, others had been put up with simply a thin partition of lath and plaster. Such was the wall between Miss Norford's pantry and the classroom in which Miss Maud Byers taught the senior girls. In her pantry Miss Norford could quite plainly hear the lessons which Miss Maud gave to her pupils.

In that case, poor Miss Norford's brain told her, the pupils could as easily hear what she had to say. To make doubly certain, while 'the Church Mice' were at Evensong one Sunday, Miss Norford excavated a little hole in the thin wall. When she had done that, she must have nipped through an open window or an unlocked door into Sun Court and cleared up the plaster that had fallen through.

She was now ready for the dénouement: which came directly after school prayers on Monday morning. No sooner had Miss Maud got her pupils in their places and was about to begin the first lesson of the week, which was Scripture, than Miss Norford came into action. The class, ready to be bored by Miss Maud's re-telling of the story of Ruth and Naomi, was thrilled and then horrified by a piercing voice which appeared to come from the very wall itself.

And what a tale that voice had to unfold.

The pre-marital adventures of parent after parent were retailed with glee and a wealth of detail, until Miss Maud ushered the children into another part of the house.

Soon after that the Misses Byers bought Dr. Norman's old house in the High Street (where my own father had been born) which they re-christened Overall House. Not, I must add, because the pupils wore overalls, but because John Overall, one of the Translators of the Authorised Version of the Bible, had been a native of Hadleigh.

The battle of the rates continued: but, with the departure of the Byers, all the battle seemed to go out of Miss Norford. When her harmonium was sold, she quite calmly took her little dog to Mr. Lemon, the vet, and had him destroyed.

Presently they came and took her to the Asylum and the Board of Control administered her property to her brother's chagrin.

7. Peyton Hall

IF some of the incidents described in the last two chapters have given the impression that my childhood in Hadleigh brought me into contact with much sadness, that is by no means all the story. There were many, many golden hours and days far outweighing what was tragic. But the tragedy and the joy were so closely linked together that it would be impossible to disentangle them: so that, although it would be wrong to give the impression that my childhood was made up of all blacks or all whites, it would be equally mistaken to think of it as an indeterminate grey. The highlights of joy and grief merged insensibly into long eventless days that were, for the most part, very happy.

I think I was lucky in that I did not go away to school until I was ten and a half: nor, until I was that age, did I start Latin or French or Algebra or Geometry. I was eleven when I started Greek: and, although I have no recollection of being 'crammed', nor, indeed, of working harder than I was inclined to, when I was thirteen and a half I won a scholarship to my public school. Most of the other boys at my prep. school had gone there at the age of seven or, at the most, eight, so that they had at least two or three years' start of me: but, on the whole, in those two or three years, they do not appear to have absorbed very much.

This, of course, is going far beyond the scope of this present book which takes me only to the age of ten.

From the age of eight until I went to my prep. school I was taught at home for two hours a day, from ten o'clock to twelve o'clock in the morning. I do not remember being taught to read. Indeed, I seem to have been reading all my life: but, at the same time, with the exception of *Black Beauty* and *Beautiful Joe*, I cannot remember any of the earliest books I read or that were read to me.

By the time I was ten, however, I had read nearly all Scott's novels in a uniform full-length edition, which I bought from Mr. Fred Emeney. I have now forgotten them entirely, as I have *The Black Tulip*, which was, at that time, a great favourite. But I do know that I was reading, reading, reading night after night. I had an enormous bedroom to myself with windows to the south and the west. There was an old-fashioned gas bracket above my bed, and, after my mother had kissed me goodnight and put out the light, I would wait until I was sure the grown-ups were downstairs before lighting up again and reading until my eyes would keep open no longer. But what I read I have no idea.

This reading in bed was, however, a very small and unimportant part of my life, for I was always out and about in the daytime, taking the dogs up on to the hills by Holbecks Park or visiting the old people in the Row Almshouses where Mrs. Parker, who was over ninety and quite blind, would pass her hands over my face—as she did to every little boy who came to her cottage—before I spoke and then, from the contours, proclaim triumphantly the name of her visitor. Another person whom I regularly visited was Teddy Norford (Miss Norford's prosperous market-gardener brother) who kept a parrot, which was a great talker, and some very fat, very sleek ponies. I spent many happy hours with Norford's ponies, grooming them and feeding them and mucking them out, because from the very beginning of the war until almost the time I went to my prep. school, our own stables were taken over by the Army and we children were not very welcome there.

Mrs. Heckford was another old friend. She had had a very hard life, being brought up by her grandmother in some village near Clacton. When I knew her in her old age she was permanently deformed, having one shoulder higher than the other. This, she told me, was from carrying heavy buckets from the village well when she was a child. She became one of my grandmother's servants when she was about eighteen and would tell me with gusto how she had slapped my rather terrifying father's bottom. After she had been with my grandmother for some ten or fifteen years she married Mr. Heckford who was, I believe, a basket-maker.

Anyway, Mrs. Heckford had never had the good fortune to rear any of the children she so regularly bore and this failure on her part embittered her husband who—so I was told, though never by Mrs. Heckford—beat her unmercifully. He died suddenly and prematurely, leaving her without any means at all and with, though she did not know it, half a century to get through. When I knew her, Mrs. Heckford had a largish house —No. 10 Queen Street—where Miss Barlow, one of the schoolmistresses, had rooms on the first floor and an exceedingly disagreeable old lady, named Mrs. Vince, had the ground floor. They paid very little, and they were waited on hand and foot. To make ends meet Mrs. Heckford took in washing at a ridiculously low charge. She was still doing this when she was approaching seventy and a friend of hers, Agnes Green, began to lose her eyesight. Agnes Green, who was a born grumbler and most cantankerous, could not persuade any of her relations to take her in. So Mrs. Heckford stepped into the breach and added Agnes to her ménage. For the next twenty years Agnes had the best seat in the kitchen, the best bits of food, the best cups of tea. Through it all she grumbled non-stop. She was still grumbling when Mrs. Heckford gave up her house and her lodgers and, taking an almshouse, moved into The Row. Agnes, now practically blind, hung on like a limpet, her cracked voice complaining all the time about the unfairness of things and how everybody had always let her down.

In the end even Mrs. Heckford let her down, by dying when she was nearly ninety and leaving Agnes, for the first time for twenty years, to look after herself. The Trustees of The Row, however, realised that she could not be left alone and found another woman to share her house with her. This new partner had not the angelic patience of Mrs. Heckford and it was not long before Agnes learned that her grumbling and complaining were getting her nowhere. Strangely enough, when I last saw her, she had become quite cheerful. Her new partner's harsher methods had succeeded where Mrs. Heckford's kindness and real saintliness had failed. Yet, in spite of all that she had suffered—her shoulders that were not the same level, her husband who had beaten her up, her grinding poverty and her back-breaking washing and mangling—I never once saw Mrs. Heckford unhappy. Nor once did I hear her complain. Her kitchen, with the kitchen fire going full blast on the hottest summer days, always had fresh flowers from her garden in it. She always had an amusing story to tell—about Tinter Cutting and his donkey or about one of the curates who had lodged with her and who frequently came home from visiting a married lady, whose husband had a blind eye, so drunk that she had to put him to bed, or about the wonderful parties that my grandmother had given when she had been a housemaid there. Times, Mrs. Heckford gave me to understand, had changed and I gathered that, although her young life had been terribly hard, they had not changed for the better. She never spoke of her husband, who was reputed to have ill-treated her, but his enlarged photograph dominated the room and she had, somehow or other, scraped together enough to put up an impressive stone over his grave in the cemetery.

No visit to Mrs. Heckford was allowed to pass without suitable refreshment, for biscuits and home-made wine were always produced and she and I munched and sipped while Agnes grizzled. My mother, knowing how dreadfully poor she was, told me I must not accept this hospitality. She might as well have told Niagara to stop plunging onwards and onwards, for Mrs. Heckford would take no refusal, and would, I believe, have been very hurt if I had persisted in it.

. . . . .

Another of my friends was old Mrs. Rand who lived in quite a large house in Benton Street. Mrs. Rand was considerably over eighty when I knew her and had never been able to write or read: so, on many an afternoon, I sat on a hard stool at her side, reading her *The Pilgrim's Progress*. This was an enormous book, bound in heavy leather, with brilliantly coloured pictures of Bunyan's characters. This book, together with a Family

Bible, weighing what felt like half a hundredweight, were kept on the round centre table in Mrs. Rand's best parlour. On reading afternoons *The Pilgrim's Progress* was carried through to the room Mrs. Rand sat in. And this was a very extraordinary room indeed.

When Mr. Rand had been alive (I can remember him, an old man of ninety, very tall and made much taller by a black silk hat) he had combined the businesses of fishmonger, bookmaker and innkeeper: so that when I went in at the Rands' front door I entered a stone-flagged passage which had on its left the now unused shop where the fish had been sold. The passage went straight through the house to another door that led into the quite considerable garden: but halfway down the passage, on the right, there was an entrance with no door to it. To the left of this entrance was a very small room with a high counter in it that had been a combined bar-parlour and Mr. Rand's bookmaker's office. There *was* a door—glass-panelled—to this, so that the select customers who used it might have a bit of privacy: but opposite it, only separated from the two draughty passages by high-backed settles which reached halfway to the ceiling, was the Public Bar or, as they are still called in some Suffolk pubs, the Kitchen. It was here, in the piercing draughts and among the ghosts of the drinkers of sixty and fifty and forty years ago that Mrs. Rand sat, her paper thin hands resting in her lap, her memories stretching back to the 'forties and 'fifties of the last century.

And what memories they were! For the Rands had been the gayest young couple imaginable! Not only had they been gay, but they had worked very, very hard and everything to which they had put their hands had turned to gold. The fishmongering flourished, for Mr. Rand patronised the new railways and had his fish sent direct from Lowestoft and Walton-on-the-Naze and Dovercourt, while other less enterprising tradesmen relied on the carriers. The bookmaking prospered and the pub, conducted most decorously, unlike some others I could mention, was a little gold mine.

One of the reasons the pub was so prosperous was Mr. Rand's connection with the Turf. Naturally, people went there to put their shillings and sixpences on their fancies: but other people—and these the more prosperous sort—went there to get information, for Mr. and Mrs. Rand were regular visitors to Newmarket races and the stables in that town, which was about thirty-three miles from Hadleigh.

Now, in my own young days, Newmarket was an almost impossible journey from Hadleigh. You could get there by motor-car, but very few people had motor-cars. You could get there by train, but you had to go halfway across Suffolk and Essex to do it. How on earth, I wondered, had Mr. and Mrs. Rand done it half a century before? The answer was *by donkey cart!*

When he was a very young man, Mr. Rand developed a passion for horses. He spent all the time he could spare in stables, grooming horses, feeding horses, barrowing muck for horses and just looking at horses. For years he dreamed of owning horses: but he was a perfectionist and he was also a realist and he knew that the kind of horses which he would be *able* to keep would, no matter how brightly the sun shone, never be the kind of horses he would *like* to keep.

So, being a very wise man, Mr. Rand put all thought of keeping horses himself out of his mind. He did what seemed to him the next best and most obvious thing. He began to breed donkeys. And, unlike all the other donkeys that were kept in the countryside in those days, Mr. Rand fed his donkeys as though they were Newmarket thoroughbreds. They had corn and cake and the best hay. They were kept at the peak of condition and, generation by generation, he bred each lot for a little more speed than its parents. After fifteen or twenty years he had a strain of donkeys that could trot at ten or twelve miles an hour, *for one hour.*

That, he considered, was the maximum that he could ever attain. So, driving a pair of donkeys tandem, in a very little chariot, built by Mr. Thorpe, the coach-builder, almost entirely of cane, Mr. and Mrs. Rand would leave their house in Benton Street at 5 a.m. in the morning and trot the first pair of donkeys the ten miles to the first posting station. I have forgotten where that was: but, I believe, somewhere just beyond Lavenham. Here the donkeys were changed for the next pair, who trotted on to Bury St. Edmunds where the second and last change was made and the third pair of donkeys pulled up at one of the Newmarket pubs before nine in the morning, where they were taken out of the little chaise, watered and fed and rested, until, in the evening, they set out on the first stage of the return journey. For all these donkeys, kept at the two inns on the road between Hadleigh and Newmarket, Mr. Rand paid full livery charges and woe betide the ostler or stable man who let one of them get out of condition. And the great thing about donkeys, Mrs. Rand used to tell me, was that they were so sure-footed. They never had a donkey that stumbled or let them down in any way: and, if at any place on the journey, they found an obstacle in their way, a tree blown down or the road flooded, they turned in at a convenient gate and went careering across country in the little cane-chariot.

Thus it was that Mr. Rand was such a regular visitor to Newmarket, so that he was on terms of great intimacy with jockeys and trainers and owners, learning all manner of stable secrets, who was 'expected' and who was 'being kept back'; and it was these secrets which his wealthy patrons, who backed in the Silver Ring, came to learn in the Parlour of 'The Fishmonger's Arms'.

So, to the tinkle of the feet of these little asses, echoing down half a century, I read *The Pilgrim's Progress* to old Mrs. Rand. Very often she gave me a shilling, which was, to me, a tremendous sum of money. She died just before I went away to school, sitting in the draughty kitchen where the old settles stretched halfway to the ceiling and where, as a young woman, she had, no doubt, sat, eating her supper, while Rand stabled the donkeys, after one of their trips to Newmarket. Though she had never been able to read or write, she had made a will, in which she left me her Family Bible and *The Pilgrim's Progress* from which I had so often read to her.

. . . . .

These visits to Mrs. Heckford and old Miss Parker and Mrs. Rand, to Teddy Norford and old Miss Cousins, who had an enormous beard and moustache and whose little house had the kind of smell I always imagine Lord Carnarvon and Mr. Howard Carter smelt when they opened Tutankhamen's Tomb—so long was it since the windows had been opened—all had to be squeezed in in the afternoons, after my morning lessons were over and if I did not go to Peyton Hall; for, for some years after the death of Mr. Lane and, indeed, even when Mr. Lane was alive and I was, unhappily at home and not at Whatfield Rectory, Peyton Hall claimed every moment that could be snatched from other duties.

In those days Mr. and Mrs. Harry Waller lived at Peyton Hall, which was a farm of about five hundred acres, with one of the most beautiful long, low farmhouses, on the banks of the River Brett, and with a mill, a millhouse (in which I always wanted to live) and two or three cottages.

Mr. and Mrs. Waller had not started life as farmers: but, very early, they had decided to become farmers. Mrs. Waller had been the village schoolmistress at Rattlesden and Mr. Waller had, I believe, held a number of appointments as agent for different insurance companies, agent for various kinds of cattle and horse cake and things of that sort. As a young man, he had been a neat, dapper little chap, whose littleness was accentuated by his wife's enormous size. She was a terrific woman in her middle age who, heroically, walked across the fields from Peyton Hall twice every Sunday to come to Hadleigh Church where, much to Dean Carter's annoyance and Mr. Stephenson's, the organist's, distress, she insisted on sitting in the choir-stalls, where, in the days of Dean Blakiston, a number of ladies had sat. Dean Carter, who had 'High Church' notions, disliked the chancel being occupied by any but a surpliced choir, but Mrs. Waller stuck to her seat on the Cantoris side, while old Dr. Norman and his family regularly plumped themselves down on the Decani side. Nothing—save death—would shift them. Poor Dean Carter predeceased them.

Mrs. Waller was not actually the fattest woman in Hadleigh, for she was easily eclipsed by Mrs. Postans, who, for all her bulk, managed to get up into a four-wheeled dog-cart, and Mrs. Twidale, who succeeded Miss Spooner at 'The Lion', but Mrs. Waller had had a much harder life than either of these and her legs troubled her a great deal as, indeed, was to be expected, considering she was never off them.

She herself told me, as she churned away in the dairy, how she and her husband had promised each other they would not marry until they had saved five hundred pounds. When they had got that amount behind them they would do what they had wanted to do all their lives and buy a farm. So they saved every

Peyton Hall

penny they could lay their hands on. In addition to teaching in Rattlesden School, Mrs. Waller—before she was married—gave piano lessons to the children of the farmers whose society she hoped one day to enter. For a very few pounds a year she was organist at a village church and tramped six miles a Sunday—wet or fine—to keep her part of the contract. All pleasure, except the greatest pleasure of all—the anticipation of one day having their own farm—was cut out of their lives, so that, for a long time, they did not even attend the whist drives which they both loved. But it was all worth it, because one day they were able to go to the Bank and see their balance and it was over the five hundred pounds.

In 1959 five hundred pounds does not sound very much: but seventy years ago it was a tremendous sum and an especially tremendous sum when it had literally been saved in sixpences and shillings.

They bought Peyton Hall, a mile out of Hadleigh and two miles from Kersey. As I said, it had a charming farmhouse: but that meant little to Mr. and Mrs. Waller, who were farmers first, last, and all the time. It was the land that counted: the land and the buildings. And the land, two-thirds arable and one-third pasture, was perfect. The pastures lay all on one side of the little River Brett, so that they were always fresh and moist and the driest summer did not affect them: and the arable land nearly all lay on gentle slopes so that, although it was heavy clay soil, it never got waterlogged, as did the clay fields in the valleys.

The farmhouse stood at the end of the farmyard with the horse yard and a cattle yard and the great barn on the right as you approached the house: and, on the left, the store houses for beet for the cattle and mash for the pigs. Behind these was a range of sties for the breeding sows and behind the sties the yards for the cattle that were reared and fed there ready for the butcher. The stackyards were scattered, so that, in case of fire, not everything should be lost, and there was one in front of the house, one away to the east of the house and another beyond the iron bridge over the river behind the house. Having a mill, Mr. Waller could grind his own meal for his pigs without paying a miller to do it for him. The mill was a water mill: and memory sometimes now makes me shudder as I think how near to death and how unconcerned by death my brother and I often were as we paddled our home-made canoe in the sleeping waters below the mill. We could neither of us swim, but it never occurred to us that there was anything the least bit dangerous in dodging up and down the river in a little canvas canoe. And it cannot have occurred to my father or mother either, for they knew what we were doing and never expressed any concern.

We were exceptionally lucky in that way: for, so long as we were not *too* late for meals (and, in a doctor's house, meals were never very punctual) and so long as we did our lessons from ten to twelve every morning, the rest of our time was our own to do what we liked in, so we paddled the canoe or we borrowed the Dean's boat, which leaked abominably, or I rode any horses that I could get hold of (Angela rode a little, but my brother was not fond of horses), so that, when I was eight, I remember riding Diamond, a great Suffolk mare, bare-back to Mr. Hazell, the blacksmith, to be shod. When I got to the forge, there was a queue of hunters waiting and I had to wait. Growing tired of waiting, I trotted poor Diamond up and down the High Street, while I bobbed about like a ping-pong ball on top of her.

At Peyton Hall everything was living and wonderful. I rode the horses in the harvest field with the binder behind them. Three horses drew the binder. I rode the middle one. If I had fallen off nothing could have stopped me getting cut to pieces, as, indeed, happened to another small boy. I strode purposefully about in the long, sunlit stable where, in the evening, the horses came, after their watering, to feed on the crushed oats and mash that was their supper. None of Mr. Makin's starvation diet for Mr. Waller's horses! Like Makin's horses they worked hard: but, unlike Makin's horses, they got the best.

Each horseman always—so far as it was possible—worked the same horses, so that the three of them became a perfect team, the horses seeming to understand what their horseman wanted them to do before he even spoke to them. Thus, King, the head horseman, worked with Gipsy and Brag: and Ginn, the second horseman, with Tinker and Captain: and Double with Matchet and Maggie: and Stanley Ginn with Sharp and Shorter and Spot Oxford with Diamond and her son, Stormer, who was named by that name because he was born on the terrible night of storm in 1916 when half the trees in Holbecks Park were blown down. And, as though he had been frightened of the noise of the thunder and the lightning had put the fear of the world in him, Stormer was born a white horse. It was not till he was just two years old that he finally turned the mahogany brown that he wore for the rest of his life.

The horsemen had a special language for the horses, so that 'Whoo-dee' meant 'Turn to the left' and 'Coop-wee' meant 'Turn to the right'—and the horses knew this language and the man with his hands on the plough did not have to take his hands off the plough handles to guide them with the reins.

In the evening, after the horses had eaten their 'bait' in the stable, they were, in the winter, turned out in the covered yard, where the racks had been piled high with hay and, in the summer, they were taken to one of the meadows that bordered the river. And in all the years that I went backwards and forwards to Peyton Hall I never saw a stick used to a horse, nor, indeed, do I believe that there was such a thing as a whip on the premises.

It was different in the cowhouse, for here the cows were thought little of, being the woman's part of farming, so that, in the traditional way, the money from the eggs and the milk and the butter, which Mrs. Waller so vigorously and endlessly churned, was regarded as her share of the takings.

But the cows at Peyton Hall (I don't think there were ever more than six or eight) had a poor time of it, for although Mrs. Waller made butter once a week and a few people bought milk from her, there was no regular milk-round and the cows were more or less there on sufferance or because they, as it were, rounded off the completeness of the farm. Unlike the bullocks in the stockyards, that were being fattened for the butcher and were fed on mangolds and chaff and other good things, the cows lived entirely on the lush grass in the water meadows during the spring and summer and hay in the winter months.

Even as a child I compared them with Mr. Wilson's pedigree Red Polls that grazed on the cricket ground, and found them, with their protruding hips and gaunt sides, sadly wanting.

And they were such sad beasts, with great doleful eyes looking out on a world that regularly, year after year, as their loved calves were born, weaned them as early as possible so that all their milk could be sold or go into the butter making. Cows, unlike goats which have an indefinite lactation, must be mated every year. Otherwise they go dry. In those days all cows calved in the spring and it is only of late years that the practice has grown up of calving in the autumn, so that the full flush of milk comes about Christmas time.

Years later, when I was waiting in the dark on Arundel Station one Christmas Eve, I heard a cow calling for her calf which had just been torn from her and over the meadows, which separated them, I heard the little calf calling back to its mother. Had they not both been securely shut up in yards, with the gates bolted and padlocked, the cow would have stormed, regardless, through ditches and hedges until she found her lost calf.

I wrote a verse for that cow at Arundel, as I waited for my train.

> '*Yes*, just before Christmas they took him away,
> That darling child you had laid in the hay;
> And they broke your heart, come what may,
> That *they* should have milk on Christmas day.'

Just so, every spring at Peyton Hall, Blossom and Tulip and Nancy mourned their calves that had been taken from them: and I think, perhaps, it was better that the calves should be taken when they were a fortnight or so old than the abominable cruelties which have recently been practised in cattle markets, when cows with calves at foot have been brought to market early in the morning, unmilked, so that the prospective purchasers may see their swelling udders. And their little calves—two or three days old—'strangers and afraid in a world they never made'—have had muzzles put over their mouths, so that they could not suck the milk that was oozing—so full were they—from their mothers, making little white pools on the muck-heaped market stones. All day long have the little calves lain there, being prodded and poked about, their little bellies crying out for food: and all day long have the wretched cows roared their agony as their udders grew tighter and tighter and the milk—that the calves needed so badly—oozed out on to the ground. That was a thing that the farmers of my childhood would never have done, for, in a very real and intimate way, they were nearer to their cattle and horses and swine and sheep than the farmers of this machine age can ever be. The animals who worked for them and on whom all their prosperity depended were not in those days generally—though, of course, there were exceptions—regarded as creatures without rights. Today the farmer's first concern is for his precious machinery. Yesterday it was for the beasts who toiled for him.

Again, in those days, the abomination of sending little calves, with the wetness of birth still on them, to market was not practised. This has, I believe, been now stopped through the good offices of the R.S.P.C.A.: but, in the years immediately following the last war, when there was a premium on milk, the calves were hardly licked over by their mothers when they were chucked into a van or the back of a car and chucked into the market and there, too exhausted to stand, they lay until they were auctioned for a few shillings to manufacturers of meat pies.

It is not many years ago—some five or six—that I was in a cattle market where a cow and her calf were brought into the ring together. The cow was sold first: but, when it was the calf's turn to come under the hammer, the purchaser of the cow did not want it. Another bidder bought the calf: and, in the ring there, the drovers began to hustle the calf out of the ring, out of its mother's life, never to be seen again, and the calf gave a piteous cry as these rough men banged it about, and then, when the mother heard that cry all her mother love burst out of her and she came running across the ring to succour her calf. But she reckoned without her human masters, who knew nothing of her mother love, for (one of them still holding the calf by its tail which he appeared to be twisting unmercifully) they turned on the desolated cow and began beating her about the head with their great sticks. Their beating was the senseless beating of frightened, ignorant men and only when they had knocked out one of her eyes so that it lay in the straw of the ring and sealed the other, so that she could not see at all, did they let up. I am glad to say there was a prosecution about this case and these men were fined, though that seems an inadequate enough punishment.

Although Blossom and Tulip and Nancy, the cows of my childhood, were not subjected to such suffering as this, there were times when their lot was very hard. The cowman was, I believe, a Dutchman. He was very tall and very thin and he was called Fons. Whether he was a refugee or had been taken prisoner and had escaped to England I do not recollect: but he had settled down in Hadleigh and married a local girl and, when he was employed by Mr. Waller, he went to live in a small farmhouse, which belonged to Mr. Waller, on the Aldham Road, called Bat Hall. Bat Hall was one of the last of the Suffolk houses that I remember to have been tarred all over, so that it presented an uncompromising blackness to the world. This tarring was done for cheapness. When the bricks had got porous, the whole house was painted thickly with tar and given a new lease of life.

Fons, I think, actually hated the cows, for he kept the handle of a garden fork in the cowshed and if one, as cows will, switched its tail during milking, Fons would beat it unmercifully with this weapon. The cows, who had their heads wedged in a kind of thing like a guillotine—only it was horizontal and not perpendicular—could do nothing. There was no escape from the flail descending on them. And how we children hated Fons. We shouted at him. We swore at him. But he always pretended not to understand us, so, in the end, I kicked him as hard as I could and got the fork handle laid across my shoulders. I do not know why we never thought to tell Mrs. Waller (for, at this time, Mr. Waller was very ill) but I can only imagine it was an ingrained part of our natures that we did not sneak, particularly on people whom we regarded as our social inferiors. I can think of no other reason for our silence: and this may well have been made more pressing by my own memory of the coalman who, when he lost the horse he had beaten, had to go into the workhouse.

Fons was also, so far as I remember, the only workman at Peyton Hall who regularly carried a stick. No matter what animals he was attending—cattle or pigs—he was never without this stick, with which he laid about him willy-nilly: and it was only later that I discovered that he actually *hated* animals and was also very frightened of them. That, now, makes his behaviour understandable though not excusable: but, then, I put it down to the fact that he was a foreigner and I supposed all foreigners were cruel. I suppose, too, though this I had not

Peyton Hall

worked out at the time, that Fons, a stranger in a strange land with an English wife and children, simply had to take whatever job was going or that he was sent to: and, although I am sure he would have been much happier in a munition factory, it may have been that, as a foreigner, he was not allowed into such places.

Anyway, he was still at Peyton Hall when I went away to school. I do not know what happened to him in the end.

. . . . .

Mr. Waller's eldest son, Percy, who lived at Semer Dairy, had a Shire stallion. It was not a particularly good one: but, in those days, you saw very few stallions other than Suffolk Punches in Suffolk. Of the Punches there were famous studs— Sir Cuthbert Quilter, at Bawdsey Manor, had two hundred or three hundred Suffolks in his stables—the Bawdsey Stud. Then there was the Sudbourne Stud and Lacey Stud and the Mistley Stud. But these were all Suffolks which, being our native breed, was, quite rightly, the most popular.

There was always a class for Shire stallions at the Agricultural Shows: but I never remember there being more than three entries—more often there were only two—and, whether there were two or three, Percy Waller's stallion, whose name I have forgotten, regularly came bottom of the judging. However, old Mr. Waller used Percy's stallion for mating with his mares, and this was an annual ceremony, for, as the horses grew older, there had to be replacements to carry on the work. At the time of which I am writing Short and Sharper and Kitty were all getting on for twenty and were no longer much use for work on the fields. Old Short, as a matter of fact, did very little except pull a two-wheeled tumbril backwards and forwards to the mill. Kitty and Sharper, who were both over seventeen hands, went in double harness in a waggon, but they had to be kept on the roads where the waggon would not sink in the clay, and they would be unable to pull it out.

One year Matchet, who was a dark brown Shire mare of a very uncertain temperament, so that she stood in a stall by herself, and Maggie, who was pitch black, came into season at the same time and a boy was sent on a bicycle to have Percy's stallion come to perform his offices.

My brother, my sister and I were very excited, for, when

we heard that the stallion whom we had thus far only seen at shows was being fetched, we decided to stay at the farm and see him, although it meant we should be very late for tea.

We heard him coming from a great distance and, when finally he came into the lane leading to Peyton Hall, we saw him teetering about on his great feathered feet as though he were a ballet dancer and we heard him giving shrill neighs and whinnies which were answered by the excited Matchet and Maggie from the stable. The man who was in charge of the stallion was having a very difficult time hanging on to his halter, so that I remember wondering if he had forgotten to put his 'devil's dung' in his pocket.

I do not know to this day what 'devil's dung' is, but every man who walks an entire horse always carries a bit—rather like a very large, very black broad bean—in his pocket. The thing is supposed to have some virtue which will stop an excited stallion savaging his groom, so long as he keeps it on him: and there must be a truth in it, for these men rarely get hurt, while strangers would, if they went near a thoroughbred stallion at these times, be knocked over and savaged by the horse stamping on them again and again with his front feet.

On this evening the stallion was, still jumping about and making his courting noises, eventually led into one of the stack-yards, while we children watched entranced, not yet knowing what it was all about. Meanwhile someone else had gone to fetch the two mares. They were brought out together and kept on the side of the stackyard gate where we were while an urgent discussion took place as to which should pay its visit first. Eventually, as Matchet was well known as a 'refuser', whatever that was, King took Maggie through the gate and cautiously approached the stallion, who was making the very devil of a noise and jumping about like one possessed. I noticed that the man with the stallion, while still keeping him on his halter, had also attached a very long running rope to his bridle. At present it was not clear what its use was.

Maggie, in the meanwhile, was taking no interest in the stallion at all and King had great difficulty in persuading her to come near him. But, at last, he did get her near enough and managed to get her hindquarters towards the stallion's head. The groom, at the same time, was hanging on like grim death to the stallion's halter and gradually letting out more and more of his line. At last he let go the halter, only holding the line, and the stallion mounted Maggie and everything looked set for a satisfactory conclusion when Maggie bucked, rushed forward, kicked up her hind legs in the stallion's face and bolted. The stallion reared backwards to avoid those iron-shod feet and now the use of the long line was clear for, had the groom only had the halter to check his horse, the stallion would have gone over backwards and broken his back (which did happen now and again with inexperienced grooms). As it was, he let out his line and managed to pull the rearing horse on to his four feet again, where he stood, for a moment, quivering with frustrated desire.

They had two more tries with Maggie, but the same thing happened each time, so, at last, they took her away and were all very gloomy. If Maggie, on whom they had relied, would not be served, there were small chances with the irascible Matchet. Nevertheless, while everyone held their breath, Matchet was now led in through the gate. And then the most beautiful and extraordinary thing happened, for the stallion and Matchet, their necks arched and their tails standing aloft like plumes, danced round each other in a kind of ceremonial dance for a while (though the groom still kept a hold on his long line), until they sidled up to each other and began, in an entirely human way, kissing each other on their necks.

Presently, all the beautiful courtship completed, the moment of bliss and sheer ecstasy followed and the stallion mounted old Matchet and I heard King mutter to himself: 'Well, would you believe it! That's a b——, that is!'

Everyone was full of praise for Matchet and the stallion who, now that it was over, took no further interest in each other and began placidly pulling oats out of the stack. We children felt as pleased and proud as the men: and, when Percy Waller's groom began his journey back to Semer, we accompanied him to where our ways parted on Porter's Hill.

After that we had to hurry, for we were very late indeed. We fairly ran down Gallows Hill and past the cricket ground, where Mr. Wilson's Red Polls grazed, until we reached the Iron Bridge. To our delight, we saw Mrs. Wickham, the curate's wife, coming towards us. She was pushing a pram in which her son Michael was travelling.

This charming picture of human maternity persuaded me that Mrs. Wickham would be as pleased as I was that another baby was soon to come into the world. With a wealth of detail I described all we had seen: the abortive attempt with Maggie; the stallion nearly coming over backwards; the love-making of the stallion and Matchet and the highly satisfactory conclusion.

So enwrapt was I in my description that I did not notice the alternate looks of horror and consternation on Mrs. Wickham's face. But I do remember telling her a bit of information that I had picked up that afternoon. 'King says', I said, 'that mares take longer than women. It's nearly a year before the baby is born.'

And, having thus widened the scope of Mrs. Wickham's knowledge, I trotted on to rejoin the twins. Somewhere on the road home—though I cannot remember where—we must have been further delayed, for there was always some new wonder to be seen and admired—but we must have had some delay, for, when we got home, Mrs. Wickham had got there first and had given my mother a most inaccurate account of what I had told her. I was, it appeared, a dirty-minded little boy. I had thoroughly shocked Mrs. Wickham and I, as the eldest, was entirely responsible for Angela witnessing this shameful affair.

It did not make any difference how much I protested that the rabbits and the guinea-pigs that we kept did it—even the little mice in their cage in the nursery, which had a horrid smell, did it—anyway, I demanded, how did I come into the world?

But it was no use. These things, it seemed, *did* happen and, apparently, no one was supposed to know about it, especially people like Mrs. Wickham, which seemed very odd, as she had just produced that pudding-faced Michael. How I hated that woman as, most unjustly, I was sent to bed without any supper!

. . . . .

One of the nicest ways of spending a day at Peyton Hall was carting muck. This only happened once a year, in the period immediately after the harvest had been gathered in and before the ploughing began. The magnificent muck-carting of those days is gone for ever now, for, save where cattle are fattened in yards, there is no muck to cart. And cattle manure is a poor substitute for the ripeness of horse dung. Today the land is artificially fed on artificial manures and fertilizers, which overheat it and, in the long run, takes more goodness out of it than it puts back.

Forty years ago nearly all farms of any size supported a flock of sheep which was folded on crops of kale and, as the sheep consumed the kale, their droppings nourished the land which, in the following season, was put down to corn. It was to the fields from which corn had been cut that the muck from the horse and stockyards was carted and, in due course, spread.

Forty years ago, too, when a farmer came to buy a new farm, one of the things that he looked for on his first visit of inspection was the depth of the muck in the yards. If it was less than a foot deep, he generally thought again before he bought the farm. At Peyton Hall, in old Mr. Waller's day, the muck was a good eighteen inches to two feet deep before it was carted. Yet the top layer was always sweet and clean straw for, every week throughout the year, except in the hottest days in summer, fresh straw was pitched into the yards, loads and loads of it, and roughly spread around so that there was no part where the old straw was still actually uncovered. The horses themselves were the best agents for spreading the straw for, when they were turned out of their stable after their 'bait' in the evening, it was no uncommon sight to see all the twenty or two dozen of them rolling on their backs, flattening the straw out. In this way they rubbed freshness into their skins: but, as the week went on, and the straw became fouled by their defecations and urinations, you would notice that the horses did not roll so frequently as when the straw was first fresh. And all the time they were stamping their ordure and urine into the straw where it sank through to the bottom, rotting it all thoroughly, so that when the time of the muck-carting came, all the lower part of the once golden straw had assumed the rich colour and consistency of an old-fashioned plum pudding.

Generally, there would be about half a dozen single horse tumbrils in use at a time at a muck-carting. That meant six horses were being used and eight to a dozen men, for two men at least were needed to pitch the muck into the tumbrils while only one man was wanted for the unloading on the actual field. This unloading was always started by a very long and unwieldy two-pronged fork which the men used to pull the muck into little heaps, at intervals of about ten yards, on the ground. A good tumbril-load produced about four little heaps. At the last heap, however, the fork was not used, but a pin, which held the body of the tumbril in a level position while it was in place, was pulled out, the horse was told to 'git up' and then 'whoa!' and the body of the tumbril turned vertically sideways and the remaining muck fell on to the last of the four piles.

It was at muck-carting and the carting at harvest home that even such a small boy as myself could be of real use, for very often each load had to be carried as much as half a mile or a mile from the yard to its destination: and a load of well-rotted sodden manure might weigh almost a ton, so that the speed at which it could be hauled even over fields that had had all the summer sun on them was never more—and often less—than four miles an hour. Consequently, if there was a boy handy who could take the load from the yard to the field, he released a man who could either stay in the yard loading or on the field unloading.

This was where I came into my kingdom.

I had always been quite fearless of horses, having spent my whole childhood nipping under their bellies, fastening girths; standing on tiptoe to get cruppers under their tails: even trying though, thus far, unsuccessfully with the farm horses, to get their great collars over their heads and ears and insert the bits into their unwilling mouths. Consequently, I was never nervous of riding on the horses that pulled the tumbrils up to the fields. To my chagrin, the labourers would not allow me to sit sideways on their broad backs and always put me astride, almost on the animal's withers, between the saddle and the collar. The collar had the hames sticking up on either side and to these I could clutch if anything caused the horse to start suddenly and throw me off balance. (Had I been sitting sideways and anything had caused the horse to shy, there would have been nothing to stop me overbalancing and the wheel going over me.) Vaguely, I suppose, I must have realised that, but, when I was well away from the vigilance of the men, I would do this forbidden thing and feel myself no end of a fellow for doing it. There was never an accident: but, as I found this sideways seat definitely less comfortable than sitting astride, I soon reverted to the orthodox position. The horse was guided by the hame rein, which is a little rein normally thrown over the hames. All these farm horses had the most delicate mouths and the least touch on the hame rein was sufficient to guide them to right or left. Indeed, I think that with some of the older horses when they had made the journey from the yard to the particular field that was being mucked once or twice, they would have needed no driver at all, but for one thing:

That thing was the bridge.

As I mentioned earlier, the house at Peyton Hall stood on the banks of the Brett and the land was fairly equally distributed on either side of the river so that, on almost every journey, the river had to be crossed by the little iron bridge, with a gravelly surface that had neither room for two carts to pass each other nor strength for two carts to follow each other, head to tail as it were, thus doubling the weight.

The horses, however intelligent they were—and, indeed, they *were* intelligent—could not be expected to know this, so someone, even such a small boy as myself, had to go with them: to halt, when necessary, if an empty cart was returning from the field and you were going up with a full one, until one had crossed the bridge: or, should two loads have been filled almost simultaneously, to prevent the horse pulling the second load from getting on the bridge before the first load had cleared it. This was, for a small boy, the most difficult thing to accomplish because the second horse *always* wanted to be as close behind his companion as possible, and though one shouted 'whoa!' with as gruff an intonation as one could and pulled hard on the hame rein, it took more than a bit of doing. In time I learnt that the best thing to do was to use guile and guide my horse to the side of the track where there was grass growing. When he got there he stretched his head towards the grass only to find that the rein, still attached to the hames, prevented his getting his head lower than his knees. This always seemed to me horribly unkind, so I would let the rein go and the horse could then eat the grass.

But, having done that, there was, of course, no possible way of getting the rein—by this time up by the horse's ears—back again. So, time and again, I had to dismount, climbing along the shaft of the tumbril and then jumping to the ground. Once

I was on the ground, I could get hold of the rein and, by standing on tiptoe, manage to pull the horse's head up again and get the rein back where it belonged.

So far so good.

The most difficult thing and—though I never realised it—most dangerous, was mounting again. This, for a boy of my size, could only be done by *climbing up the spokes* of the wheel, shouting all the time, 'Whoa, there! Whoa now! Whoa!' until I could scramble from the wheel to the shaft and then, edge myself along till I reached the narrow part of the horse, up by his withers, on which I could sit astride. It was not particularly dangerous, I see now, if the horse reared off when once I was on the shaft because then there was the harness to clutch on. But, as did happen once or twice, it was dangerous if the wheels began to go round when you were standing on one of the spokes. The only thing to do then was to yell 'Whoa!' and fling yourself backwards as far from the tumbril as you could get.

But what a sense of power and responsibility one had sitting on the highest part of Kitty, who was seventeen hands two at her withers: or Sharper, who was the same height. What a difference from the flat broad back of Mac, the Shetland pony at Whatfield, who now seemed like a toy! You were now so high up in the world that you became almost like that king of old days who lamented that there were no more worlds to conquer!

So, proud as though you were the very owner of Kitty or Sharper or Diamond or whoever it was, the small boy rode on the great horse to the field to be mucked. In your nostrils was the lovely ammoniac smell of horse, the living horse on which you were riding, and the warm, comforting smell of the horse-dung that you were carting.

My legs—between the knees—where I gripped the bare skin of the horse were, at this time, always rather sore from the dampness of horse-sweat and having to hold on with them tightly as we went over the ruts where, sometimes, the load behind us would shift and the old horse would stagger a bit before he balanced himself and his load again and threw himself once more into the collar.

So to the narrow farm gate into the field (for farm gates were always narrow seeing that every foot of land was of value; though they have had to widen them now, what with their combines!) where, with a touch on the rein, you guided your horse through, never scraping either gate-post, though you did really know, deep in your heart, that your touch on the rein had accomplished nothing, for the old horse kept the wheels in the deep tracks made by other wheels in the years that had passed, when other horses and other small boys had gone on the same Odyssey, carting the splendid muck to the headland and then down the lines from one little muck heap to another, making sure, all the time, that your line was absolutely true from one end of the field to the next. The best way to do this was to take a tree or a certain shaped bush in the hedge in front of you and keep on straight for that, no matter how the horse might want to deviate to right or to left.

If you had that as a kind of plumb-line you could not go wrong; that and the co-operation of your horse and the song that was, all the time in your heart, though your knees were chapped with sweat and your bottom was sore from damp on the bare back of the horse and, by the evening, your hands were half frozen and aching with clutching on the hames, for it would be late in October and November itself before the muck was all carted and the horse yard that had been like a great cushion to walk on had once again been bared to its base which you found, every year, to your astonishment, had a bottom of bricks and cement, thus preventing the precious urine from running away into the earth where it would serve no purpose.

. . . . .

It is natural that the ingathering of the harvest should hold the predominant place in the countryman's calendar, because it is, for this alone, that the whole cycle of the year has been preparing. The muck-carting, the muck-spreading, the ploughing, the harrowing, the sowing, the harrowing again when the little plants were established, the blessing of the fields and the prayers for the crops on Ember Day, the prayers for rain and the prayers for fine weather, all these were but the preparations and the preliminaries to that day when, at last, the Lord of the Harvest and his men brought home the last sheaves and it was time for the thatchers to get to work, making the stacks watertight and, not being content simply with doing that, proudly adding to their labour by making their thatches decorative and surmounting them with intricate and beautiful models—all in straw—of such things as a windmill or a plough or, occasionally, a cross.

When I was a child, although all the sowing of seed at Peyton Hall was done by a drill, there were frequently to be seen men 'broadcasting' the seed, just as they had done in Bible times. And I remember how every year we used to make special journeys to a farm in Layham where this method was always employed. We were told how old-fashioned it was and how wasteful and I remember the scorn in the voice of our informant: but that, I suppose, made us all the more fascinated, because we were seeing something that, by the very nature of progress, was being got rid of for good and all.

The fields we went to when in search of this sower were remote from any metalled road, which was, I suppose, one of the reasons why the seed was cast in this way: but, in those days, no one thought anything of walking three, four or five miles over country paths: and so, after we had left the lane that ran up the back of Sir Joshua Rowley's park at Holbecks, we got on to a farm road, which finally petered out at Mr. Miller's farm. Thence it was nothing but footpaths over four or five arable fields until we reached a meadow that lay on a steep hillside, leading down to a marshy bogland, with a stream running through it.

But if, at the top of this very steep meadow, we turned from the path and cut across to the left, we came to a ruined cottage (how long since it had been lived in, no one seemed to know) with an orchard of old gnarled apple trees and phloxes and fuchsias and valerians that had all run wild and a well with the well-head gone, but some boards roughly thrown over the mouth, so that the unwary might not fall, and there, from the end of this wild garden, we could watch a very old man broadcasting the seed: just as the man in the parable had broadcast seed and, like that man, the birds of the air followed him.

I would, I remember, stand for long minutes, watching him, his slow rhythmic tread, the regular dipping of his hands, alternately, into the poke that was strapped round his shoulders and hung about his middle, and the graceful sweeping movements of his hands. Although I believe that there are a very, very few places where this is still done, I myself have never seen it since I watched that ancient man in that remote field in Layham.

The ruined cottage was a thing of wonder and delight. In those days, though the windows had all long since been knocked in and the doors flapped on their hinges and the bats and owls slept in the corners of the ceilings, the stairs, although broken here and there, were still in place, and one could climb up to the bedrooms and, from the unglazed window frames, look out over the marshy valley beneath.

How one longed to be able to live in this lovely remote place, with the bats and the owls for company: and the cattle in the marshes below to look at and the rabbits, so tame were they, that they came and sat in the ruined garden to watch us, not afraid in the least that we would hurt them, for this place was as deserted as any in Suffolk . . . only an old man broadcasting seed and a little boy with eyes of wonder and delight.

And so the little boy decided to move house and go to live in the deserted cottage, among the gorse and the lace-patterns of the cow-parsley and the rabbits and the shrill-calling jays and the occasional bark of a fox.

I cannot remember much about my actual planning for this removal from my home: but there must have been a certain amount of planning for I remember my ignominious return only too well, which I made in three journeys (about eighteen miles in all), carrying on the first two journeys a black and shiny gladstone bag, which was a tremendous weight and forced me to rest very often, what with the bread and the jam and the ginger beer bottles and the onions in it: and lugging home a great rug on the third journey, that I had taken against the cold nights. But I cannot remember getting the things there, so that it would seem that the excitement and the happy anticipation of what was going to be my Swiss Family Robinson life had far outweighed any physical fatigue I may have felt carting my supplies along those country footpaths and storing them in the bedroom up the broken stairs.

I had done it all with great secrecy, extracting the gladstone bag from a part of our house called 'The Tunnel', which was a long narrow and rather low passage leading off at the top of the stairs to the maids' bedrooms, which we knew as the 'Tunnel Rooms'. I imagine I stole the jam and the bread and the other commodities when the kitchen and pantry were deserted and the great tartan rug must have come out of the day nursery, for it was regularly used for picnics, which was a great come-down for it, as it had originally belonged to my grandfather (who died in 1877) and had then been used as a carriage rug.

But I have never been able to keep a secret: and it was my hopeless loquaciousness that put an end to my plans for emigration.

I had—in the course of a week—done two journeys with the gladstone bag and one with the tartan rug—and I was really established as a hermit in the ruined cottage (that night was to be the night of my disappearance) when I remembered—for food was of paramount importance—that the apples on the trees in the cottage garden would not be ripe till the autumn and that I should need fruit of some sort. Accordingly—for this was a matter that could not be discussed with such a big man as Teddy Norford—I kept my eyes and ears open until I heard the little hand-bell that, tied to the handles of his hand-cart, merrily heralded the approach of fat Charlie Cousins, some of whose business was done selling, from door to door, in the town.

Now Charlie Cousins I did not want to see, for he had never been known to give anything away, save once when he presented me with an apple, half of which had been eaten away by the wasps! Worse than that, if Charlie Cousins were at home, his little bearded sister Kate would not have dared to give anything away either. So the sound of the merry little bell announced that Charlie was on his rounds and that, for an hour at least, Kate would be alone in the house and would—I had no doubt—supply me with apples.

The gladstone bag was already in the ruined cottage and, as I had to have something to carry my apples in, I took the next best thing. This was the 'Surgery Basket'. In those days, before the advent of the Welfare State when few doctors dispense any medicines and the sick are sent with a prescription to be 'made up' to the chemist, who tells them to come back in a couple of hours, my father had 'a Club' and he also had some patients 'on the Panel'. Many of his more old-fashioned patients did not believe in 'The Panel'—it smelled too much of Liberalism and Lloyd George and writing things on paper—but they did believe in 'The Club', which my grandfather had run long before my father.

The essence of the Club was the same as the Panel or the National Health Service. The difference was that it was a purely personal relationship between doctor and patient, without any Lloyd George or Government muck. Members of the Club paid three shillings a quarter, sick or well, and got medicine at, I think, sixpence a bottle. Pills were about the same price. These medicines and pills appeared to work wonders, but we were living in one of the Ages of Faith.

Now, when my father was called out to see a patient who had been taken ill, he clearly could not carry his dispensary round with him, so, on his return to his surgery, he would make up the medicines, wrap them all in beautiful white paper—which was sealed with red sealing-wax—and address them to the patient. (He used the old-fashioned double 's'. It took me a long time to find out what Mifs meant. When I did, I was so delighted that I used it myself for a long time.) If the patient was able to send someone to collect the medicine, that was much appreciated, but usually he or she was not able, so we had a succession of surgery boys—George Sisson, Fred Briggs, Fred and Charlie Willis, Ernie Green, their names come down the years—who popped the medicines into the Surgery Basket, shut down the lid and went on their deliveries.

At other times, when the basket was not being used to sustain the sick, I borrowed it to take my rabbits to be mated or to the market or my guinea-pigs, with which I was accustomed to do a great deal of bartering: so it was no unusual thing for me to be seen with this particular basket: and it was the very usualness of it on which I relied.

Now, with Charlie Cousins busy at side and back doors in the town, bearing my basket, I nipped round by the churchyard through the market place, to Duke Street where the Cousins' lived. Katie—that tiny woman with the luxuriant beard—came to the door and, to her, under a pledge of secrecy, I explained my requirements. No sooner said than done. Poor Katie, who had been a prisoner in the house for years (I never remember seeing her out of it, though there was nothing physically wrong with her at the time. It was, I think, the beard that kept her at home, and, remembering the treatment the Hadleigh louts gave Dummy, one is not surprised), entered into the spirit of the thing with gusto: so that I got the impression that, had it been possible, she would have joined me on my expedition. She filled the basket with apples. She even added a pastry pie of some sort (which got broken up and the dogs ate it) and bade me God speed.

Now, if I had, from Katie's house, gone straight to my new home, all would have been well. But this was impossible: for I had to return the basket to the surgery and transfer my goods to another container.

It was, as I came bustling through the Kissing Gate by the churchyard, that I met nemesis. Her name was Mrs. Vince, that disgusting old lady who lodged with Mrs. Heckford. What, she wanted to know, had I got in the basket? A rabbit? No, not a rabbit. Some more of those horrid guinea-pigs? No, not guinea-pigs. What was it? she asked again and again.

And then, I suppose being flushed with the enthusiasm dear Katie had expressed for my pioneering adventure, I let Mrs. Vince into the secret. I was, I told her, going to camp in the deserted cottage. I told her where it was. I told her what I had already carted over there. I told her that it was a deadly secret, which she was to keep to herself. Then, indeed, were the flood-gates of Mrs. Vince's eloquence opened. Then did I hear what a naughty, selfish, inconsiderate, disobedient little boy I was. Had I thought of the worry my parents would suffer when they found I had gone?

I had not!

Had I thought of what people would say and I would be pointed to as the boy who ran away from home? And, when boys ran away from home, what did people say?

I did not know!

They said the boys had been ill-treated: that their parents had beaten them: that they had not had enough to eat. Were my parents like that?

They were not.

And there I stood at the Kissing Gate, listening to how awful I was and promising myself that—because, even then, I knew old Mrs. Vince, whom I hated, was right—I would abandon the idea of the cottage and the Swiss Family Robinson existence and the lovely companionship of the bats and the owls and the white bob-tailed rabbits and, with the same stealth that I had taken them out there, would bring my supplies home.

But it was not to be so. There was to be no easy way out. The way of the transgressor was to be made as hard as possible: and, with dragging footsteps, with Katie's apples in the Surgery Basket each weighing a ton, I followed Mrs. Vince to my home, where the whole plot was exposed to my mother and my new world that had not yet been even properly built, toppled in ruins about me. My mother was quite adamant that all the stuff was to come back. She explained that, had I been missing, she and my father would have been very worried indeed; and that one rug, even the old carriage rug, would not have been sufficient to keep me warm on a summer night.

To Mrs. Vince's most obvious disappointment my mother was not angry, for which I was most grateful: and, to Mrs. Vince's equally obvious indignation, she promised that, as soon as all the provisions had been brought back from the ruined cottage, I could have a camp-bed and sleep in the tent on the lawn.

All this came to pass: and I did sleep in the tent in our garden, but it was not a success, for all the time I was still dreaming of and longing for a lodging in that ruined cottage in the fields.

To get back to the harvests. In the same way that the man broadcasting the seed was a sight that would soon be vanished for ever, so, on some farms, where the Lord of the Harvest led his men with their scythes, they were, too, the last of a dying race. First the ordinary reapers had come to take their place. These were simple cutting machines, drawn by two horses, that mowed the corn and left it lying in swathes for the women who followed the reaper to pick up and tie in sheaves, which they stooked, ready for the men on the waggons to cart away. The reaper, however—although it is still used on grassland—had a very short life on arable land, for it was quickly succeeded by the self-binder, which, drawn by three horses, both cut the corn and then, conveying it into its own belly, tied it up with binder twine and spewed it forth in regular rows at regular intervals. The self-binder was the last perfection on the farms of my childhood: and the next and, up to now, the final development in the harvest fields has been the Combine, which is, really, a little factory on wheels: and quite unsuitable for our small fields, though it is excellent in the great expanses of Canada and America.

Harvest which, to the farmer, was the apotheosis of his year, and was looked forward to, with the happiest anticipation by everybody whom I knew, was always clouded for me by the realisation of what happened at the end of it. As I have related before, I rode on the horses pulling the binder and, when the day's work was done, rode one and led another down to the river to drink and then home to their stables: but every circuit that the binder made of the dwindling corn brought the thing that I dreaded nearer and nearer.

The smaller that square of corn standing in the middle of the field became, the larger grew the crowd of men and boys and girls with great sticks in their hands and loud laughter on their mouths and lean lurchers at their heels. All the less reputable people from Angel Square and Benton Street and The Green and the Bessels congregated on the field when the square of uncut corn in the middle became very small. And there was a horrid air of expectation over everything. There was a hush and a silence as the binder went on round and round, round and round, reducing the standing corn all the time. In that everdwindling square of corn the rabbits were waiting, eyes ablaze with terror, their little sides heaving up and down with their ghastly breathing . . . as the binder and death came nearer and nearer.

All day long what had been their home had been falling about them and all day long they had crept further into the standing corn away from the noise of the binder, the clonketyclank, clonkety-clank and the heavy, unhurried regular tread of the horses that, to these little beasts, must have shaken the earth. And still, all day long, they crept further into the corn until they were huddled in a quivering mass of dozens and hundreds waiting—and maybe they knew it—for death.

The ritual was always the same. At some stage when the noise of the binder had almost paralysed them with fear and the square of standing corn had become no bigger than a tennis court, the rabbits were able to see through the few remaining rows of corn to be cut. Before them they saw open country and the friendly hedges where were their burrows and the paralysis of fear gave place to an urgent need to run and run and run. Always one rabbit only broke cover first and always the rest of them, terrified, hearts thumping, eyes ablaze, followed that one who had taken the first plunge.

Then was all hell let loose, as the dogs went into action and the men and the boys and the girls, armed with their great sticks, ran after the rabbits who, had there been only one or two men after them, would have escaped: but now, no sooner had they dodged one than another and another and another appeared, knocking them on the head with their sticks. Those few who escaped the men were caught by the lean lurchers.

When the butchery was over, the men and boys and girls went round the field collecting the rabbits. They chucked them all in a great heap in a corner of the field. Some of them had only been stunned. Some had only had bones broken. The eyes of these still looked out, terrified and afraid, as the men with their pocket knives slit dead and still living down their stomachs and pulled out their guts, which the lurcher dogs ate. Sometimes, one saw, if one was not afraid and ashamed to look, the eyes of a rabbit, that had had its guts torn out, looking for the last time on a world where he had always been afraid . . . of the foxes and the stoats and the owls and the weasels and the shiny traps of the farmers and the wire-snares of the poachers . . . and the inexorable noise of the binder.

. . . . .

When the sheaves had all been carted from the fields one sheaf was left standing in the middle and, until that, too, was taken away, the field was still 'out of bounds' to the public. This single sheaf was left standing to show that the horse rake had not yet been over the field. In the days before the introduction of the self-binder, when men and women followed the reaper and tied the loose stalks of corn in sheaves, a tremendous lot of the crop was left behind and the horse rake pulled this all into long narrow lines across the field, to be carted later.

The self-binder meant that there was less wastage: but still quite a considerable amount of stalk was left with the ears full of corn. Mostly this was rather short stalk, which the binder had failed to pick up, so, until the horse rake had been over the field and the rakings carted away, a sheaf was left standing to warn the gleaners not to go there.

As soon as the final sheaf was removed, the gleaners came in dozens. I don't think I ever saw a man gleaning, for the very old men, who could have done with a few ears of corn, were, by the time they gave up work, too crippled with rheumatism to be able to stoop and pick up the bits of straw the rake had missed, but the women and children came in numbers.

They generally made a day of it, bringing some bread and cheese and cold tea in bottles and moving from field to field as they systematically combed each one. The real experts brought buckets and sacks. They cut the ears of the corn off the stalks and put those in the buckets. When they had got a good bundle of stalk, they crushed it up and shoved it in the sack. In this way, some of them were able to get enough corn to keep two or three chickens the year round (and the chickens were better fed than they are on all this manufactured stuff today) and enough straw for the nest-boxes and for the tame rabbits which, at this time, seemed to be kept by almost everyone of the poorer householders in the town.

Rabbit-keeping in Hadleigh was, in fact, during and just after the 1914 war, the main hobby and occupation of the working people just as, in the north, all the miners used to keep whippets. The rabbit-keeping must, I think, have been more profitable than whippet-keeping, because, apart from the money prizes to be won at Village Shows for miles around, the rabbit skins were worth money (a man named Chandler, who lived at the bottom of Tinker's Lane, made his whole living, apparently, by dealing in rabbit skins) and the rabbit, after the skin had been sold, made a good meal.

And they *were* rabbits in those days! There were Flemish Giants, with lop ears, weighing between twelve and sixteen pounds. There were Belgian Hares, which looked exactly like the hares one saw in the fields but were not hares at all, being rabbits! There were English rabbits, which were white with black or brown spots on them, the spots being arranged symmetrically or the rabbit was no good for show purposes. Dutch rabbits, which could be black and white, blue and white or brown and white: but the division between the two colours must be clear-cut, quite straight down the middle. Angora rabbits, that had fleeces which were six or eight inches long and had to be combed out every day, and the combings kept until there was a pound or two when they were sold for quite a good sum. The Angora rabbits had to be kept in warm places, because, with their long white fur, they could not be bedded on straw

Peyton Hall

which would get stained with urine and discolour the fur, so they lived on wire netting bases and their droppings fell through the netting and did no harm. Blue Beverans were just coming in. They did not become really popular in Hadleigh until after I had gone to school.

Without the gleaning, it would not have been possible for the poorer people to have kept the same number of rabbits or, indeed, chickens and pigeons and guinea-pigs, for nearly every cottage had some kind of livestock then, just as nearly every cottage now has the radio and many of them the television, and there are fewer and fewer hours spent in the sheds at the back where, when I was a child, you could always find the man of the house.

Harvest, with the gleaning and the Harvest Festival, was not quite the end of the year, because the farmer now had to sell his corn and, to do this, he had first to get it threshed. So far as I can remember, Percy Nunn from Whatfield was the only owner of threshing tackle at this time, though, a little later, both Arthur Emeney and Edwin Clarke, returning from the war, set up as threshing and ploughing contractors; but, of course, to do that was a very expensive business as both threshing and, increasingly, ploughing was being done by the old traction engine. In threshing only one engine was used. For ploughing two engines were needed, one at either end of the field. A steel cable, on a thing like an enormous cotton reel, connected the two engines and the plough, which had five, I think, ploughshares on it, was dragged up and down the field on the cable. By the time I went away to school, Mr. Waller was using this steam plough on his big fifty-acre fields on the Aldham and Whatfield roads, and though we did not know it then, the days of the horses were already numbered.

The threshing machine is, of course, still in use, though now most of the old steam engines have been scrapped and petrol or oil engines are used, while men standing on the corn stack feed the sheaves into the drum of the threshing machine where, miraculously, the grain goes into one compartment, the husks or chaff into another and the straw is bundled out on to an escalator that, being adjustable, can tip the straw at whatever height it is required. Thus, throughout the day, the corn stack dwindled and the straw stack grew bigger and bigger. Sometimes the men let me go on the stacks with them, but they were not very enthusiastic about it, for although they did not have to move fast, they did have to keep up a rhythmic swing with their two-pronged forks, and if a small boy got in the way, he was likely to get a nasty cut with the sharp prong of a fork.

The escalator, at this time, was operated separately from the actual threshing machine which worked the drum and was worked by one of the older horses—usually Short or Kitty—who, left entirely alone, walked in an eternal circle all day (like the horses at Felixstowe when they pulled up or let down the bathing machines into the sea). The circle round which the old horse moved was a very large one indeed, so that there was no danger of the poor thing getting giddy. But it was a very sad sight to see this kind of hopeless and endless mechanical movement by a creature of flesh and blood.

The times of threshing varied from farm to farm. There being so few threshing machines, the little farmer (who, probably, had no storage space either) had to take the machine when it suited the contractor. If the job was only going to take a day or two, he fitted it in when he was at another farm in the neighbourhood (for it was a costly business moving threshing tackle along the roads) and that meant that, with little or no storage space, he had to sell his corn as soon as it was threshed at whatever price was ruling in the Corn Exchange at the time. This very inequitable system meant that most of the little farmers remained little farmers all their lives. A few of them made a success of their farms: but, later on, when the depression came and successive governments let the farmers down, most of them went bankrupt.

Things were very different on a big farm such as Peyton Hall: and, at one time, when prices were not what was expected, I was told that no barley was threshed there for three years. At the end of that time the price of barley boomed. A message was sent, post-haste, to Mr. Nunn and the threshing tackle was there in double-quick time. The result was a profit of many hundreds of pounds, while the smaller farmers, who had been forced to have their grain threshed whenever the contractor was ready to do it, had, many of them, sold at a loss.

So, in the four or five years that I went to Peyton Hall, I was privileged to see each year's work through all the seasons—the ploughing, the sowing, the harvest, the threshing: the root crops and the kale on which the sheep were folded: the mating of animals and the birth of the young animals and, sadly, the slaughter of those whose only reason for being was that they might be slaughtered.

They were happy, happy years: so that today I can still tell you the exact order in which the horses stood in the stables and the cows to be milked in the byre, yet as in everything, tragedy was closely linked with all the joyous and golden hours: for little Mr. Waller himself, who had, with such ruthless determination, such singleness of purpose, saved the money to buy Peyton Hall, had little pleasure in it.

In middle age he became a depressive and, as the years went by, his periods of depression became longer and more acute so that, for nearly all the time that I knew him, he sat by the fire, weeping hopelessly on his very bad days, interminably reading the dictionary when the days were not so black.

There was in those days nothing to help him. Electro-convulsive therapy had not been discovered and insulin was still only used for diabetics. His last attack lasted, I am told, almost exactly five years—and then, one morning, Mrs. Waller told me he suddenly announced he would have two boiled eggs for his breakfast. It was the first time for years he had shown any interest in his food. After breakfast he went out in the yard. By the end of a week, he had been over every acre of the land that he had hardly seen and had not considered for years. He was alert and alive, the same self that had, years ago, determined, come what might, he would be a farmer.

It was not very long after this, while he was still in full and happy possession of his faculties, that he had an accident in his mill. When they got him home in a tumbril drawn by old Short, they did not need Dr. Everett to tell them he was dying.

But it is good to think that, after all the struggle and suffering, he had some weeks given him at the end when he was once more a young man as he hurried about his fields, seeing that gates that had been broken were mended, that hedges that were overgrown were cut back and that Peyton Hall had become the place he had dreamed of when he courted his bride half a century before in the days at Rattlesden.

8. The River

WHEN my father was a boy in Hadleigh in the 'sixties and 'seventies of the last century there was much more of what is known as 'social life' in the town than we, as children, enjoyed: and, in the same way, the social life that we knew forty years ago would astonish children of today by its variety and abundance.

Children of today are accustomed to such things as motorcars and television sets and travelling by aeroplane. No house seems complete without a radio set but all these things were either unheard of or in their infancy before I left home for school. As we had never had them, we could not have known what we were missing. But, anyway, we never had time to 'miss' things or to be bored with things. The days were never long enough to cram everything into them that needed to be crammed and the nights—especially in the summer, when we camped out—were full of excitement.

My father had been the eldest son and fifth child of a family of thirteen. If my grandfather had not died at the early age of forty-seven, he would probably have had more children, though he could hardly have equalled the remarkable record of *his* father, my great-grandfather, who sired twenty-three children (by three different and successive wives), seventeen of whom lived to be old people.

Naturally, I never knew my grandfather, who died in 1877 and my grandmother died two years before I was born, but, from all accounts, in their short married life of less than twenty years, they were wildly gay and wildly extravagant and bore absolutely no resemblance to the Victorian parents whose prototype is Mr. Barrett of Wimpole Street. Both of them coming from families renowned for their longevity, they can never have had any forewarning that my grandfather was to die as a young man, leaving a hopeless muddle behind him for his young widow, with children varying in age from eighteen to two, to disentangle.

My father was about seventeen when my grandfather died and the hard times that he and his brothers and sisters had to go through after his death, never eradicated in him an indifference to money that he had inherited from his parents. His habits would have been, had he been able to indulge them, very extravagant. He loved books and pictures and good furniture. I am sure that, all through his life, he never wore a suit or a pair of shoes that had not been made for him. As he grew older and poorer, I think he grew more and more puzzled by the world and the ever-changing values of money and the ever-changing habits of people. He found it quite impossible—in his last years—to understand why it was impossible for children attending the primary schools to walk there. For anything over, I think, two miles, the Education Authority paid for a bus to go round and fetch them in the morning and deliver them again in the evening. If, by any chance, a child lived in an out-of-the-way place where the bus, for some reason, could not go, the Authority provided the child with a bicycle, free, gratis and for nothing.

These bicycles, like all things given away free, were subject to very rough usage. At about the time that my father died, just after the 1939 war, I knew one boy who had, in five years, been supplied with three bicycles.

To my father, remembering his own schooldays, that proved that there was something wrong somewhere: for, as he told me, he, as a boy of eight years old, had ridden his pony, daily, winter and summer, the eight miles to the school in Dedham that he first attended and, in the evening, the eight miles home again. When he was a little older and went to Ipswich School, he rode his pony backwards and forwards daily.

His ingrained extravagance was an extravagance not only of money, when he had it, but of strength and spirit and generosity. He squandered his life (though he lived to be nearly ninety) by giving more of himself than was necessary to all kinds of causes. When he took any action, he took it not only spontaneously, but, as soon as he knew what was needed of him, he dropped every other pursuit and went bull-headed. Besides his practice, in which he was always single-handed and which covered about a hundred and twenty square miles, he was, at one and the same time, Chairman of the Urban District Council (this for twenty-five years), a Magistrate, for about the same period, Correspondent of the Church Schools (both boys and girls), Churchwarden, Chairman of the Grand Feoffement, a member of the Council of Panel Doctors, a Governor of Sudbury School, and a member of innumerable committees whose concerns ranged from archaeology to Anglo-Catholicism. All of these activities were unpaid and, indeed, all of them cost money in the time that he had to give to them.

Yet, in addition to all this, he found time to be President of the Bowls Club and there was hardly an evening in the season when he was not to be seen on the green behind the 'White Lion'. He was Vice-President of the Cricket Club and attended their matches regularly on Saturday afternoons, though, I believe, cricket bored him intensely and he only went there because he wanted to see Hadleigh win. For years he was Chairman of the Committee that ran the Deanery Fêtes and the Athletic Sports and he even visited all the local Agricultural Shows and the meetings of the Fur and Feather Society.

Add again to this that he was a great reader. His day started with the *East Anglian Daily Times*, which kept him informed of anything that he had missed in the county itself. From the *East Anglian Daily Times* he moved to the *Morning Post* (and what an outcry there was when that magnificent organ of opinion was absorbed by the *Daily Telegraph*!). After lunch he read the *British Medical Journal* or *The Lancet* or *The Church Times*. When he had finished his rubber of bridge in the evening, he took up his serious reading—archaeology, Church history, the autobiographies or biographies of leading Churchmen, the *History of the Great War*, in God knows how many volumes, the pseudo-scientific outlines of H. G. Wells, he ploughed through

The River

the lot! And only after he was seventy, in the last twenty years of his life, did he take to fiction.

This happened in a most extraordinary way. When Thomas Hardy, the Wessex poet and novelist died, his obsequies followed a somewhat dramatic and, to many minds, not altogether tasteful pattern, for, after the heart of the dead poet had been removed, his body was cremated. The ashes were buried among the poets in Westminster Abbey: but the heart was sent back to be buried in the Dorset he had lived in and loved.

Cutting Thomas Hardy to pieces could not upset a man who had performed hundreds of post-mortems, though my father did intensely disapprove of the publicity and drama which attended all this. And he also disapproved of the burying of the ashes in Westminster Abbey, because, so he understood, Thomas Hardy, though a fine poet and novelist, had been an agnostic. And my father was a very devout, though never a militant, Anglo-Catholic. His saints and heroes were Edward King of Lincoln, Charles Gore, Lord Halifax and William Temple (though he could not approve of Temple's politics) and he was convinced that none of these people could possibly approve of the burying of an agnostic in the Abbey. But, with typical fairness, he set about reading Hardy's novels, starting, as it were, at the top and going downwards: that is to say, starting with *Tess* and *Jude the Obscure* and ending up with *Under the Greenwood Tree* and *Far from the Madding Crowd*.

He had, of course, never been to Wessex, which differed in every respect from his beloved East Anglia, but he was captured entirely by and surrendered completely to Hardy's novels. After that, he read modern novelists with great pleasure. He read Hugh Walpole—whose father, the Bishop of Edinburgh, he had known—and disapproved strongly of them: but he went on reading him. H. G. Wells, Arnold Bennett, the impossible George Meredith, Philip Gibbs, all came as grist to his mill and, in the end, he joined a fiction library and drove the librarians nearly mad by changing his books so frequently.

The only way in which he got through all this work and extraneous business and pleasure and bridge and reading was by living, for all the time I knew him, to a rigid time-table. His life was—so far as a doctor's can be—entirely governed by the clock. He rose at exactly the same time every morning. He had his meals (except luncheon which was very movable) at exactly the same time. He spent exactly the same number of minutes on the bowling green every evening. His bridge was so arranged that it finished almost exactly at half-past nine: and his bedtime was the same every night.

Yet, somehow, he managed to teach his children to ride bicycles, running beside us, although he was between fifty-five and sixty at the time, as we wobbled down Holbecks Lane. And, when the annual Athletic Sports took place every year, he insisted that we all competed in them (a thing which none of the children of the other professional classes did) and coached us, in races round the churchyard, before breakfast. These before breakfast outings were things which we learned to dread: but they could not be avoided. No matter how cold the weather—nor how wet—at seven-thirty we set out with our dogs—the chief of which was a St. Bernard, named Bruce—who were taken to the river for a swim. After that we trudged drearily halfway up Holbecks Lane where, when we reached a certain tree, we were turned about and, getting as far on the road home as Toppesfield Bridge, set off at a gallop, dogs and all, until we arrived, out of breath, on our own doorstep.

As though these physical exertions were not enough, he also taught us to row. Although, in his childhood and boyhood his own parents had had a boat on the river, we never owned a boat, as our house had no river frontage: but the little lazy Brett was still the scene of much activity and we were allowed, whenever we liked, to borrow the Deanery boat. It was in this boat that we learned to row. And a heavier, more cumbersome craft it would be difficult to imagine.

In the early days our activities on the river were bounded by Mr. Alderton's mill, which was just beyond Toppesfield Bridge to the south, and Mr. Cocksedge's mill, which was just beyond the Iron Bridge to the north. Boating and fishing still being among the recognised activities of many of the townspeople, the river was regularly cleared of weeds and, in those early days, there was no trouble from the discharge of waste matter from the factory known as the Brett Works. But not many years were to pass before this became a very serious threat to the amenities. First of all, the river began to be coated with brightly coloured slime, which presently began to stink and then the fish died and

The River

floated, bellies upwards, on the surface, and finally, even the buttercups and the rushes in the meadows on either bank began to fade and wilt.

The factory, naturally, had everything in its favour. The nuisance began during the war and was, rightly, blamed on the war: and, as we were all filled with patriotism, we suffered the spoliation of our river if not in silence, then with resignation, assuring ourselves that, as soon as the war was over, the factory would stop spewing all that muck into the river and the fish would return.

But, unfortunately, it never happened like that at all: for, by the time we were celebrating victory, nearly all the boats on the river had been left for so long in the boathouses that they had begun to rot: and as, for most people, life had become much more earnest and difficult than it had been before 1914, the boats were left in the boathouses and the river was deserted.

At the same time, I must make it clear that it was only that stretch of the river, below the Brett Works, that was affected. This was only a very short stretch, but it was the part that concerned us and concerned my father particularly as he remembered the time when nearly every family in the town had had a boat on the river. When we first took out the Deanery boat, however, that and the boat from Toppesfield Hall and one from Hadleigh Hall and one that Mr. Scarfe's daughter, Mona, owned—a much more up-to-date craft than any of the other three I have mentioned—and the canoe belonging to Eily Gayford were the only craft on the navigable part of the river between the two mills.

This part of the river was very beautiful. The river itself ran exactly parallel with the High Street and the east bank of the river was, from Toppesfield Bridge to the Brett Works, bounded by the gardens and orchards of Toppesfield and the Deanery and the Hall. Beyond the Hall lay that abomination, the Brett Works, but beyond that again there were the greenest and most beautiful meadows I have ever seen. All year round they kept their greenness unless they were covered with snow in the winter, while, in early spring, they wore the dazzling gold of the kingcups which were succeeded by the equal gold of the buttercups. Each bank of the river was lined by pollarded willow trees: and, on the west bank, there were cattle grazing:

and I particularly remember two Alderney cows that had a very superior brick-built cowshed. I do not know—I never knew—to whom these cows belonged. There was no farmhouse near them. The nearest habitation of any sort was the cottage in the Brickfields where the head brickmaker lived, but I am sure he did not own those cows.

Another most interesting thing on the west bank of the river were the osier beds, where, in the hunting season, hounds regularly found a fox. The osier beds belonged to Mr. Markwell (I believe his family still owns them) and sometimes I would go and watch Mr. Markwell and his men cutting the osiers, which were as pliant as whipcord. When they had cut all they needed or all that were ready for cutting, they were carried into one of the large sheds that adjoined the osier beds. I believe they were partly dried here—though not dried so much that they would snap—and, when they were in the right state, Mr. Markwell would, with incredible speed, twist the osiers into all manner of shapes, so that what had been growing on the banks a day or two earlier, turned, almost before our eyes, into hampers and baskets of all shapes and sizes—shopping baskets, garden baskets, bicycle baskets, even hideously uncomfortable basket chairs (for years we had one in the garden that was a torture to sit in!) and anything else that could possibly be made of basket-work. In those days, before the introduction of plastics (which, incidentally, was manufactured in the early days—and still is—at Mistley, less than six miles from Hadleigh), the uses of things made from basket-work were legion and Mr. Markwell and his men were always very busy: for, in those days, no one would have thought of buying a basket from Ipswich or any other big town when they were made in Hadleigh itself.

Beyond the osier beds was a plantation of willow trees that belonged, I believe, to Mr. Charles Grimwade of Toppesfield Hall. These trees had been planted with the intention that, when they were ready, they should be cut down and made into cricket bats and, before the 1914 war, this was an annual part of the year: but that war put an end, for the time being, to the making of cricket bats, and when it was over and the manufacturers came to have a look at the trees again and mark those that were suitable, they found that, with hardly any exceptions at all, the trees had grown too big and tough and hard to be of any use. A very few were marked and cut down: but the rest were left there. As the years passed they fell down—for they were no use for firewood, being dangerous things that spattered sparks in all directions—and were left there to rot, so that the last time I was that way, the plantation presented a sorry sight.

I mentioned Mr. Charles Grimwade just now and he, along with my father's cousin, Willy Evans of Ely, were the last two of the old type solicitor that I remember. They both, when I was a child, had only just given up wearing top hats every day. But they still wore them on Sundays. They both had all their letters copied by hand and kept in great presses. The offices of both were remarkable for the traditional dust and apparent muddle. But the muddle can only have been apparent to the uninitiated, for both Mr. Grimwade and cousin Willy were most competent people with tremendous reputations for soundness and integrity, which continue today in their firms.

Mr. Charles Grimwade, who was a little short red-faced cherubic man, drove about in a brougham, drawn by a single bay horse. He had a large family of sons and daughters; the eldest son succeeding him in the practice. When I was a child, I heard of a very kind and imaginative thing that he did. Like all Hadleigh people, Mr. Grimwade believed firmly that there was no place in the world that was the equal of Hadleigh, and he pitied anyone greatly who, by force of circumstance, was forced to leave our little community. People who went of their own accord were fools. There was, however, one exception, in Mr. Grimwade's eyes, to this rule. Years earlier a man from Hadleigh, named Bacon, had been ordained and 'gone for a missionary'. I think that he went first to India and then to China. Periodically, he came home and stayed with his sister who lived in a remarkably gloomy house in Church Walk. On these visits, Dean Carter regularly invited Mr. Bacon to preach in the parish church, when he would tell us all about his experiences as a missionary and how badly more missionaries were needed: and the collection at this service was always given to Mr. Bacon to help him to build a new church or buy a lot of medicine or anything else that his people would need.

Now, all this seemed very excellent to old Mr. Grimwade, but the more he thought of it the more awful it appeared to him that Mr. Bacon, a Hadleigh man, should have no stick nor stone in Hadleigh. True, Miss Bacon had a house in Church Walk. But Mr. Bacon himself had nothing and was giving all his life to making Christians of Indians and Chinese. Mr. Grimwade thought—he was convinced—that if Mr. Bacon had some roots in Hadleigh, he would not feel so lost and remote in those dreadful places where he spent his life. So, with great kindness and generosity, he gave Mr. Bacon a large field, that was let, first, to one of the Aggises and then to Eric Slater. The rent was now paid to Mr. Bacon, though everyone was pretty sure that he spent it buying more necessities for his people. But Mr. Grimwade was well pleased, because Mr. Bacon now had a permanent root in Hadleigh.

On the west bank of the river were also the brickfields. These, I believe, belonged to Mr. William Wilson and, as children, we were taken sometimes to watch the bricks being made. It seemed to me a singularly boring process, so I took little note of it, but I mention it here as a further example of how, only half a century ago, a small town like Hadleigh was almost completely self-contained. There were brickmakers and glaziers and maltsters and coopers and wheelwrights and farriers and blacksmiths and horsebreakers. There were basket weavers and stay-makers and milliners and tailors and dressmakers. There were millers and farmers and brewers: and Mr. York, the Bank Manager who preceeded Mr. Gale, even coupled the business of managing a bank with the job of 'manure merchant'. This has always seemed to me a very odd thing that, in those days, when the roads and the lanes and the fields were covered with horse-droppings, it should have been necessary to have a 'manure merchant'. So I have been forced to the conclusion that Mr. York was the predecessor, in his own small way, of Fison's and I.C.I.

I remember Mr. York coming to tea. He was a tall, rangy man, of well over sixty, made taller by wearing a top hat. He had grey sponge-cloth trousers and a double-breasted frock-coat, such as Sir Winston Churchill sometimes wears. He sat and had nursery tea with us and let drop, in the ordinary course of conversation, that he had just walked to Bury St. Edmunds and back. We had, of course, all been to Bury St. Edmunds, which was twenty-two miles there and twenty-two back: and we wondered how many days Mr. York had taken for this

The River

amazing achievement. A little later in the meal we heard that it had all been done that day: for Mr. York had left at five o'clock in the morning and had reached Bury at half-past ten. He had then 'done a bit of business', and walked back. When he left us after his tea, he announced that he would walk round Layham Church (about four miles) to give him an appetite for his supper.

We did not believe him: but my parents told us it was all quite true. What with Mr. and Mrs. Rand driving their donkeys to Newmarket and Mr. York walking to Bury and back, they were giants in those days!

We were allowed to take the boat to any part of the river between the two mills and, after my father had been with us three or four times, he apparently thought we were all quite safe, because he never came with us again and no doubts were ever expressed as to our chances of running into danger, though, at this time, none of us could swim. It never seems to have occurred to either of my parents that some of the things we were doing might easily have led us to all sorts of disasters. Fortunately, they never did: though once my brother, who was of an inventive turn of mind and had been given a box of chemicals 'safe to use in the home', caused quite a considerable explosion and burnt off all his hair and his eyebrows.

But this singular belief that we, as a family, were immune from all kinds of disasters to which the rest of the world was subject—for, I am convinced, it must have been just this—brought my father into conflict with the Government over the matter of poisons.

For a long time the new Panel Service, introduced with stamps, by Lloyd George, was suspect not only by the medical profession, but by all the Friendly Societies (Odd Fellows, Buffaloes, Foresters, and so on) and by a very fair percentage of the public for whose benefit it was intended. My father, however, while retaining his Club, with its members, which I have already mentioned, did eventually join the Panel doctors and his surgery became, in time, subject to inspection. Actually, his surgery premises were among the best that I have ever seen, if only he could have been persuaded to use them for the purpose they were intended: for he had a magnificent waiting-room with a door straight on to the street, a very large and well-equipped dispensary and a consulting room which looked on to the garden. Rarely could he be persuaded to use the consulting room, for he had been brought up in the old school of medicine which ordered, 'Look! Listen! Only, as a last resort, Touch!' He asked questions and, as the patients were not afraid of him, he got truthful answers. But he rarely had occasion to ask a patient to undress. When that did happen, he was forced to use the consulting room: but he much preferred the waiting-room, for that, leading straight on to the street, with the door very often open, meant he could see everything that was going on, and when people passing saw he had no patient with him, they would drop in and give him all the local gossip.

The Panel Committee—or whatever it was called—did their best to put a stop to this. They had a very small measure of success. Well-meaning people, they had no idea of the pride with which country people in those days would relate their symptoms and aches and pains of the most intimate sort before a mixed audience. They simply could not understand that, to all these simple country folk, their bodies were no more mysterious than the bodies of the animals with which they worked . . . And, if there was a bit of a mystery, you talked it over, with plenty of detail, with the doctor. If there were other people in the room, it did not matter, because, if they had not been there, they would have got the full details in the street afterwards: so the well-meaning efforts of the Panel Committee, in this respect, accomplished very little. They were probably not very surprised or disappointed as they must have come across similar cases in other country surgeries.

But they did blow up about the poisons: and, looking back, I am sure they were right, though, I am equally sure that, just as my father can never have dreamed of any of us being drowned or cut to pieces under a self-binder or kicked by a horse, so he can never have imagined anyone taking a dose of any of the poisons which were kept openly on the shelves in the dispensary with all the other bottles. (Incidentally, as the house was lit by gas and there were no pilot lights, he had got into the way of knowing exactly the position of every bottle on his shelves and frequently dispensed in the dark.)

The sight of strychnine and antimony and tartar emetic and hyoscine and morphia and many other poisons jostling, cheek by jowl, with formalin tablets, cascara tablets, castor oil, syrup of figs and other less harmful agents of his trade, sent the Panel Committee nearly mad with rage.

They said nothing at the time. Maybe, they were speechless with horror. But the morning after their visit, a registered letter arrived, informing him that, unless he took immediate action and had a poison cupboard—which must be kept locked—made at once, he would be reported to the British Medical Council: and—who knows?—his licence to practise taken away.

I think his immediate reaction was one of surprise. It must have seemed to him ridiculous that such a fuss should be made about nothing: but, as the Panel Service had come to stay and as he had joined it, he supposed he had better do as they had ordered.

Now in his dispensary, which had, originally, been an enormous pantry with all the walls lined with shelves for the storing of preserves, the shelves against one wall had been left while the other walls had been stripped to make space for his desk at which (like his relation, the Reverend Sabine Baring-Gould) he always stood: and the piece of furniture, rather like a Welsh dresser without a back, where he kept his drugs. The shelves, which had been allowed to stay, contained an odd assortment of things from scales to measure out drams and minims and mortars and pestles and the stuffed head of an eagle which his father had shot in the Deanery wilderness (I wonder where it is now?) and his great-aunt's dolls and a vast accumulation of papers of archaeological or ecclesiastical or scholastic interest. Surmounting all this were some prints of St. Bartholomew's Hospital.

So, after what must have been mature consideration, my father cleared a little space at the end of one of these shelves so that the wall of the room made one end to what was to be the poison cupboard. He then, with his ruler, measured the part which he had to enclose at the front and at the other end: for the shelf above formed the top. This operation completed, he and I then went down to the stables where, very inexpertly, we cut up two pieces of wood that, we hoped, would fit in the two spaces to be filled. When we returned to the house with them, we found they did fit. Our next job was to go to Mr. Taylor, the ironmonger, where a pair of hinges with the requisite number of screws were bought, as well as a padlock with key. We had some nails at home already.

The piece of wood to form one end of the cupboard was nailed into position. The hinges were then screwed on one of the longer sides of the long piece of wood and the other screws on the other side of the hinge were screwed into the shelf which was to be the top of the poison cupboard. The flap now went up and down quite successfully and it only needed the padlock to be screwed on to the lower end of the flap and its staple on to the shelf that was to be the bottom of the poison cupboard and the job was done.

We regarded it with considerable pride and satisfaction and began to move the bottles of poison into their new home. As we were doing this, I had the misfortune to knock over and break a bottle of ammonia. The pungent smell forced me to flee and run outside. My father who had, many years ago, lost both his sense of taste and that of smell in an accident, had, for a moment, the last very faint sensation of smell he was ever to experience, until he, too, was compelled to leave the dispensary because his eyes were watering.

He had, however, got his poison cupboard and duly reported this to the Panel Committee. They appear to have been satisfied. At any rate, no one ever told them that the key of the padlock that closed the cupboard had its permanent home on the mantelpiece of the waiting-room, where it shared this honour with a bust of my great-grandfather that had at some time lost its nose, the family crest, a clock that kept very erratic time and a dreadful collection of foul pipes.

. . . . .

Boating in the Deanery boat was, to our minds, a somewhat dull business: and it was certainly very laborious, for the boat was heavy and the weeds, year by year, grew more luxurious and we had explored again and again the reaches of the river between the two mills. There were, besides, times when we were forbidden to go on the river. One of these was the disappearance of an elderly gentleman in the town (who, I believe, never was traced) and there was a not unnatural feeling of alarm that we might come across his body in the rushes. Nor were we allowed to take the boat out when there was an angling competition, though single fishermen we disregarded. And if the *East Anglian* announced that there was to be a meet of the otter hounds on any part of the Brett near Hadleigh, the boat was definitely taboo; so that, eventually, we grew tired of it and my brother, who was much more of a handyman than myself, built himself a canoe of plywood and canvas, in which he paddled in those parts of the river that were beyond the bridges. In this canoe he travelled many miles, but I do not remember ever going with him, because at about this time I took up fishing with my friends, Mr. Emeney (who kept the second-hand bookshop and collected rates and rents) and Mr. Stephenson, the undertaker.

. . . . .

This sudden and most unexpected enthusiasm for fishing had its genesis in the discovery of my grandfather's and uncle's rods which had, many years ago, been stowed away in the lofts over the stables. Before the soldiers with their horses took over the stables, we had never been specially interested in all the junk that was stored in the lofts: but as, at the beginning of the war, all this stuff had to be shifted to make room for the hay and the corn, endless possibilities were exposed.

I can remember the fishing rods perfectly, although I was never, in the true sense of the word, a fisherman, for they were exceedingly beautiful things which had all the suppleness of the willows that grew on the banks of the river. After I had found them and pieced each one together and tried my hand at casting a fly on the lawn, only to get the end of the rod hopelessly caught up in one of the Spanish chestnut trees, I asked my father if I might learn to fish. Could he teach me?

This, however, was too much for him to undertake. Nor do I know if he had ever been a fisherman. I doubt very much if he had, for in his younger days his tastes and habits were of a more vigorous kind. But if he could not—or would not—teach me to fish, he did what turned out to be a far better thing, for he suggested that I went to see Mr. Fred Emeney.

'He'll teach you all you want to know', my father told me, but whether he meant about fishing or something else he did not enlighten me.

Mr. Emeney lived at the very bottom of High Street, at No. 128, which was opposite the large house in which Mr. Maitland Mason, the miller, who was also an artist, lived. Just beyond Mr. Emeney's house the High Street forked left to Kersey and Lavenham and Bury St. Edmunds and right to forgotten little villages as Whatfield and Aldham and Elmsett. At the junction of these three roads, standing fair and square to the High Street, was Mr. Hazell's blacksmith's shop, from which, when I lay in bed at home in the morning, I could hear, as early as five o'clock, the clink of hammer on anvil. It was to Mr. Hazell's that I had regularly ridden Diamond and Captain and the other horses from Peyton Hall to have them shod and seen Mr. Hazell rip the old shoes off them and pare their hoof and, heating the new shoes over the forge fire till they were red-hot, hammer them into shape on his anvil and then, after plunging them into his tank of water to cool them, put them to the horse's feet.

You never had to *wait* for a set of shoes to be made at Mr. Hazell's, for, knowing all his customers as well as Mr. Elliott, the bootmaker, knew his human ones, Mr. Hazell made their shoes, as it were, in advance, so that, except for the short time taken in the actual fitting, there was never any waiting at The Forge. If there had been, Mr. Hazell would have lost many customers: for time meant money to the farmers and the aggravating, but quite natural, thing was that the horse's shoes always wore out more quickly at the busiest seasons of the year.

Waiting with the horses at the forge, I had often looked in Mr. Emeney's window, but, until my father himself suggested it, I had never been into his shop. The window and its contents were of interest, for lying in rows, with their spines at the top, there were numbers of books, gradually getting faded by the sun, so that the gold of the titles were washed out and it was almost impossible to tell what the names were. Lest one should be in any doubt about what Mr. Emeney sold in his shop, there was a piece of cardboard on top of the books, on which the single word, BOOKS, was printed in capital letters and in red.

The front door was to the right of the shop window: and, on my first visit, I made the mistake of opening the door and walking straight in, as one would in any ordinary shop. I soon saw that this was no ordinary shop, for the door led straight into

The River

Mr. and Mrs. Emeney's 'front room', which was the epitome of gracious living and the result of much satisfactory hoarding.

Let me try to recall some of the objects between which one moved, with such circumspection, in this room. There was a large square table in the middle, which may have been of a polished mahogany had one been able to see either the top or the legs, but it was covered—shrouded might be a better word —with a heavy green cloth that reached to the floor and that had a fringe with little green and red bobbles on it. Round the table, their seats pushed in under it, were six tapestry covered chairs: and, against the wall, was a Recamier shaped sofa, covered in the same kind of cloth. This sofa had been turned into another storing place for books which, in their piles, reached halfway to the ceiling.

There were against two of the other walls cabinets of some inlaid material which had, it transpired later, been taken over by Mr. Emeney in lieu of outstanding rent or rates from those of the people he called on who had got into arrears. No doubt they were well worth the consideration.

The mantelshelf had, as its centre-piece, a marble clock of a singularly modern design, flanked at either end by glass cases, one of which housed a couple of red squirrels and the other a kingfisher. At other convenient places in the room there were other glass cases. These contained preserved specimens of some of the mightier fish which Mr. Emeney had caught, from time to time, in the Brett. There were a lot of flower stands with ferns on them and, incongruous among the dead squirrels and kingfishers and fish, two very lively canaries. I had been told that canaries only sang when kept in solitary confinement. This is quite untrue, for Mr. Emeney's canaries sang all the year round except when they were moulting. The walls of this room were, I suppose, papered, for distemper had not yet been accepted as a covering for walls, but it was impossible to tell with what they had been papered, for every square inch was covered by water-colours, mostly views of Hadleigh, by local artists who made up in quantity what they lacked in quality. Their sense of colour, too, was particularly strong, for never has there been such green grass, such blue skies, such red brick and such grey stonework. At any rate, the room could not have been called dull.

Finally, in a thing shaped like a drainpipe—it may have been one—were several dozen walking-sticks, carriage whips, riding crops, and umbrellas. A number of fishing rods stacked in the corner by the door that opened into the street, showed that Mr. Emeney was a devotee of the piscatorial art.

On this first occasion that I entered this room, I was too bewildered to take in the full splendour of its furnishings. I remember that, for a moment or two, I really did not know what to do. Should I just stand there and wait for someone to come to see me? Or had I got into the wrong house, for this was no bookshop? I felt very nervous and self-conscious, as though I had secretly penetrated into a private part of Mr. Emeney's life: and I would willingly have turned and run home, had I not realised that, if I did that, I should only be sent to the same place another day, when, probably, I should be faced with the same dilemma.

So, hoping that no one had heard me, I backed out through the front door on to the street again and, closing the door behind me, I rang the bell. I remember hearing it jangle a long way away and, after a long time, Mr. Emeney himself came to answer it.

I had, of course, often seen Mr. Emeney in the street as he walked up and down with what I can only describe as a *measured* tread that must, I am sure, have put a mighty dread into the hearts of the rent and rates defaulters. In his smart brown suit, with his brown boots and his brown trilby hat and his pearly tie-pin stuck in his reddy brown tie, Mr. Emeney appeared the very embodiment of reasonable property. And I use this word 'reasonable' advisedly, for there was nothing flamboyant about Mr. Emeney. He could never have given anyone the idea that he was not a man with the same troubles as his victim. Rent and rates, his reasonableness proclaimed, were abominable things, but, my dear sir, they were reasonable things as well and you, as a reasonable man, must know how reasonable it was to pay them. Thus, no matter in what straits the family was on which Mr. Emeney, in the course of his business, had to inflict his presence, I am told that it was a very rare thing for him to have to report failure. The rent and the rates were nearly always forthcoming and the contents of Mr. Emeney's own house increasing. He obliged, by removing the defaulter's pieces of furniture, with the greatest condescension and good humour so that, as they saw the little rosewood card-table being trundled away on a barrow, they—one and all—realised how singularly lucky they were to have such a decent fellow, such a reasonable fellow, as Mr. Emeney to collect their rent or rates. Other less human collectors might have let the thing go to Court, with all the added expense and publicity, instead of paying the bill himself and taking that trumpery bit of furniture in exchange.

I have said that, in the streets, Mr. Emeney wore a brown trilby hat and I suppose that, on this first occasion, seeing him for the first time in his own house, I did not expect to see him wearing a hat at all. Whatever I may have expected, I remember that his appearance surprised me, for Mr. Emeney at home —though still neat, save as regards his headgear—was a marked contrast from Mr. Emeney in the street. The clothes he wore were of the oldest. The suit had been new perhaps twenty-five, certainly twenty, years earlier and had, through the decades, fulfilled its various purposes. Originally used only for visits to Ipswich or to funerals and other occasions like Edward VII's Coronation festivities on Holbecks Park, it had, after ten years or so, come into use for the regular business of rent and rate collecting. Worn every day—and a large part of every day was spent *sitting* in it—a certain shininess had developed which, with an undeniable bagginess in the wrong places, relegated it to the suit in which to attend sales. This may seem an odd thing to the uninitiated who will argue that, as everyone for miles round knew Mr. Emeney and his circumstances, what difference did the age or quality of his suit matter when he appeared at a sale, hoping to get a bargain. But the matter did not appear in such simplicity to the wearer of the suit. In his utter reasonableness, Mr. Emeney told himself that his rival bidders at sales must be influenced to a certain extent seeing him in such poor clothes and, even if the extent was only a matter of shillings saved, it was worth it.

After some years of attending sales, the suit that had once graced the Coronation festivities was taken over for garden wear—for digging and hedge cutting and sawing wood—and it was, in this its final state, that I saw Mr. Emeney at his door on this first visit. As I say, I was surprised. But I remember that I was much more surprised at his headgear, for the splendid brown trilby had been discarded and the good man now wore the most disreputable of cloth caps. Later, I was to learn that, when Mr. Emeney was parading the streets in his brown trilby, his wife, who was a dim little woman who lived somewhere 'at the back', wore the cloth cap. She handed it back when her husband came home and removed his trilby, for Mr. Emeney was completely bald—as bald as the late Alfred Drayton—and went in mortal terror of catching cold. I used to wonder if Mrs. Emeney wore the cloth cap when her husband was out, so that it would be kept warm against his return, lest that precious cranium should suffer a sea-change from any contact with a covering not sufficiently aired.

I forget how our first, as it were, official interview went, though I am pretty certain we did not talk much about fishing, for Mr. Emeney, treating me with that deference that he might have extended to Archdeacon Hodges, ushered me into the shop which, so individual was he in his way of living, could only be approached through the front room of whose contents I have already made a catalogue.

The shop was really a kind of rather wide passage and it was precisely the same width as the window in which the notice 'Books' was displayed. Here Mr. Emeney had what, I realise now, can only have been five or six hundred volumes, but, to my delighted eyes, those humble volumes might have been the British Museum Reading Room and the London Library knocked into one. I think this feeling of the immensity of Mr. Emeney's stock came from a sudden overwhelming realisation that, if I had enough money, all these books could be mine. This must sound pretty precocious, but, maybe, in the sequel, the reader will be able to follow the reasoning by which I reached this conclusion.

Every room at home had books in it. My father's waiting-room and consulting room were book lined. The dining-room was full of books. There was a bookcase in the drawing-room. There were others on the upstairs landing. Bookshelves had been put up by Mr. Wright, the carpenter, in our day nursery and they were well stocked with all kinds of books: but it was in Mr. Emeney's draughty little shop, with its tiled floor, that the idea of possessing books of my own first came to me: and, as you will see, I soon took steps to make the idea and the ambition an accomplished fact.

That visit was only the first of many, many visits that I paid to this little shop, where, for my delight, Mr. Emeney produced volumes embellished with steel engravings, volumes decorated with woodcuts; novels of such authors as Rider Haggard, Ouida, Mrs. Humphrey Ward, George Eliot; uniform sets of 'Standard Authors', an appalling number of volumes of the dullest sermons that their authors had been justified in preserving by the astonishing demand for such reading matter in the last century; fortnightly numbers of the *History of the Boer War*; an extraordinary production, in several volumes, called *Women of All Nations*, and so forth and so on.

Not only was the number of the books to be wondered at, not only was the variety of their contents a matter of the highest gratification, but their prices were most reasonable. Book after book could be had for a penny. Twopenny books and threepenny books abounded. Nothing, so far as I ever knew, was more than a shilling: and anyone could buy six numbers of the *Boy's Own Paper* or *The Children's Newspaper* for a single penny.

Very shortly after my introduction to Mr. Emeney's shop, I had set my mind on acquiring two sets of volumes. The first was the collected novels of Sir Walter Scott in a marbled binding and with marbled tops and printed in the smallest print imaginable. This was, I think, in about thirty-two volumes and might be had—the lot, I mean, not a single volume—for a couple of shillings. The other—and, to my mind, a much more urgent acquisition—was *The Shire Horse Society Stud Book* in twenty-eight volumes from 1880 to 1907. They were enormous books and the lot could be had for one and sixpence, for as Mr. Emeney was good enough to explain, he would have to let them go cheap, as he wanted the space.

But the job was to collect the money. I believe that my pocket money had at about this time been increased from threepence to sixpence a week: but even if I went without all the necessities that could be bought at Mrs. Kettle's (which would cause comment that, for some reason, I did not want) it would take at least seven weeks to be able to buy these two enviable sets. And when one is less than ten, seven weeks is more than a lifetime. At least it was to me then: and I have no reason to suppose that it still does not stretch to infinity for present-day children of comparable age.

There was, too, another trouble: and here Mr. Emeney, with his reasonableness and his splendid salesmanship, was my undoing: for if, for a couple of weeks, I, on Saturday morning, handed him my weekly sixpence on account, sure as fate, he would, from some sack or other hiding place, whip out a little volume marked at the modest price of one penny. In this way and for this price, I acquired *The Greek Anthology*, *The Rubá'iyát of Omar Khayyam*—who, so Mr. Emeney told me (and I am sure he believed it), had lived at Woodbridge—'a wonderful rum chap, he was too—heathen, you know'—and *Lyra Apostolica*.

Another week I bought, for threepence, a beautiful book, named *Ancient Collects*. I had this for many years. It disappeared some time during the last war and I have not been able to find another copy since.

But these casual purchases—while excellent in themselves—delayed, week by week, the purchase of Sir Walter Scott and The Shire Horse Society, which still, to my shame and humiliation, took up space which he could badly afford in Mr. Emeney's shop.

Something had to be done and done pretty quickly, if I was not—as I was convinced would happen—to lose the whole lot.

I consulted my friend, Teddy Norford. Looking back, I am pretty certain that I hoped that Teddy Norford would give me the necessary cash, which goes to show what a poor judge of character I was, for Teddy Norford, for all his prosperity, had no patience with book learning.

It was he, however, who planted the seed of the idea that was, it is true, going to get me the books: but was also to get me into the most hideous disgrace with my family.

'What you want to do', Teddy Norford told me bluntly, 'is to earn it.'

It seemed useless to tell the fat little man that I could not dig, but that I was not in the least ashamed to beg. He gave me an apple, very kindly allowed me to water his ponies, staggering under the weight of the heavy buckets from the pump to the stable: and left me to work out, in my own mind, how I was to earn the vast sum of three shillings and sixpence. On one thing, at this stage, I was determined, for I had learned my lesson—I

The River

would not visit Mr. Emeney again until I had the whole three and sixpence. I knew, from bitter experience, that, if I took sixpence at a time, I should only come away with a penny volume of unreadable sermons, in a pretty binding, by an Eminent Divine, a twopenny volume of *Views on the Danube* and a pocket edition of Tennyson's *In Memoriam*.

Another friend, Hasty Double, who was at that time clerk to Mr. Cecil Grimwade, the auctioneer, and to whom I explained my dilemma, put me into the way of earning a living.

'Why not', said Hasty Double, in effect, 'pick up the money in the market?'

He did not, of course, mean I should find it lying about on the cobbles: but that I might, by acting as a porter, earn here a little and there a little.

Consequently, on Monday morning I joined the other urchins, who hoped to earn a copper or two, outside Mr. Slater's shop on the market corner. This, as I was to learn in a week or two, was the recognised spot for those who wanted to be hired to wait, for nearly all the traffic for the market came round this corner, only farmers from Layham and Shelley slipping in by, as it were, the backway past the 'Ram'. Here, outside Mr. Slater's shop, regularly on Mondays, men and boys of all ages congregated, from an ancient with one eye and, so far as one could tell, one tooth, who dribbled endlessly, to the swarming children from the Towns and Goody and Clarke families. The doyen of this little army was Drover Baker who, in the forty years I knew him, seemed not to alter a bit. Short and stocky, with a little clay pipe jutting from the corner of his mouth, always wearing a long holland coat that covered him almost to his ankles and brown boots of the 'officer type', Drover Baker must have walked tens of thousands of miles, with cattle going to market or cattle coming from market, for in those days there were no great lorries that would take a dozen or more bullocks in a load. The only alternative to using men of the stamp of Drover Baker was the railway: and this was very expensive and not always reliable. Besides, on railway journeys, horned cattle were apt to injure each other, so, on both counts, it was cheaper for them to be driven, by easy stages, from or to their markets.

The only regular exception to this rule were the bulls which, when they changed hands, travelled in state in a single-horse cattle-float. I remember one enormous grey bull, that weighed so much, that a trace horse had to be harnessed to the float in addition to the shaft horse.

Sometimes, men like Drover Baker were needed to go to the Midlands—places like Northampton and Leicester—where the farmers had bought herds of young cattle, that were to be collected on the Midland pastures, to be fattened in the yards. These journeys meant that the drovers might be away for anything up to a week, for they did not hurry their cattle—one drover walking in front of them and the other, and senior one, with his dog, bringing up the rear—letting them browse on the verges of the roads and travelling at not more than three miles an hour. Before night fell, the junior drover was left in charge of the cattle while his colleague sought information of a farmer with an empty yard. The farmers always helped each other in this way—for, perhaps, next year they might be coming to the great lamb sale at Ipswich or the sale of Red Polls and Dairy Shorthorns at Stowmarket, when this mutual aid system worked in reverse. When there was no yard vacant the farmers would tell the drovers of a meadow, not too far off the main road, and warn them of the weak parts in the hedge or fence through which the cattle might stray. When they had learned where these places were, the drovers, having driven their charges into the field, stationed themselves and their dogs at the gaps or weak parts and stayed there, as sentinels, all night.

Rarely did a bullock stray. If one did get away, it was always sought and recovered before the cavalcade set out again in the morning.

With such as Drover Baker, then, on this Monday morning, I took up my post and waited to be hired. I soon found that that was of no use at all: for, time and again, when all the other little boys and men had disappeared and were carrying chickens and rabbits or driving frightened pigs and sheep and I was the only one left and was telling myself that the next job would be mine, one of the boys, who had just had a job, would come running back on his bare feet, and, just as I saw my intended victim coming round the corner with his crates of chickens and rabbits, would rush forward with 'Here y'are, Mister', and, before the consignor of chickens or rabbits could protest, had seized the crate, dragged it off the back of the cart and, plunging his hand in among the squawking chickens or the rabbits huddled up in the corner, had them transferred from crate to market pen in no time. The crate was returned to the farmer. Twopence or even threepence changed hands and the ragged, bare-foot boy was darting about looking for another victim.

So, in desperation, seeing the morning slip away and the market filled up and myself without so much as a penny in my pocket, I began to dart about, looking beseechingly into the eyes of tough characters that looked back blankly at me, running forward to try to untie the cords that held the crates shut, only to hear a loud voice say, 'Here, get on. You 'ont untie that that way': and, pushing me roughly aside, accomplishing, as though by magic, what I should have fumbled at for ten minutes and then made a mess of it.

I was in despair. I could get no work. Worse than that, I got in the way of people who were busy. Perhaps, worst of all, was the fear that someone—some respectable person—would spot me and hurry home with the news of what I was doing, as the curate's wife had hurried home after the mating of Matchet.

At one o'clock, still without employment, I had to leave the market, for although my parents were very easy-going about the times of meals, one could not miss them altogether. At the same time, if we had something exciting or important to do afterwards, they did not make us sit there until my father, who might have been late, had finished: so, on this occasion, I excused myself with some muttered fable and hurried back to the market.

But this time, I was determined to be a success. The reason why I had failed so far was that I looked too respectable: for I had realised, just before I went home to dinner, that I was the only boy plying for hire wearing shoes and stockings. All the other boys had bare and extremely dirty feet and legs. Although there was no time for me to dirty my legs satisfactorily, it was an easy matter to get rid of my shoes and stockings.

I took them off in the churchyard and put them behind one of the loose flat tombstones. It is sad to relate that, when I returned to collect them, someone had got there first. But, by that time, the enormity of my conduct had been pronounced so utterly past excusing that the loss of shoes and stockings was but a small additional peccadillo.

Off I trotted through the Kissing Gate, past the Fire Station, to the market. But I did not trot for long. Those boys must have had feet made of steel, for never have there been such sharp pebbles to bruise and cut my own feet. The grit got in between my toes. I tried putting my feet down flat. I tried keeping religiously on the pavement, but the grit and pebbles had got there as well: and then, just as I was going to give it all up as a bad job and hobble back to the churchyard, an enormous man —whose name, though I did not know it at the time, was Barney Whyatt—seized me by the shoulder and yelled, 'Here, boy, lend a hand' and I found myself tugging and lugging and heaving at one end of a crate full of chickens, while Barney Whyatt shifted the other end as though it weighed no more than a shopping basket.

It was no good. I could not shift the thing. I was a failure in the market. I might as well go home and give up all hope of Scott's novels and *The Shire Horse Society Stud Book*.

'You can't do that', said Barney Whyatt. 'You're not big enough.'

I let go of my end of the crate. It was all over now.

But, miraculously, it wasn't.

'I ought to have got someone bigger', he said. 'Tell you what you can do', he said.

I waited.

'See them empty crates over there', he pointed to them and I nodded.

'Fill them up', he said. 'Two dozen birds to a crate. Not more', he said, looking at me closely. 'Can you read?'

'Yes, sir', I said.

'Here you are then', he told me and handed me a long slip of paper, with the auctioneer's name and address at the top and the auctioneer's receipt at the bottom: and, one beneath another, a list of numbers which, I knew from selling my own rabbits in the market, were the numbers of the pens that Barney Whyatt had bought. All I had to do—and this was simplicity itself—was collect the chickens, two at a time, from the pens carrying them over to the crates, stuff them inside and, when there were two dozen in any one crate, tie up the little opening through which they had gone.

For the next twenty minutes to half an hour I worked like a

slave. The hens were fat and heavy and determined, first, not to come out of the pens and, second, not to go into the crates. But I knew, from watching, what to do. You get them out of the pen, you lifted the door which, once you let it go, automatically dropped into the closed position again, and plunging your hand in among the birds, seized the leg of whatever you could. You dragged this screaming, squawking creature out and, as you did it, the door fell shut, so that the other chickens were still penned in.

Once you had the chicken outside you transferred it to your left hand, plunged your right hand in again, seized another leg and dragged that one out. Then, your hands full of chicken, you raced over to the crates where, sitting on the crate, you transferred the right hand chicken to your left hand which now held two chickens, four legs in all, which was quite as much as you could manage. With your freed right hand, you lifted the door of the crate and, now using both hands, shoved the squawking, indignant chickens in, shutting down the opening as soon as the chickens were inside. Then back to the pens for the next load.

I remember I lost one chicken. It flew out of the pen as I put my hand in and was last seen flying over into The Lawns garden. I did not tell Mr. Whyatt about this. No doubt, I should have done, but what was one chicken among so many?

When I had emptied all the pens whose numbers were on my list, I sat down on the last crate and waited. Presently Mr. Whyatt came rolling along the market. He was in great good humour. I do not think he was ever known to be otherwise. He slapped people on the back as he passed them, shouting greetings and having jokes, until he came to me sitting on the last of the crates.

'Got 'em all in?' he asked.

I nodded and handed him his bit of paper with the numbers on it. I wondered if I would get twopence or threepence. Thank heaven, I thought, he did not know who I was or he would not give me anything.

He looked at me for a long time. Then he said, 'I never thought you'd a done it—you're a rum young b———, you are. But you'd best get away now, or you'll be in trouble. Your dad's in 'The Lion' and do he see you doing that, he'll tan the hide off you. Here,' he added, as I was about to run away, 'here's your wages, though God knows what you want it for.' And he shoved his hand in his pocket and pushed a coin into my sweaty hand. One coin! He had only given me a penny! A penny for all that work. Still, it was a start.

'Here, hop it,' he said, 'you don't want to get caught with no shoes or socks.'

I hopped it. I limped through to the churchyard, to the tombstone behind which I had left my shoes and my stockings. They were not there. Perhaps I had gone to the wrong tombstone? So I looked behind others and I was, indeed, very troubled to lose my shoes and stockings for a miserable penny! And Barney Whyatt with all those chickens!

I sat down and pulled the penny out of my pocket. And then, miracle of miracles, it was not a penny. It was the biggest coin I had ever possessed. A half-crown! A whole half-crown! The loss of my shoes and stockings did not matter. I was more than halfway to getting Scott's novels and *The Shire Horse Society Stud Book*. . . . But Mr. Whyatt's generosity brought back very guilty feelings of the chicken that had got away. . . . Ought I, I wondered, to go back and tell Mr. Whyatt? But then, perhaps, he would ask for the half-crown back.

It was in this mood of indecision that I was found by one of our maids who had been sent to look for me: for though my father had not seen me in the market, other people had, and in their kindly busybody way had gone post-haste to tell my mother.

'The mistress wants you', said Florence Gant, who was really a very nice girl and sometimes took us to tea with her parents on her Sundays out. 'What a mess you are in! Where on earth are your shoes?'

I think I did my best to explain. I know I stuffed the half-crown away in my pocket and I remember hobbling painfully after Florence through the churchyard and through our back gates and in at the back door. I remember, too, that Florence, with great kindness, put shoes and stockings on me, before I went into my mother's presence. And then, indeed, did the heavens descend, for my mother was very angry indeed, because I had disgraced myself and gone and mixed myself up with a lot of 'common people'. I must learn to think of my father's position in the town. I must remember I was a gentleman's son and was going to be a gentleman myself. Why—here my mother grew really indignant—people who had seen me carting those chickens about in the market, might have thought I was like the Towns children and doing it for money!

After a good deal more of this, I escaped, still clutching the great silver coin in my sweaty little hand. That night, in my bath, all the skin seemed to come off my feet where I had walked on the pebbles and I could not sleep for the pain they gave me. But I was consoled and comforted by feeling the lovely silver coin with its milled edges. Before I finally went to sleep I put it in the lower part of the soap dish, where no one would look for it.

The next morning—for this was in holiday time—I was down at Mr. Emeney's early, soon after nine.

Mr. Emeney himself answered my ring at the bell and, without speaking, ushered me, ceremoniously, into the shop.

'I have not got all the money,' I told him, 'but I have got most of it.'

Mr. Emeney, I remember, regarded me for a long time without speaking. His sharp, little eyes, which had spotted many an antique in some rent defaulter's house, seemed to bore right into me, as though he would search out all my secrets.

'I saw you in the market yesterday', he said at last. 'Did the Doctor know you were there?'

I told him nobody had known I was going to be there, but that somebody had gone round to our house and sneaked on me.

Did I know who it was? Mr. Emeney said.

I was able to tell him, quite truly, that I had no idea who it was, for I had not been told, whereupon Mr. Emeney shook his head and looked very wise. He could, he said, have a guess and he would not mind betting he would not be far out. But that was as far as he would go. It was, he assured me, better that I should not know, though whether this was that he feared I might lay violent hands on the informer or not, I do not know.

Finally, he asked how much I had got: and, on my producing the half-crown, he looked at it for a long time, before he said that the price he had mentioned had been three and six and that was cutting it to the bone. 'But there,' he added, his sharp little eyes seeing right through me, 'I was always a soft one. You can have the lot for what you've got.'

I was so staggered that it was some time before I was able to thank Mr. Emeney sufficiently for his generosity: and when I had done that—for it really was very kind of him—the most distressing thought occurred and, diffidently, I tried to explain the position. How was I, I asked, to account for more than fifty volumes suddenly arriving at my home? Where could I say I had got the money from? I explained my mother would be even more angry than she was already if she knew I had earned the money in the market.

For a long time Mr. Emeney was silent. He filled his pipe. He lit it. It bubbled. It went out. He lit it again, for Mr. Emeney was, I believe, having a dreadful fight in himself. He had already, because, apparently, he admired the way I had gone to work carting chickens, sacrificed a shilling. Now he was struggling with himself as to whether he should go further and sacrifice his reputation for being a reasonable no-nonsense-about-him business man. He kept lighting his pipe and the pipe kept going out and the tiled floor of the shop became strewn with matches, while the battle raged within him.

At last, while I still stood there, worried and irresolute, I heard Mr. Emeney say, 'Leave it to me. You wait a minute', and he went out to 'the back' where he lived with his wife. I remember looking at the steel engravings and the woodcuts. I remember looking at *my* volumes—my volumes now—of the Stud Book. But were they my volumes? How could I explain how I came to possess them?

At last Mr. Emeney returned. But he did not come from 'the back'. He came in by the front door, through the front room, and I saw at once that he was wearing his brown suit and his brown hat. The suit and the hat in which he paraded the streets, the reasonable no-nonsense-about-them suit and hat: and, although his eyes were still sharp and beady like little pin-points, there seemed now to be a twinkle in them.

'Here,' he said, 'you can load chickens for Barney Whyatt, so you can load books for me. But', he added, with a kind of pawky humour, which I had never seen previously and was never to see again, 'you won't get paid for it this time.'

He pointed at the books—my books. Then he pointed to the street where, outside his door, he had drawn up his little hand-cart that had transported so many little antiques.

'Put 'em in there', he said, and waited until I, carrying three or four at a time, had got the whole lot on the hand-cart.

He then covered them with a couple of sacks, explaining that we did not want everyone to know our business. He still had not explained what explaining he was going to do to my mother when we got home.

When the books were all neatly covered, so that no one could tell what precious cargo we carried, Mr. Emeney indicated that I should trundle the cart along, while he, measuring his pace to my alternate mad rushes and full stops (for I had never pushed this kind of cart before), proceeded on the pavement.

We came at last to my home where we stopped at the front door. Mr. Emeney now dropped his grand manner and began to address me, with great servility, as 'Master Jack', and insisted on carrying the books into the hall where we piled them on the table that one of my aunts had carved from a piece of wood that had come from the ship in which Adelaide of Saxe-Coburg, William IV's Queen, had been brought to England by my great-great-uncle.

When we were pretty nearly finished and the piles of books reached nearly to the ceiling, my mother appeared. I was petrified, but Mr. Emeney, only pausing to touch the brown hat which he had, up to now, kept firmly on his head, continued the unloading and piling.

What on earth, my mother asked, had we got here?

And then Mr. Emeney told her the whole story which he must have worked out while he was 'at the back'. He had heard, he said, what a fine little chap I had been in the market, helping one or two of the old rheumaticky chaps loading their chickens —a real little gentleman's act it was—and as he knew they would not have been able to reward me for my services, and as he also knew what a little man I was for reading and such like, 'his father all over again', he had given me some books. He hoped, he said, my mother would not mind, but it was not often, indeed it wasn't, that in these days you came across a young boy with such kind intentions. And, puffing and blowing, he continued piling up the books, until, at last, he had finished and I heard my mother say how very kind it was of him and she was sure I would like the books.

'Not at all,' said Mr. Emeney, 'I'd do the same again. Good deeds like that deserve their reward.'

'Have you', my mother asked me, 'thanked Mr. Emeney?'

'Indeed, he has, Ma'am', Mr. Emeney told her: and then, before anything further could be said, he was out of the house and, with deliberation, had turned the hand-cart round and was wheeling it away. He never once looked back: and I remember feeling nervous that my mother might cross-examine me about his story.

I need not have worried. She picked up one or two of the books—the Stud Book was all on the top—looked at them with extreme distaste (she was, perhaps, remembering Matchet, the stallion and the curate's wife) and then remarked, 'What an extraordinary kind of book to give to a boy. I suppose', she added crushingly, 'he wanted to get rid of them to make room for something else.'

It was, at that moment, touch and go whether I blurted out about the half-crown! Extraordinary books, indeed!

But I was stopped from any such indiscretions and the consequent discrediting of Mr. Emeney's story, by her telling me, 'Well, they can't stay here. You'll have to get them upstairs into the nursery.'

. . . . .

My friendship with Mr. Stephenson was not of such an intimate nature as that with Mr. Emeney: but, here again, Mr. Stephenson and I shared a secret, just as Mr. Emeney shared the secret of the half-crown with me, for it was with Mr. Stephenson that I had my most memorable day's fishing.

At the time of this expedition, Mr. Stephenson must have been in his sixties, a tallish man with a mottled complexion, a very watery eye and a nose somewhat out of the straight. He had, too, a slight impediment in his speech, not quite enough to call it a stammer, but just enough to suggest that he had only that moment come out of the 'snug' at the 'White Lion'.

Mr. Stephenson was our undertaker: and on my grandparents' tombstone in the cemetery, neatly inscribed in the bottom left-hand corner, was the name of his firm 'Downes and Stephenson'. For a long time, knowing that my grandparents lay beneath, I had assumed that the 'Downes' part was a

The River

misprint, and that the legend should have read 'Downed by Stephenson'.

Later, it was explained to me that Mr. Downes had, at one time, been, first, Mr. Stephenson's master and then his partner. When Mr. Downes died, the business had passed to Mr. Stephenson and the widowed Mrs. Downes. As though to make doubly sure of it, Mr. Stephenson, after a decent interval, married Mrs. Downes who was some thirty years his senior. At the time that I went fishing with him the former Mrs. Downes and the present Mrs. Stephenson was a little over ninety. I do not think she had been out of doors for years. The only glimpses I ever caught of her were through the uncurtained dining-room window, propelling herself round the room by holding on to the backs of chairs. Whenever Mr. Stephenson spoke of her it was with a kind of reverence, as though he had not yet got over the shock of finding himself the husband of the widow of his late master. He had, as it were, gone up in the world: but, unfortunately, he had failed to keep both feet firmly on the ground. For there is no doubt about it, but that Mr. Stephenson liked the bottle.

In Hadleigh, when I was a boy, a very large number of the men—and a smaller number of the women—had this failing and only in exceptional cases were they thought any the worse for it. Nevertheless, there were exceptional cases: and I am afraid that poor Mr. Stephenson was one of them.

He was forgetful, so that coffins did not always arrive at the right times, and had to be sent for, when we had the exciting spectacle of Mr. Stephenson driving his beautiful grey hackney at full pelt down the High Street, with the old-fashioned coffin carrier bumping along behind, as he hurried to keep some forgotten appointment.

Perhaps the worst performance Mr. Stephenson ever put up was at the funeral of a very distinguished member of our community. The most stringent precautions had been taken that nothing should go wrong. The coffin had been delivered in good time. The mutes had been warned and issued with their ill-fitting frock-coats and top hats. Makin had had it drummed into him again and again that the hearse and six carriages would be wanted. The bell had been tolled at the right time. The Dean and the Curate had conducted the first part of the service in the church and a solemn procession had then formed up, in which were representatives of the Urban District Council, the Freemasons, the various Friendly Societies and, of course, the family, for the mile-long journey to the cemetery.

Here, with the company solemnly assembled round the open grave, the undertaker's men stood ready to lower the coffin to its last resting-place, while the Dean read the Committal sentences. At the appropriate place the boards beneath the coffin were pulled aside and the undertaker's men took a hold on the cloth bands which were secured round the coffin, so that they could lower it gently into the grave. They waited, holding these cloth bands, for the coffin, deprived of the support of the boards beneath it, to give a pull as it began to descend.

But nothing happened.

Dean Carter, still reading the service, made frantic signs with his hands to indicate that, by this time, the coffin should be out of sight.

The undertaker's men did their best. They gave the coffin a poke and a push. One of them tried to shift it with his boot. The result was disastrous. The smaller end of the coffin, where the dead man's feet were, slipped into the grave and was only pulled back with difficulty.

At last everyone realised that some hitch had occurred, which had better be left to be sorted out by the grave-diggers, and the undertaker's men afterwards. So the service, with the coffin still above ground, came to its end. The mourners, the members of the Urban District Council, the Friendly Societies, the Fire Brigade and all the rest of them left the cemetery. Only Mr. Stephenson and his hirelings remained standing, puzzled, at the graveside.

It was, at that moment, that Mr. Stephenson took his white silk handkerchief out of his black silk hat and a piece of paper fluttered to the ground. Mr. Branch, the cemetery superintendent, retrieved it and handed it back to Mr. Stephenson, who, peering at it from his watery eye, suddenly announced in a voice of considerable relief:

'Well, that explains it. I must have sent you the wrong measurements. I've got his here.'

Thus, the matter having been satisfactorily explained, Mr.

The River

Stephenson and his men set to work to enlarge the grave which had been dug for a corpse two or three inches shorter.

I have mentioned Mr. Stephenson's grey horse and it was this magnificent animal which was the immediate cause of my getting to know its master: for it was, I think, with the exception of Lady Alexander's Monarch and Margot and Edwin Cooper's high-stepping hackney of which he was secretly afraid, the finest carriage horse in the town. It was not a thoroughbred hackney, being too tall, but it had splendid action and carried its head perfectly, better, I think, than Lady Alexander's Margot, for Stephenson's horse—which was the only horse I knew that had no given name—was driven without a bearing-rein, the sight of which, holding Monarch's and Margot's heads unreasonably high, used to distress me.

As I say, it was this horse which effected my introduction to Mr. Stephenson: for one day he drove up to the Post Office, opposite our house, left the horse standing outside and went in to transact his business. Whatever the business was, Mr. Stephenson was a mighty long time and, presently, having regarded the horse from our dining-room window, I went out into the street the closer to observe its finer points. In this way, ten or fifteen minutes passed until, presently, I peeped in through the glass door of the Post Office. There was no sign of Mr. Stephenson. Indeed, there were no customers at all. I must, I think, have argued with myself that, perhaps Mr. Stephenson was on the telephone, for I went in and asked Miss Ellisden, our postmistress, where he was.

Miss Ellisden, who *rustled* in black satin and a magnificent coiffure, told me he had left twenty minutes earlier: so I went out again and stood waiting by the grey horse, who by this time was getting restive.

Still no Mr. Stephenson . . . and the horse was stamping his front legs in a very restless way. Perhaps, I thought—for I had heard of Mr. Stephenson's forgetfulness—perhaps he had forgotten the horse. In that case, the best thing I could do, the *only* thing I could do, was to drive the horse back up the High Street to its stables. So, having no fear of horses, even so magnificent a horse as this one, I climbed up into the four-wheeled dog-cart and took the reins. It had been my intention to turn the horse and cart round in front of the Post Office, but, though I tugged hard on the right-hand rein, nothing happened: and the splendid grey horse moved sedately to the top of Church Street, turned to the left and then, at a pretty stiff trot, took me all the way round the churchyard. When he got back to Church Street, he turned left again, turned right at the obelisk and broke into a canter, which soon became a gallop, till he swung into Mr. Stephenson's yard and stopped dead outside his stable. Luckily I had hold of the dashboard or I should have been shot over his head.

This was the first time I had met a horse with a mouth like iron. Later, I was told that Mr. Stephenson drove him in a port bit. But, port bit or not, I had not driven him at all.

So far as I remember someone presently came and took the horse and asked no questions as to where his master was, simply remarking that he had probably forgotten him—which, indeed, proved to be the case—and I went home, pondering on the hardness of the horse's mouth.

That evening, my father told me that Mr. Stephenson was most obliged to me for taking his valuable horse home and, as a reward, if the morrow was fine, he had invited me to go fishing. Would I like to do this?

Yes, I most certainly would: and at some time the next morning Mr. Stephenson, driving the grey horse, arrived at our house, where I was waiting for him, fully equipped with rod and basket and another basket of food, in case Mr. Stephenson had not brought any.

'What's that?' he asked, as I proceeded to stow my things away.

'Our dinner', I said.

'You won't want any dinner', he told me. 'I have got the dinner, a special one. You leave that at home.'

I remember I longed to ask him what the special dinner was: but, obediently, I took my own basket back into the house and dumped it in the hall. Then I climbed up into the high cart and took the seat next to Mr. Stephenson. Watching him drive, I began to understand why I had not been able to guide or steer the grey horse yesterday, for Mr. Stephenson was forced to hold one rein in each hand and he kept the horse on the bit all the time, using so much energy and concentration that he was quite unable to make any kind of conversation.

The River

We went down the High Street, past the blacksmith's, over the Iron Bridge and up Gallows Hill, where the horse condescended to walk. At the top of Gallows Hill, however, the road begins to descend the long slope of Porters Hill, and there are wonderful views (now spoiled by the erection of a lot of Council houses) over Aldham and Whatfield and Kersey. But with this horse in the shafts there was no time to look at views, for he set off at a canter down the hill, Mr. Stephenson tugging hard at both reins, and myself clutching to the back of the seat. Presently Mr. Stephenson was able, for a moment, to get both reins into his left hand and jab on the brake. The suddenness with which he did this brought the grey horse almost to his knees and me almost over his head: but, somehow, we both kept in our places and, the brake locked on the wheels, got to the bottom of Porters Hill.

'Too much corn', Mr. Stephenson remarked affably: and, at the bottom of the hill, pulled the grey to a stop, while he produced a flask from his pocket, uncorked it, put it to his lips and gurgled rapturously.

'Cherry brandy,' he explained, 'finest thing for a cold morning', which seemed an odd thing to say as it was the middle of August and very hot. I remember, however, that I was most concerned and worried as to what was going to happen when we got to the very steep hill that led down to Semer Post Office. This was known as 'a dangerous hill' and there had been several accidents on it and if the grey decided to treat it in the same way as he had Porters Hill, our hours were numbered.

But, as there was nothing I could do about it and I was entirely in Mr. Stephenson's hands and he, it appeared, was entirely in the horse's hands, I tried not to think of it and to sit up straight, proud of being behind such a fine animal.

We passed the 'White Horse', known to the local people as 'The Donkey' or 'The Half-way'. We passed the corner to Kersey Church, with Mr. Mason's pretty mill set back in its orchard. We passed the Kersey and Cosford cross-roads and saw the farm where Percy Waller's shire stallion lived. We went on at a steady trot that ate up the miles until we came to Semer Workhouse, which stood at the bottom of a long, gently sloping hill. And here it was that I realised that Mr. Stephenson had also been having thoughts about that long steep hill to the

Post Office: for now, instead of letting the grey fall into a walk, as had clearly been the grey's intention, he flipped the reins on its back—he carried no whip—and kicked his boots against the dashboard and made fiercely threatening noises from his twisted mouth.

The gallant grey responded. Without breaking his trot, he came to the top of the long hill—and when we had passed the turning to Monk's Eleigh, Mr. Stephenson told me that, if it had not been for the hill we were just going to descend, he would have put a tombstone in the back of the trap 'to take the liveliness out of him'. However, the thought of the tombstone landing on top of us if the horse bolted down the steep hill had decided him against the idea; but the measure of trotting the horse up Semer Hill had certainly cooled his ardour: for now, though he did not slacken that purposeful trot, I noticed that Mr. Stephenson had not to use both hands on the reins and altogether everything was very much relaxed.

So it was that, when we reached the top of the hill, he pulled the horse up, put on the drag and, as sedately as if we had been one of Makin's own turn-outs, reached the bottom and the little brick bridge that goes over the Brett that here is so tiny.

On the bridge we stopped for a little while Mr. Stephenson got out his flask and, when he had gurgled away a bit more, announced that we were nearly there—and, sure enough, in about half a mile, he turned the horse into a farm gate into a meadow where we descended and, while I was unloading my rod and basket, Mr. Stephenson had the horse out of the shafts, his harness off him and, putting a headstall on him, turned him loose in the meadow.

'Will you catch him again?' I asked, for I was beginning to have a very great awe for this horse who, it seemed, mostly went his own way.

'Indeed, I will', said Mr. Stephenson. 'As a matter of fact, I don't have to catch him, he'll come when I call him.'

So, leaving the horse and carrying my rod and basket while Mr. Stephenson carried *his* rod and basket, we walked across the meadow until we reached the river bank. Now here the Brett is really no more than a stream, so that grown men can walk across it without getting wet above their waist: but, in the shadows under the roots of the ancient willows, there used, in

The River

those days, to be plenty of fish sleeping and it was here that Mr. Stephenson proposed we should have our lunch before the business of the day started.

He selected a suitable tree and set about 'laying the table', for I remember he had actually brought a cloth which he laid on the grass and then proceeded to cover it with the food he had brought.

And what food there was!

A cold chicken, cut neatly in half. Salad, with a most delicious cream, that, Mr. Stephenson said, his wife had had the secret of from her grandmother or some equally remote person. And bananas and grapes and a box of sweets and a large bottle of whisky for Mr. Stephenson, 'just the thing for a picnic', and a bottle of ginger pop for me.

He had forgotten to bring any cutlery, which was a good thing, so we each seized our half chicken and bit fiercely into it, but we got into a bit of a mess with the salad and Mrs. Stephenson's grandmother's salad cream which, liberally spattered all over me, gave a very odd taste to the sweet. I drank the ginger pop and Mr. Stephenson glug-glugged away at the whisky and made comfortable remarks like 'this was better than measuring corpses' and that it was a good thing the whole of Hadleigh did not know this little spot or the place would be crowded with people who had made fishing a business.

That, I remember, was what Mr. Stephenson had against his fellow fishermen—that many of them had made it a business—and I thought of Mr. Sisson and Mr. Gregory, our fishmongers, and old Mr. Rand, who had had the donkeys, and I could not reconcile the business of their shops with any business that might be conducted on this bit of river.

But, by this time, I think I must have been too full of chicken and ginger pop and grapes and sweets that tasted of salad dressing to pay much attention to what Mr. Stephenson was saying, until, at last, I heard—as from a great distance, so sleepy was I—him announce that it was about time we got to work.

We packed up the remains of the lunch—except the whisky and the ginger pop: and Mr. Stephenson, his face, by this time, almost puce, his eyes watering freely, the impediment in his speech troubling him more than ever, led me a little higher up the stream where, he announced with both authority and generosity, I should find the best fish.

As for himself, he would take the lower reaches: and, with this fine gesture of self-sacrifice, Mr. Stephenson left me to assemble my rod, select my bait and get on with the business of the day which, according to himself, must be never allowed to become a business at all. And I am sure that had he returned to watch my progress, Mr. Stephenson would not have been disappointed at the way I was behaving, for, having got my rod together—and it was far too weighty a rod for a small boy like myself—I lay down on the bank, the better to digest the chicken and all the other good things.

I watched the dragonflies and I remember seeing the lazy fish lurking in the shadows: and, once or twice, the thin line of bubbles that showed an otter was swimming under water. I noticed, too, that the fish which, I should have thought, would have panicked at the presence of the otter, did no such thing. They simply froze. Even their tails, which had, up to now, been moving gently from side to side, stopped altogether, until, from their beginning to move again, I guessed the otter had passed.

Sure enough, she had: for, as I lay there so silently watching, I saw the dark, sleek, almost black body, dripping with water, come out on the far bank of the river and, for a moment, she stood there, long and low on the ground, with the water dripping off her and the sun lighting up her dark body, so that it sparkled like diamonds, until, across the meadow, in little dashes and then freezing quite still, another otter—much smaller—came to join her.

It was charming. It was very beautiful, as the two otters, their lips drawn back as though they were laughing, began gambolling and playing on the river bank. They chased each other backwards and forwards. They leapt over each other and gave each other playful little nips. They—in that summer afternoon on the river bank—had not a care in the world, while the little boy watched and the fish slept and the grey horse—when I could see him from the corner of my eye—grazed on the lush grass.

And then, in a moment, there was a fearful splash and an inhuman stuttering yell and the otters had gone as though they had never been there and the fish had fled and the grey horse had his ears pricked.

The River

I jumped up.

I looked for Mr. Stephenson: but he was not where we had had lunch. There was no sign of him on the bank. What had been the splash then and why had the otters fled and the fish disappeared and the horse had his ears cocked?

It was then that I saw him, struggling in the water and he gave then another of those stuttering cries. Even as I saw him, Mr. Stephenson managed to struggle to his feet and the fear I had felt that he might be drowned was dispelled, as I saw the water came no higher than his middle. But, for all that, he continued to shout for assistance, and I ran to help him, though there was little a boy of my size could do to get him out of the water.

When I reached the bank opposite him, Mr. Stephenson was groping at the roots of the trees, trying to find a way to pull himself out, but he never had much success for he could only use one hand, as, in the other, he was still clutching the now half empty bottle of whisky.

In the end—but I don't remember how—he did get out of the stream and lay down with the greatest good nature in the sun to dry his clothes.

From time to time he took a swig at the whisky and his spirits returned as he pledged me to secrecy, for, said he, it would never do if Mrs. Stephenson knew he had fallen in the river. She would be worried to death that he caught a cold.

Cold, he repeated, and, indicating the bottle, assured me it was the finest thing in the world to keep out a cold.

It was evening before the whisky was finished and Mr. Stephenson's clothes were sufficiently dry for us to go home.

But, by that time, the grey horse had given us up as hopeless and had disappeared. We stood on the side of the road, hopeless and disconsolate, and were very lucky when a farmer driving into Hadleigh gave us a lift.

Mr. Stephenson promised he would collect the rods and baskets the next day: but I was not to say that, in case I was misunderstood.

I didn't.

9. Church

YET, with all these excitements and distractions of those early years, the thing that took precedence over everything else was the Church: for the Church was always, day and night, with us. Living almost in the churchyard our waking and sleeping hours were regulated by the chiming of the quarters and the striking of the hours themselves.

At seven-thirty every weekday morning the bell was rung for Holy Communion. At six o'clock every weekday evening it was rung again for Evensong: and it rang at intervals all day on Sundays and Feast Days. Living so near the church we always heard the Passing Bell and could tell, before we ran out into the street, if it was tolled for a man or a woman. We heard the muffled peal as the Old Year was rung out and the glorious crash of sound that welcomed the New Year that was so full of promise. On special days in the year bell-ringers assembled from distant parts of the county and, for hour after hour, the bells thundered out over the old town, so that their echoes were caught up in the ancient roofs and tossed hither and thither and the whole world was a medley of glorious, delirious sound.

Today there seems to be some kind of prejudice against church bells and I have heard people say the sound of them makes them depressed and morbid: but, to me, the ringing of bells is the purest, most entrancing music, taking me back, in memory, to those winter nights when I *forced* myself to keep awake, so that I might hear the farewell to the Old Year and the joyous greeting to the New.

Oh, the resolutions that, in secret, I made on those long ago New Year's Eves: and the remorse and the tears that were shed as, one by one, they were broken!

But the Church was more than the bells just as it was more than home and Peyton Hall and Whatfield Rectory and the excitement of the market and the different excitement of Mr. Emeney's bookshop: and, in this chapter, I will try to recapture some of that faith and wonder that was mine as a small boy and of which so much has been lost today.

So I remember that first solecism when, at my own earnest entreaty, I had been allowed to go to Sunday School on the afternoon of Christmas Day (for children of our class did not, as a rule, go to Sunday School) and I sat among all the other children, stuffed with Christmas dinner, while Dean Carter stood among us in the nave.

'And what', he asked, in that silver voice of his, 'was God's gift to us on Christmas Day?'

And in the silence that followed, while all the other children were looking at their feet, I heard myself say 'Turkey and Plum Pudding'.

But that was not the answer at all: and my shame was boundless, so that I never went to Sunday School again: for, afterwards, when we were out of the church, after the Dean had explained what God's gift had been, the other children surrounded me and mocked me with their repeated cries of 'Turkey and Plum Pudding', as though I were the only one of them who had had those things; as, indeed, I was, though I had not known it.

Our whole home life was centred round the Church, for my father had been reared in the full fervour of the Tractarian Movement, that had been hatched, under the chairmanship of a Hadleigh rector, Hugh James Rose, in the library in the Deanery Tower: and I feel that I must, at this point, try to show, however inadequately, how near, as a child, I felt myself knit, not only to the ordinary people of the Hadleigh of the present, but to the legendary people of the Hadleigh of the past.

And this was not as difficult for me as it may sound, for my father had been over fifty when I was born: and his father had had for uncle that sea-captain who brought Queen Adelaide to England and who had, as a young man, fought under Nelson on the *Victory*. My seven-times-great-grandfather, who had been Archdeacon of Norfolk, was the son of a man who had fought with his king at Naseby and that man's mother had been the daughter of Sir Richard Grenville who went down in the *Revenge*. My father's room was hung with portraits of these people and prints of their various exploits, so that, through hearing so much of them and always seeing them on the walls, they became much more *real* to me than my living relations who were away in such places as Rugby and Tunbridge Wells.

But much, much more real than the presence of these ancestors of mine was the presence—an almost tangible presence—of the great men of our town. Of these my father spoke with a greater pride than of his own forbears and it was the memorials of these in the church to which, when I was very tiny, he introduced me.

First among these—in the Lady Chapel (known then as the South Chapel, for fear of any hint of popery)—was the carved bench end showing the wolf holding in its mouth the head of the martyred King Edmund, after whom our Cathedral city is named. And the story goes—and those who lived in the ages of faith never doubted it—that when the boy king, St. Edmund, had been martyred by the Danes in, some say, Hoxne Woods and others on Sutton Heath, and after the Danes had withdrawn, his faithful subjects came to carry away the body to give it Christian burial. The King had been shot to death by the Danish arrows and then he had been decapitated: and the English could not find his head anywhere.

They had, indeed, almost given up hope and were ready to depart with only the torso and limbs to be given Christian burial when, through the trees, they heard a voice calling, 'Here! Here! Here!' So, half fearful and wondering if it might not be a trap set by the Danes, yet not daring to disobey the summons, they went in the direction that the voice came from: and they had not gone very far before, through an opening in the forest, they saw a wolf trotting towards them, bearing something in its mouth. And some there were of them who would

Church 151

have shot the wolf out of hand: but there were others who restrained them, seeing that the wolf showed no fear and advanced resolutely towards them.

And it was only when this fearless wolf came right up to them that they saw that it carried in its mouth the head of the royal martyr. Then, indeed, did those who had wanted to shoot the wolf thank God that their hands had been stayed in time, as the wolf laid the head of the king at their feet and, making an obeisance, faded away into the forest, to become immortal as St. Edmund himself is immortal, so that, to this day, Suffolk boys and girls who wander courting in the Hoxne Woods or on Sutton Heath have no fear of any wild beast.

There may be other representations of this act of piety than that on the bench end in Hadleigh Church: but this is the one I knew best from seeing it as a child and hearing the story of that long ago day.

Then there is Guthrum, the King of the Danes: and he, my father told me, had been the real founder of our town, because, as far as was known, before Guthrum settled here, there was no town at all. Whether that is true or not—and anyone's guess is as good as anyone else's—the fact remains that the first recorded mention of Hadleigh tells how it became the burial place of Guthrum. Guthrum had been a Danish king, into whose camp at Eddington, you will remember, King Alfred had penetrated, disguised as a harpist: and, sitting there, as far away from the light cast by the leaping flames as he could, he listened while the Danes, full of good food and drink, discussed their plans for battle.

When the Danes were all asleep, the harpist Alfred crept away into the night and made his plans accordingly, so that, in the great battle that followed, the Danes were defeated and Guthrum was captured, and, on condition that he laid down his arms for good and became a Christian, his life was spared. More than this for, when King Alfred saw how sincere he was in his acceptance of the Christian faith, he made him King of East Anglia: and, according to Asser, the Monk of St. Davids, who wrote the Annals of that time, Guthrum took the name of Athelstan, when he became a Christian: and he first ruled over the East Anglians after the martyrdom of the holy Edmund. The death of Edmund took place in A.D. 870 and, fourteen years after his own baptism, Guthrum died at Hadleigh 'in SUFFOLCIA, ubi palatium ejus erat: obiit ibique sepultus est'—which means 'where there was his palace and there he died and was buried'.

In the church at Hadleigh they will show you a great and ornate tombstone that, for centuries, has been known as Guthrum's tomb. It cannot, of course, be his actual tomb, as it was put up at least four to five hundred years after Guthrum's death: but there is no reason why it should not have been erected as his memorial in the prosperous Middle Ages when Hadleigh was a centre of the great wool trade. At any rate, the importance of our little town does really stem from the time when the Danish king-convert made it his home and it became a royal town that was to be of undiminished importance for nearly a thousand years.

In the church, too, there is a memorial—a kind of palimpsest on bronze—to Dr. Rowland Taylor, who is quite the most famous of all Hadleigh men, for here he was Rector in the reign of Queen Mary Tudor and, for his intransigent protestantism, he was martyred. I think, from all I have read about him, that Dr. Taylor must have been a most lovable and holy man, of the world of men to which St. Francis belonged, but I am afraid that my childhood's memories of this great man are entirely dominated by the periodical descents on the town of various extremist Protestant societies who, first of all, regularly slipped pieces of paper into our letter-boxes, assuring us that, as there were candlesticks on the altar in our church, we were heathen and idolaters: and that our dear Dean Carter was neither more nor less than a Roman: and that, if we weren't careful, Rowland Taylor's blood would have been shed in vain.

On occasions, too, these people had the impudence to hold a kind of drumhead service in the nave of our church. Be it noted that they would not go into the chancel, for fear, one supposes, of being contaminated by such Popish things as the cross and the candlesticks! Be it noted, also, that such were their manners that, like the Rector of Aldham who had said mass in the church in Taylor's day without asking permission, so they, borrowing a leaf out of their opponent's book, never had the manners to ask permission of the present Rector. Having been allowed to finish their service, unmolested and undisturbed, having made the most slanderous allegations against the present incumbent, these good people—for good they were—though disgustingly bad mannered—marched, with fearsome banners flying and more pageantry than had been seen in Hadleigh since their last visit, through the streets to the place of martyrdom a mile outside the parish on Aldham Common.

Here more tub-thumping took place, though to a diminished audience, for the place of martyrdom could only be approached up a steep hill and many of the weaker brethren had fallen by the wayside: and various resolutions were passed, a whacking great tea was eaten on the verges round the memorial and the beano was rounded off by an orgy of handshaking, which—so the Church people always maintained when I was a child—was the surest sign of 'Chapel'.

I realise that I was and am still very prejudiced against these militant Protestants: and I think my prejudice in those days was largely engendered through sheer jealousy, for it seemed to me that these 'foreigners'—and precious few local people took part in these affairs—were trying to steal Rowland Taylor from us and make him a part of a bigger, less lovely, less comprehensible 'movement'.

When there was no one else there and all the flag-wagging Protestants had gone home, I went myself to visit Dr. Taylor's stone which stands in the middle of a ploughed field off the Hadleigh to Ipswich road. At the time that Dr. Taylor was martyred, this place had been part of the common land of Aldham: and, soon after his death, a rough unhewn stone had been laid on the site on which these words had been rudely cut:

'   1555
D. TAYLER in de
fending that
was good at
this plas left
his blode.   '

For nearly three hundred years this was the only solid memorial to Dr. Taylor that his townspeople had erected. They had, however, in another and very beautiful way, shown their veneration for this previous Rector, for, in July 1729, a resolution was passed that 'the land be not ploughed within a rod round Dr. Taylor's monument'.

This and the 'rude stone' seem to me a more fitting memorial than the obelisk, with its rather ornate verses by a later rector, which was erected in 1818.

What manner of man, then, was this Dr. Taylor, for, from the remarkable performances of the Protestants who came to Hadleigh for their celebrations, I had, as a child, come to regard him as a kind of John Bunyan, a man as rough and unpolished as the stone on Aldham Common: and it was only after I had found a book of my father's that I got any clear idea of him.

He was *not* a rough, unhewn peasant as some of his champions would have had me believe, for he came of gentlefolk from the West Country, with an estate at Upton-on-Severn. He went to Cambridge where he studied Law, eventually becoming Doctor of Laws: and Master of Borden Hostel, which was, at that time, a part of Caius College.

His knowledge of law and his quite exceptional theological knowledge brought him to the notice of Archbishop Cranmer, who made him his Chaplain, and with whom he lived at Lambeth Palace. In 1544 Cranmer appointed him to the Rectory of Hadleigh. Seven years later he became Archdeacon of Exeter and, in addition, Canon of Rochester: and, in that year and the year following, he was one of two people authorised to hold episcopal jurisdiction in the diocese of Worcester when, for a time, there was no Bishop. Rowland Taylor held all these posts, as we should say, in plurality, though he does appear to have lived, for the most part, at Hadleigh: where, we are told, during his time the town seemed rather 'an university of the learned than a towne of cloth-making or labouring people'.

His chief characteristic—so far as his parishioners were concerned—seems to have been his abounding cheerfulness. He had, the martyrologist Fuller says, 'the merriest and pleasantest wit of all the martyrs' and he was always 'smiling pleasantly'. Somebody else described him as 'pleasant Taylor'.

He does not, indeed, from contemporary records, seem to have borne any resemblance to the awe-inspiring, dour, spoilsport conjured up by those militant Protestants who came to Hadleigh when I was a child.

His pleasant wit, his learning, his cheerfulness had procured him innumerable preferments and there seems no doubt that he would have become a Bishop but for the untimely death of Edward VI, for, however pleasant he was, however good his company was, Dr. Taylor believed in Edward VI's Prayer Book and the newly established Church of England. He was, too, by the time Queen Mary came to the throne, married and with a family.

The death of the boy Edward VI was the end of all preferment for Rowland Taylor. Though, had the King lived, he might have become a Bishop, even an Archbishop, with his name in the history books, the death of the King and the succession of Queen Mary brought him something infinitely greater and more precious, the crown of martyrdom.

For soon after Queen Mary's accession, Dr. Taylor, being in his library in the Deanery Tower, heard the bell ringing for a service. Thinking that perhaps he had forgotten this particular service (as has happened to many a parson both before and after) Dr. Taylor hurried from his library to the church to see what was happening.

To his astonishment, he found the Rector of Aldham celebrating the Mass.

For once his pleasant wit seems to have deserted him, for he and the Rector of Aldham had 'words' which were reported to Lord Chancellor Gardiner, who was also Bishop of Winchester. Gardiner ordered Taylor to appear before him 'to answer such complaints as were made against him'. With Archbishop Cranmer and Ridley and Latimer already in prison, Taylor's wife and friends begged him to escape while he could. With his family connections, it seems probable that he could have lain hidden until such time as the persecution was over. Perhaps, had he known that Queen Mary would be dead in less than three years and Protestantism would be re-established under Queen Elizabeth, Dr. Taylor might have taken his friends' advice.

He did not know this. He went to meet Gardiner, to proclaim his faith in the reformed Church of England, as set forth in the Book of Common Prayer, which, it is believed, he may have had some part in compiling.

So, undaunted, Taylor set out for London and the trial before Gardiner—with whom he argued most appositely regarding the validity of marriage for those in Holy Orders—

and his long imprisonment, his condemnation and his martyr's crown.

There can have been, among those who loved him, little doubt as to what would be the outcome of it all, for his wife and children and his faithful servant, John Hull, all accompanied him, as though they would savour every moment as though it were their last together.

The trial went the preordained way of all these trials: (In the following year his curate, Richard Yeoman, 'an old man of upwards seventy', was tried and burned at Norwich): though Taylor's 'pleasant wit' never forsook him and he does seem to have been genuinely amused by the fear he had engendered in Bishop Bonner's chaplain: for this person, when Bonner was about to deprive Taylor of his orders, begged him not to strike him on the breast with his crozier, for, said he, the devil being in Taylor, there was no doubt the crozier would rebound and strike the Bishop of London the more violently.

His little son was allowed to visit him in prison, where they had supper together and 'were merry' and the good doctor begged the child not to forsake his mother when she 'waxed old', for which, he said, God would reward him and grant him long life.

It seems to have been a kindness that was bestowed on him when his jailers allowed him to see his son: but this kindness was not extended to his wife and daughters who were not allowed in the prison at all. It must be remembered, of course, that, in the eyes of Taylor's accusers, Mrs. Taylor was no wife at all: and was, indeed, one of the chief causes of his heresy.

But husband and wife were to meet again, for when, late at night, the little procession left London on that long journey to the martyrdom on Aldham Common, as they approached St. Botolph's Church, Taylor heard, through the darkness, his wife's remembered voice. The procession halted and Mrs. Taylor and her children came out from the porch of the church where they had been sheltering. For a little, husband and wife were together—together and alone—and then Mrs. Taylor, standing back, promised that she would meet her husband again at Hadleigh. Then his servant, John Hull, lifted his son up in his arms and put him before him on the horse on which Taylor rode.

His father blessed him and, delivering him again to John Hull, said, 'Farewell, John Hull, the faithfullest servant that man ever had', and rode on into the night.

The last night was spent in the cells beneath the great Wool Hall at Lavenham and here, it seems for the first time since the journey began, Taylor was chained to the wall, while the curious came to look on him. Yet never once is it recorded that he made the least complaint or was distressed at this indignity, for he beguiled the time with pleasantries: and was unaffectedly glad when he was told that, instead of going the direct route to Aldham Common they would pass through Hadleigh: so that he would see 'yet once before he died the flock whom God knew he had most heartily loved and truly taught'.

So the long journey continued until they came at last to the bridge (where is now our 'Iron Bridge'), where a small crowd had gathered to greet him. Among them was a poor man who waited at the foot of the bridge with his five small children and who now cried out, 'God help and succour thee, as thou hast many a time succoured me and mine'. The guards tried to drive the man away, but he kept up his crying, until Dr. Taylor, shackled though he was, rose in his stirrups and bade the poor man be of good cheer, for God was with him.

They crossed the bridge and travelled up what is now High Street where people must have been at every doorstep to see him pass: and when they came to the Almshouses Dr. Taylor reined in his horse at the last of them and asked if the blind man and woman that lodged there were within. They told him they were: but would not come out for fear of being trampled by the crowd. Then Dr. Taylor, removing his glove, placed in it all the money he had left and, lest others, who were not intended for it, should get it, threw it, with unerring aim, through the window.

They came up the long hill out of Hadleigh and now there had been added to the guards and to those parishioners who loved him, all the rag-tag and bobtail of the place who had come out to see a good day's sport. There was laughter and jostling and shouting and arguing until at last they came to the Common where a stake had been erected set about with faggots and kindling.

The merriment and the weeping continued. Yet, still, Dr. Taylor seemed the merriest of them all, for suddenly perceiving one Joyce in the crowd, he called him to him and, his arms now unshackled, slapped him on the back and told him to stoop down and pull off his boots, for, said he, 'you have long been looking for them'.

At last the preparations were over and he was bound to the stake, the faggots were piled against his body, the kindling was laid against the faggots; then, as they were about to set fire to the kindling, he cried, with a loud voice, 'Good people, I have taught you nothing but God's Holy word and those lessons that I have taken out of God's blessed book, and I am come hither this day to seal it with my blood'.

As he finished someone in the crowd leapt on the faggots and struck him across the mouth, so that he drew blood. Unable to wipe the blood from his face, Dr. Taylor turned his head and asked him 'Friend, what need I of that?' and the man slunk away into the crowd and the kindling took light and began to crackle and the faggots began to smoulder and then, as the flames reached the pitch in which they had been dipped, burst into a great beacon of fire.

And while they were all watching and the flames leapt higher and higher, before they could reach the body of Dr. Taylor, a brave man in the crowd, who had concealed a butcher's cleaver under his garments, leapt through the fire and split the martyr's skull, so that the agony of the burning did not reach him.

So he died and his memorial in Hadleigh Church is in the sanctuary of the Lady Chapel where is also the wolf holding the head of St. Edmund. It reads:

    Gloria in altissimis Deo
Of Rowland Taillor's fame I shewe
    An excellent Devyne,
And Doctor of the Civile Lawe,
    A preacher rare and fyne;
King Henrye and King Edward deyes
    Preacher and Parson here,
That gave to God contynuall prayse
    And kept his flocke in feare
And for the Truthe contempved to dye
    He was in fierye flame,
Where he received pacyentlie
    The Torment of the same.

> And strongelia suffred to the ende
> Whiche made the standers by
> Rejoyce in God to see theire friende
> And pastor so to die.
> Oh Taillor were Thee myghtier fame
> Uprightly here inrolde,
> Thie deedes deserve that thee good name
> Were syphered here in golde
>
> Obiit Anno dm 1555.

But, somehow, I like to think of Dr. Taylor in his simplicity and not as an exponent of this or that creed. I like to think of him saying goodbye to his wife in the shadow of old St. Botolph's Church, for we have no knowledge that she was able to get to Aldham to see his martyrdom. For both their sakes, I hope this was impossible. And I like to think of the poor man with the five little children coming to say goodbye to him on the bridge: and I like to think of that famous throw of his glove with the money in it through the window of the blind couple's house: and of the joke he made about his boots and of that last act of mercy when his friend split his skull open and sent him to join the noble army of martyrs.

I think the solemn militant Protestants of my childhood had missed the whole point of Dr. Taylor which was his essential humanness.

And, most of all, I like to remember his joy when he heard that he would—on his way to his death—pass through the Hadleigh he loved.

. . . . .

Nearly three hundred years after the martyrdom of Rowland Taylor, the Deanery library was the scene of a series of meetings that continued for four days and, from which, the Oxford Movement had its beginnings.

And this seems to me a most extraordinary thing that the same room which was used by (with the exceptions of Cranmer, Ridley and Latimer) the most famous of all Protestant martyrs, should also have been the scene of the inauguration of the most famous and most permanent of what some people would call the Return to Rome.

Of course, it was not a return to Rome: though the most

brilliant of the Oxford men, Cardinal Newman, did become a Roman Catholic.

Hugh James Rose was the Rector of Hadleigh and Dean at the time of this meeting: and it was he who summoned it: and, although it is known as the Oxford Movement, it is, I think, typical that the convener of the first meeting should have been a Cambridge man, who was either dropped or who excused himself when the others decided that none but Oxford men should take part in the movement.

Anyway, this is all a bit of Church history which was only of interest to me because of the association of men like Cardinal Newman and the great Pusey and Keble, the hymn writer, with Hadleigh Rectory, so that, all my childhood, I regarded Dean Carter, who was our Rector, as in the direct succession from Rowland Taylor and Hugh James Rose. A previous Rector, Dean Blakiston, had been one of my godfathers: while one of my father's godfathers had been Dean Knox. Dean Blakiston has always remained a dim character, for he died after a very short stay at Hadleigh: but Dean Knox (who must, I think, have been a relation of Flurrie Knox, whose chronicles have been so enchantingly written by Somerville and Ross) lives yet, though he has been dead eighty years.

We sat in the front pew at church, with the pulpit immediately in front of and above us. The pulpit had been put up in the memory of old Dean Knox and it had a fine inscription all round it, giving details of his life and ministry. But, better than that, from our seat, as it were, in the stalls, we were able to watch closely the personal habits of the preachers. Thus old Dean Brownlow, from Bocking, had the worst-fitting false teeth in the world. They snapped and rattled and, as the sermon went on, the wet patch of saliva on the front of the old man's surplice, which had started off the size of a half-crown, spread and spread and spread until it was the circumference of a soup plate. As it was only when it got to this size that the sermon stopped, we argued that, perhaps, Dean Brownlow used his spit as a kind of hour-glass! Before my time, my Uncle Eubald, who had been curate at Hadleigh, put up the most dramatic performance in the pulpit that was ever heard of.

It happened this way.

Uncle Eubald was very much addicted to the bottle, and,

indeed, on this account, he died as a comparatively young man. But while he was in Hadleigh his sermons were frequently so muddled and incoherent that no one could make sense of them. He was, however, very popular, for he had a good eye to a horse and was always asked to all the best houses. The choir boys of that day hit on a splendid plan to add drama to the Sunday morning service: so one Sunday morning, when Uncle Eubald was due to preach, a couple of them—still, happily, with us—got into church early and rigged up a kind of trip wire at the top of the pulpit steps. By an ingenious device, they arranged that the trip wire would lie concealed against the stone steps of the pulpit until Uncle Eubald was in action.

When he was well into his stride, one of the choir boys pulled his end of the trip wire so that it was raised off the ground about a foot, all ready for the moment when Uncle Eubald should ascribe all honour, might, majesty, dominion and power to Almighty God at the end of his sermon. He had a habit then of hurrying out of the pulpit as though he were afraid the congregation might yell 'Encore' and he would have to start again.

On this occasion he had meandered through his ten or fifteen minutes and he had been—I am told—even more obscure than usual, when he came to an abrupt finish, addressed the Almighty and turned sharply to come down the steps. Today he came down even more quickly than usual, sustaining a fractured collar-bone and a couple of broken ribs. In the excitement and confusion that followed the choir boys got their trip wire out of the way before anyone else discovered it, so the true reason for poor Uncle Eubald's fall was never given to the world.

Most unfortunately, my uncle being *hors de combat*, he was unable, as was his wont on other Sundays when he preached, to retrieve the carafe of water and its accompanying glass from the pulpit at the end of service. Some self-appointed busybody did this and bustled about the place spreading the news that the water was not water at all, but good, honest gin.

Shortly after this, Uncle Eubald left Hadleigh. He was, I believe, subsequently unfrocked, but my information on this is vague, as—such is the stupidity of well-bred families—they do not talk about things like this.

At about the same time as Uncle's little upset in the pulpit, Miss Hogger was the organist. This was, of course, long before the present big organ was built, which is now electrically pumped, but, when I was a child, was pumped by little Mr. Cross. Sometimes he forgot to pump it and the thing gave out in the middle of a psalm or hymn. Miss Hogger was also one who had a taste for a drop and the story is told that, in the middle of one of Dean Knox's sermons, she was so affected by his description of the death of David and Jonathan that she, impromptu, rendered the whole of the 'Dead March in Saul'.

Dean Knox himself must have been a remarkable little man. He had no great learning and had been intended for the Church as the younger brother of the Earl of Ranfurly, an Irish peer. He was ordained, both deacon and priest, by his uncle, the Bishop of Killaloe, when he was twenty-four. When he was twenty-six Archbishop Hawley presented him to the living of Monk's Eleigh, five miles out of Hadleigh: and, at thirty-four, he became Rector of Hadleigh and Dean of Bocking and also Chaplain to his kinsman, the Bishop of Down. It seemed that, for a young man with his family connections, who had already advanced so far (for Hadleigh has been the stepping-off place for many Church dignitaries), a bishopric must be waiting.

But Mr. Knox had other ideas. He was very rich. As life went on he became richer. He liked country life. He was a fine horseman and he lived, at the Deanery, in great state.

For all that, he had his fair share of tragedy. He married twice and was left a widower twice, each of his wives leaving him with a single daughter.

Although as children we looked on the Deanery with its acres of gardens, its orchards, its river frontage and its 'wilderness' as the next thing to heaven, my poor father could only ever look on it as a wretched substitute for the splendours of Mr. Knox's time, for Mr. Knox, drawing rents from Ireland and having the fortunes of his two first wives at his disposal, kept a butler, two footmen, five indoor female servants, a coachman, two grooms and four gardeners. His horses and carriages were the admiration of the whole county. The dinners he gave lasted from five o'clock in the afternoon until midnight. There were annual dances and balls. The gardens were the scenes of fêtes and all kinds of excitements: and it was in the wilderness at the Deanery that one year a pair of eagles came to nest.

Today those eagles would have been protected, I believe, but, to his eternal shame, my grandfather—who was a famous shot—went, at Mr. Knox's invitation, one morning and bagged the male bird. The corpse was carried home in triumph and the head and both feet were cut off, stuffed and mounted and were still with us when we were children.

The bereaved eagle flew off to Holbecks where she was, I am told, caught taking a lamb and was shot by the then Sir Charles Rowley.

But if Mr. Knox lived in splendour himself, he saw to it that no one in his parish went hungry. Daily, soup and rice puddings and other foods were given away to any who came for them at the Deanery side-door. And, though I am sure, the poor people of Hadleigh must have blessed him, I sometimes wonder what the poor people of Ireland, from whom he drew his rents, thought of him.

As, during some twenty years of his reign at Hadleigh, he was a widower, he persuaded my grandmother, who was—although she had had thirteen children—a remarkably active woman, to start a Blanket Club and a Clothing Club. My mother, in her turn, succeeded to the administration of this: and I well remember the excitement as Christmas drew near and it was time for the members to receive what they had paid for during the year.

In actual fact it did not always work like this because, in times of need, the goods were generally supplied first and paid for afterwards.

The principle was that any member of the club paid in so much a week, according to her means, sixpence or a shilling. Again the principle was that, when the required amount had been amassed, a call was made on one of the drapers and the stuff was bought there and handed over to the thrifty one. There were two *Church* drapers in the town: Mr. Arnold, at the corner of Queen Street, and old Mr. Spooner opposite the 'George'. As it would have been very troublesome and required an awful lot of book-keeping to deal with both these shops simultaneously, *everything* was bought from Mr. Arnold one year and *everything* from Mr. Spooner the next year.

Mr. Arnold's was a much more up-to-date shop than Mr. Spooner's. There were wire contraptions on the ceiling, like little railway lines, along which little boxes with money in them whizzed backwards and forwards from or to the cash desk, where one or other of Mr. Arnold's pretty daughters presided. Mr. Arnold was also a churchwarden and, during the war, when it was difficult always to get tobacco, he and Dean Carter regularly came to my father's surgery after Sunday evening service and had little packets of Country Life Mixture made up for them, just as though it was medicine!

Mr. Spooner's shop was *not* up to date. There were no wires on the ceiling and Mr. Spooner himself wore a black frock-coat, black trousers, a black made-up tie and a starched dickey. He was very, very fat and he wheezed painfully. But the most memorable thing about Mr. Spooner's shop was its wonderful smell of dust and serge and 'good' cloth. It was a singularly stuffy smell, which may have accounted for Mr. Spooner's wheeziness: and it was so all-pervading that it is in my nostrils now.

When Mr. and Mrs. Spooner both died within a few days of each other, my mother was halfway through a year's dealing with the firm. Everyone wondered who would buy the shop: and everyone was suitably upset when a Mr. Connell, who had retired from a similar shop in Brighton, found retired life too boring and bought it, for Mr. Connell was a foreigner and it was wrong to see local businesses going to foreigners: and, worse than that, Mr. Connell was Chapel.

It would not have been so bad if he had been a kind of passive chapel: but Mr. Connell was remarkably active and, to crown it all, his son was in the Ministry. There was nothing for it, but to take the Clothing Club away from Mr. Connell and rely entirely on Mr. Arnold, who, at any rate, was a sound churchman.

Then, without warning, while still a young man, Mr. Arnold suddenly died and mother was now faced—so it seemed —with the necessity of buying everything from chapel people. But there is always a silver lining and it was, at this time, that Miss Norford began her attacks on her rate-paying tenants and Mr. Churchyard bought himself a new shop.

Mr. Churchyard had always been Church, but mother had

not gone much to his old shop, because of Miss Norford's habit of emptying her slops on passers-by. Now that Mr. Churchyard had moved away from Tippy Norford's house, mother could take the Clothing Club there and everything was lovely again and no one was tarred by dealing with Chapel.

Mr. Churchyard was a go-ahead chap and instead of calling his new shop number so and so High Street, he called it Albion House. No one knew why: but it gave the place tone: and it had the most enormous plate-glass windows!

As I have said, my father's whole life centred round his town, but, more particularly, round his church: and when the war came and most of the young men went away, there were only the Dean and himself and old Rule left to do everything.

The curate, Mr. Gardiner, put on a uniform and C.F. after his name and Mrs. Gardiner rented a tiny cottage in Mrs. Heckford's garden and went to live there. The organist, Mr. Hockey, who was engaged to Miss Whatling, the Police Inspector's daughter, joined up and was killed early in 1915. Miss Whatling put a beautiful pair of candlesticks in the sanctuary in his memory. There was, of course, the usual outcry from the ultra Protestants about popery, but Dean Carter stuck to his guns and got a Faculty through and the candlesticks are there to this day. Then Joseph Cheek, the Deanery gardener, joined the Suffolks and there was no sexton or bell-ringer or general handyman in the church.

Miss Maud Byers took on the bell-ringing for Sunday early morning service. Old Rule—who had been retired for years—began again to keep the churchyard tidy, though he never bothered much about the north side where, we were told, all the malefactors had been buried: and my father, to his intense satisfaction, took Cheek's place at the south door and dished out hymn books and prayer books and showed people to their seats.

While my mother and the twins continued to occupy our seat at the very front of the church, my father took his seat even behind the Misses Byers, who were so humble that they sat right at the back. It was not long before I joined him. It gave me somehow a feeling of great importance being with him at the back of the church, for, on occasion, when he was showing a stranger into a seat and I was left alone, another stranger would turn up and I had the privilege of supplying him with prayer or hymn book or even showing him into a seat.

But I noticed another thing about the back of the church, which I did not like at all. There was no singing.

Our church is a very large church and we had then a very good choir, and sitting up in the front, we were able to join in the singing, the choir leading us, without being conspicuous: but, at the back of the church, there always seemed to be a deadly hush and, if I lifted my voice, I felt thoroughly self-conscious and ashamed.

It was soon after Cheek had gone to the war that the order came that, on account of the air-raids, the church was to be 'blacked out'. In the 1939 war, when black-out was universal, many churches simply abandoned their evening services and had Evensong at three in the afternoon. I do not know what happened in Hadleigh in that war: but, in 1915, we set to work to black out the church.

There are very few stained windows and these are of such dark glass and the gas supplied by the gas company at that time was so awful that it was decided it was quite safe to leave them as they were: but there still remained the clerestory windows—thirty of them—and about a dozen of the windows in the aisles. The clerestory windows were painted over with black paint, which took years to get off when the war was over.

For the huge windows in the aisles, great blinds of some dark blue blind material were made. Mr. Spooner supplied the material. Mr. Wright, the carpenter, put the blinds on runners: and, so far, so good: but these blinds only went up to where the arches in the windows began to take shape. Above them was a great expanse of plain glass in each window, which was divided up by mouldings and traceries and goodness knows what in all kinds of intricate shapes.

There were many conferences as to what could possibly be done. At last it was decided to buy quantities of thick brown paper (Mr. Coates, the Printer and Stationer—Chapel again!—supplied it) and cut this into the appropriate shapes to fit into all those intricate patterns.

It was, indeed, a Herculean task, but, somehow, with everyone, even the school children, taking part, all these little patterns were cut out and pasted into the windows and Hadleigh Church was blacked out.

There was, I remember, a curious feeling of intimacy and solidarity about those services in Hadleigh Church in the years of the first war. Whether, as a child, one was more receptive to that kind of atmosphere than in later life or whether that kind of atmosphere has never again existed it is really not possible to say with any certainty: but, for my part, I think that there was a closeness embracing us all then, a kind of brotherhood that now, it seems to me, has gone for ever.

When I was a child in this little town of about four thousand people, I think everybody knew nearly everybody else: and I am quite sure that, although people of certain 'classes' did not do things which people of other 'classes' did, there was far less class consciousness. Nobody, when I was a child, minded calling another person 'Sir' or 'Madam'. Indeed, it was a kind of point of honour always to be well-mannered: and to give a person a title to which he may or may not be entitled seems to me only good manners.

Today, although manners are, I believe, better than they were ten years ago, the only *spontaneous* good manners seem to come from people brought up in traditions—the tradition of aristocracy or the tradition of the Public Schools or the tradition of service.

Of them all the tradition of service is the noblest: and it is also the one tradition that is common to the other two.

But, as I say, these war-time services in our church had an intimacy that may not be recaptured, for, Sunday after Sunday, the Dean read out the lists of the casualties—the killed, the wounded, the missing—and, even to a small boy, each name brought back a remembered face: a face seen in the High Street, in the market, in church: Cecil Grimwade in the market; Offie Spooner in his cycle shop; Fred Foster at the Town Hall; Joseph Cheek feeding Sally, the Rectory pig; Spot Oxford at Peyton Hall; Monkey Scarfe, the butcher's son—the lists were endless: and each name meant something.

And so, Sunday after Sunday, with the spirits of St. Edmund and Guthrum and Rowland Taylor and Hugh Rose and old Dean Knox about us in that gracious building, we knelt, in our home-made black-out, and, at the end of each Evensong, sang our final hymn, the words written by one of my own forbears, who had once had a curacy not far from Hadleigh on the Essex Marshes:

> 'Through the night of doubt and sorrow
> Onward goes the pilgrim band,
> Singing songs of expectation
> Marching to the Promised Land.'

Then out into the dark churchyard, not daring to show a light or strike a match in case Inspector Whatling came after us, as we waited for Mr. Stephenson, our blind organist who had taken Mr. Hockey's place after he was killed, to lead us home.

10. Great Aunt Mary

My Great Aunt Mary was the last of my family to live in Ely. She had been born in Ely, in The Chantry House on Palace Green, in the reign of William IV, whose Queen her uncle had brought over to England. Nearly ninety years later she was to die in a little house in the Market Place to which she had moved in, I believe, the 'nineties, when her father died and his estate was split up in fairly equal shares among the surviving of his seventeen children.

Now, in order to get the relationship between my father and his Aunt Mary into some kind of perspective, I must explain that my father's father had been the oldest son of my great-grandfather's first marriage. Great Aunt Mary was the youngest child of that marriage. So far as my father and his family were concerned, the children of his grandfather's two subsequent marriages had not really counted. For one thing, they were completely outnumbered by Family No. 1. For another, when Family No. 1 was all grown up, Families 2 and 3 were still at school or in the nursery.

When my grandfather, John Thomas, died in 1877, he left a young widow with ten children of whom my father was the oldest boy, being eighteen. His Aunt Mary was, at that time, a woman in her early thirties. She had long since given up any hope of marriage: and she lived with her father in The Chantry House, her two sisters, Catherine and Elizabeth, her step-mother Avice (who was younger than she was) and her little step-sisters, who were babies. They had the usual crowd of servants, but the social life in Ely (which was often completely isolated in winter) was centred entirely round the Cathedral, the Palace, and my great-grandfather's house, The Chantry. The Canons of the Cathedral were, at that time, all old men, who spent their months in residence reluctantly and then migrated to Bath or Cheltenham, which was just coming into prominence.

When my grandfather died, *his* father told *my* father that he was making him his heir, which was, of course, in those days of masculine domination, the natural thing to do. Consequently, my father went to St. Bartholomew's Hospital where he qualified as a surgeon and duly went into practice at Hadleigh. He was helped in this by his grandfather and I believe that, when he once, as a very young man, suggested he should leave Hadleigh, he was so vigorously opposed by his mother, that the idea never re-entered his head.

Be that as it may, I am quite sure that, once he had decided to settle there, he never regretted that decision. Hadleigh became his life, his whole life, and he was very, very happy there. At the same time, there is no doubt that he was bitterly disappointed in other ways: and it is of the culmination of his disappointment—indeed, the disappointment of all our family—that I am about to write.

My great-grandfather's third and last wife predeceased him, leaving her two children, who were subsequently married, comfortably provided for, so that, for the last few years of the old gentleman's life, he lived on at The Chantry with his three daughters—my father's aunts—Catherine, Elizabeth and Mary. For a good many years before the old gentleman died, his affairs seem to have been getting into a worse and worse tangle, though he continued to live in some state and was, apparently, quite unaware that his fortune had gradually dissipated itself. When, at last, he did die, he left my father all his settled estate, which consisted of The Chantry and one or two other houses in Ely: and what little money he had to his three unmarried daughters.

There seems no doubt that it had been his intention that my father should move to Ely and take up practice there. It was the natural thing to have done, for there was a practice ready-made. There was a house and there were the three unmarried daughters, who had always lived in this house.

My father never gave me any explanation as to why he had not moved to Ely. I think, at one time or other, he must have given his reasons to my mother and I think they cannot have satisfied her, for she always had a peculiar dislike for all members of his family.

The truth, so far as I have been able to disentangle it, seems to be that his mother was not willing to leave Hadleigh: and that, by this time, he himself had become so involved in the affairs of our little town that he would have found it hard to tear himself away. But more urgent than his own personal predilections were the claims of other people on him. Although he was not yet married, he was already keeping two households going. His mother and his youngest sister, Margaret, lived in the High Street; he lived, with his sister Nora to keep house for him, in Church Street. That, in 1907, his mother would die and Margaret would join the establishment in Church Street and that, only a year later, he would marry and both Nora and Margaret have to set up house by themselves in the New Cut was all in the future and undreamed of when The Chantry became his.

The question was what to do with it. He could not go to live there. His aunts had nowhere else to live: but they certainly had not enough money to keep themselves at The Chantry. And it did not occur to Elizabeth, Catherine and Mary that they could possibly live anywhere else. It must have seemed dreadfully unjust to them that their home should be left to this nephew. It would have been bad enough if the nephew had come to live with them in that home. It was infinitely worse that they should continue there alone, relying on his kindness and long suffering and charity.

He, too, they seem to have argued, must have seen the invidiousness of their position. And, when they realised this, they went into action. Elizabeth was their captain. She was the oldest. She also had a little money in her own right and she had, to support her, her maternal uncle, old Willie Evans, the solicitor. She wrote long and long-suffering letters. She painted vivid and heart-rending pictures of these three ladies being turned out into the world. Finally, she suggested, with diffidence at first, but later, quite bluntly, that the only gentlemanly thing her nephew could do would be to make over The Chantry to herself and her sisters. At first, I believe that this was not taken particularly seriously at Hadleigh. Many of Elizabeth's letters were not even answered: but, if it was thought this would calm down the lady's demand, a rude awakening was coming, for the electric telegraph was brought into commission and impassioned appeals for justice and fair play sped over the wires of Cambridgeshire and Suffolk to come to roost at Hadleigh.

Whatever dignity my Great Aunt Elizabeth boasted was sadly lacking in these public displays of emotion and acquisitiveness. Her own and her sisters' poverty was proclaimed to the world: until, in the end, my father made over The Chantry to his Aunt Elizabeth. Having once decided to do that, he failed to protect himself in any way. It was as though the whole thing shocked him and he wanted no more of it: or it may have been, as my mother and his own sisters averred, that Elizabeth promised to leave it back to him at her death.

Whatever be the explanation, the deed was done with all expedition and, no sooner was it done, than poor Elizabeth, as though she had accomplished her life's work, caught a chill in the Cathedral and went home and died. She left her estate in trust for her two surviving sisters: and this estate included The Chantry, the return of which to my father was not even mentioned.

Very soon after this Catherine died and Great Aunt Mary became Catherine's heir and, The Chantry being too big for her, sold it and bought a small house in the Market Square, where, with a companion and two or three servants, she lived the pleasant life that ladies used to live in Cathedral cities.

I rarely met her. On the only two occasions that I can recall with any distinctness I fell into disgrace, though I could not then see—and I cannot now see—that I had committed any great breach of good manners in either case. But Great Aunt Mary's code was a very different one from the code of the 1914–18 war years. She had not really changed her outlook since the death of her father and the middle years of Queen Victoria.

Great Aunt Mary

An example of this was the plumbing of the little house in the Market Square!

There had been none when Aunt Mary bought it. There was none when she died. As she gave large sums of money to her Cathedral and to her various charities, she never had any to spend on herself—or so she would have averred: though she kept two or three indoor servants and a companion and her stables (where there was only one fat pony to draw her old-fashioned phaeton) were crammed to the ceiling with priceless furniture from The Chantry. She never saw this furniture. It was never dusted or cleaned. The worm got in it. Some of it rotted away. But there it remained . . . a kind of trust that Aunt Mary must not touch.

She could easily have sold some of it and spent the proceeds on a bathroom and lavatory. It simply never occurred to her. She had her bath in front of her bedroom fire. She used an ornate and beautiful night commode and the companion and servants went, as we should say in Suffolk, 'out the back'.

Her house which had, if I remember aright, drawing-room, dining-room, breakfast room and about six or seven bedrooms was as crowded with furniture as her stables: and, even to my childish eyes, she exhibited an utter lack of taste. Sheraton chairs stood cheek-by-jowl with dreadful wickerwork ones that gave off frightful pops and bangs. An enamel candlestick jostled against massive silver ones. Framed pictures, cut out of *The Illustrated London News* hung alongside beautiful prints and etchings. On occasional tables in the drawing-room were mountains of seals and scent bottles and antique rings and snuff-boxes and miniatures, all—to the inexpert eye—higgledy-piggledy, but, to Aunt Mary, everything in its place.

As I remember her, she was a tiny woman with very white hair and very blue eyes and the family aquiline nose and dressed in black velvet and lace. She never *lounged* in a chair. Nor did she ever move a chair nearer to the fire on cold days or nearer the window on hot ones. Although she and her companion (at the time I knew her this woman was a relation of some obscurity) lived alone (except for the three servants) in the house, they used every room (except the spare bedrooms) every day. Breakfast was in the morning-room whither they returned, after breakfast was cleared, to read the papers and interview the cook. Other meals were in the dining-room, at a table at which a dozen could sit comfortably, except tea, which was in the drawing-room, where, after dinner at night, they sat playing patience or inexpertly playing the piano until it was time to take their candles and go to bed.

Regularly, twice a day weekdays and three times on Sundays, my great-aunt and her companion walked to the Cathedral: and regularly, throughout the day, gongs sounded in the house in the Market Place and the parlour-maid announced what particular meal was to take place.

The food was awful. Small boys can generally eat and enjoy most things, but what passed as food in Great Aunt Mary's house beggars description. Served on priceless porcelain and in wonderful glass, it was raw or cooked to a cinder. And, if it was any good, there was never enough of it.

And that brings me to the first time I disgraced myself and thereby, fortunately, missed one of Great Aunt Mary's meals.

We had, during the war, a succession of very odd curates at Hadleigh while our Mr. Gardiner was being a C.F. None of these curates stayed long. Some of them, I believe, hobbled, ungracefully, into their graves, thoroughly disillusioned with the world, the Church of England and themselves. Others disappeared after a week or two, and although we were told they had gone to the Front, other people—less charitable—suggested they had been 'sent downstairs'. I was never quite sure what this meant until Inspector Whatling one day very obligingly showed me over the Police Station. The last thing he exhibited were two horrid little cells, whose walls were made of white porcelain tiles.

'This', said Mr. Whatling, 'is where they go when they're sent downstairs.'

That, of course, explained about the curates.

One of these migratory people was a middle-aged, singularly unshaven-looking man, named Hollis, who lodged with Miss Phillips at the bottom of High Street, where other people, like bank clerks, made their home. Mr. Hollis was not a particularly decorative kind of person. My mother said he did not wash, but I suppose he was the best Dean Carter could get at the time. At any rate, he conducted the services efficiently: and he had been to Cambridge and, so far as that went, he was a gentleman.

Great Aunt Mary

He early got into the habit of dropping in at our house at about tea-time, where he would frequently meet other clergymen with whom, one remembered afterwards, he seemed to have little in common. But he still came to tea and became quite a hero with my brother and myself, for he had a motor-bicycle. I cannot now remember the make of this machine, but I believe it had an engine known as a two-stroke, and it *may* have been a Lewis.

At any rate, Mr. Hollis was good enough, on many occasions, to let my brother take it to pieces. After which he (Mr. Hollis, I mean) very patiently put it together again. When he wasn't wearing a cassock, he wore a really filthy mackintosh. I do not remember ever seeing him in a jacket and trousers!

One day Mr. Hollis announced that he was going to Ely on his motor-bicycle. Would I, he asked, like to ride on the pillion? I must tell you that they were not called pillions in those days. They were called 'carriers' and they were simply a bare bracket with no upholstery and you had nowhere to put your feet, which you had to lodge, very insecurely, on the edge of the pedal which the driver was using.

I was tremendously excited and, supported by Mr. Hollis, I asked permission to go on this trip. It says much for my parents' faith in God, the motor-bicycle and the curate, that permission was granted: and that my mother sat down and wrote to Great Aunt Mary, telling her that the curate and I (unfortunately, she did not mention the curate's name) would be coming to Ely on such a date and would do ourselves the honour of calling on her.

The great day arrived and so, soon after breakfast, did Mr. Hollis. His little motor-bicycle bang-bang-banged into Church Street and I, as well wrapped up as John Gilpin on his more famous ride, came to the door. My parents came to see us off. I must say there was a look of mild astonishment in my father's eye when he saw Mr. Hollis's motor-cycling uniform, for the good man was wearing his cassock, the skirts of which he had tied up round his middle, so that they would not catch in the wheels and, covering that, he wore his filthy mackintosh.

We got off to a good start and jog-jogged along at some fifteen to twenty miles an hour. Although Mr. Hollis had made some kind of a cushion on the iron-carrier it was extremely uncomfortable. But, worse than that, was the frightful position in which I had to hold my legs all the time. To ease them Mr. Hollis stopped every half-hour or so and I trotted up and down trying to restore the circulation.

In this way we got to Bury St. Edmunds where we had to go across the great open space known as the Angel Hill, opposite the Norman Tower of the Abbey. On this particular day half the British Army seemed to be drawn up on the Angel Hill and, had we known this, Mr. Hollis would, undoubtedly, have gone another way. As it was, by the time we saw them, it was too late to turn back and, to the concentrated horror on the faces of staff officers with the most shiny of field boots and sparkling of badges and buttons, Mr. Hollis chugg-chugged across Angel Hill and between the serried ranks of infantry, who, unlike their officers, regarded this extraordinary looking person and the little boy on the carrier with open amusement.

Once through Bury, we stopped outside the Barracks for me to stretch my legs again, for we were now about to start on that entirely straight stretch of thirteen miles to Newmarket. We would be able, said Mr. Hollis, to 'let her out'.

When my legs were sufficiently un-numbed, I got back on to my uncomfortable seat and Mr. Hollis proceeded to 'let her out'. I don't suppose we went more than twenty to thirty miles an hour, but, perched on that ghastly seat, with my legs stuck out in front of me, it seemed as though we were travelling on rather bumpy wings. Fortunately, there was nothing to pass and nothing wanted to pass us, until we reached Kenton, where there are a number of stud farms and plenty of racehorses on the roads. There is—or was—also a speed limit of five miles per hour. On this account, Mr. Hollis attempted to slow down. The infernal machine gave one hiccup and stopped altogether.

I got off my perch. Mr. Hollis dismounted and looked in a puzzled way at the motor-bicycle. But there was nothing that *looked* wrong. And, sure enough, when he started it up again, the thing roared away and Mr. Hollis jumped on his saddle and I jumped on my perch and we were off! So sudden was our departure that I nearly fell off backwards, but, at any rate, there seemed nothing wrong with the engine.

Until, coming towards us, we saw a string of racehorses. Mr. Hollis braked and changed into lower gear, remembering the five miles per hour limit. He needn't have bothered. The beastly thing stopped altogether and while we were looking at it disconsolately, the racehorses passed us and the man in charge of them thanked Mr. Hollis most politely for his courtesy. Mr. Hollis took it as no more than his due.

'The trouble is,' Mr. Hollis told me, when the horseman was well out of sight, 'she won't travel in anything but top gear. And', he added, 'we've got to get through Newmarket.'

I wondered what would be difficult about that, but presently Mr. Hollis explained that this ridiculous speed limit also operated in Newmarket.

'It's the horses', he added. 'Archaic,' he added, 'quite out of date. The only way we shall do it is fly our fences.'

This meant absolutely nothing to me at the time: but I soon had occasion to remember his words.

'Hop on', he said.

I hopped on. Mr. Hollis banged about with his self-starter and we were off! Our sedate fifteen to twenty miles an hour was a thing of the past! And the nearer we got to Newmarket, the harder this intrepid curate kept his foot pressed on the accelerator. We fairly sped down the Bury Road. We fairly raced up towards the monument where the road diverges and you go straight on for Cambridge and turn sharp right round the monument for Ely.

Behind us we left string after string of bucking, excited, infuriated racehorses. Behind us we left shouting stable-boys, savage trainers, and a magnificent symphony of oaths and blasphemy and curses.

'Hold on!' roared Mr. Hollis.

I held on to the rope round his middle. My bottom was battered and bruised and sore. We swung madly round the memorial. A policeman, on a push-bicycle, yelled at us, but I still held on and we were out on the Ely Road.

A mile out of the town we stopped.

'We did that all right,' said Mr. Hollis, 'but we'll have to have her put right before we come back. They'll be on the look-out for us.'

As a matter of fact they were on the look-out for us already! I trotted up and down the road, getting the circulation back in my legs, when I saw Mr. Hollis suddenly disappear behind the motor-bicycle. For a moment, I could not think what had happened. Then there began a series of bangs and kicks and back-firing and presently Mr. Hollis stood up, more oil-stained than ever. At the same time the policeman who had tried to stop us in Newmarket came up, sweating, on his bicycle. It struck me, even then, that Mr. Hollis must have seen him before I had. How, otherwise, could one account for his sudden engineering activity behind the machine?

I kept away. Although I had no reason to fear the police, instinct must have told me that this was an occasion which was better settled without the presence of children. And instinct was undoubtedly right, for presently I spotted the surreptitious—though, at the same time, as one man to another—transfer of a piece of paper: and the policeman saluted most respectfully while I heard him assure Mr. Hollis that there would be no further trouble this side of Ely. With that comforting assurance, he pedalled away and I returned to the motor-bike.

'Well,' said Mr. Hollis, 'we got through that one all right. Always just as well to keep on the right side of the Bobbies.'

We got to Ely about half-past twelve and went straight to Great Aunt Mary's house, parking the motor-bicycle in the Market Place. As there was no place for Mr. Hollis to put his filthy mackintosh, he kept it on, simply untying the bit of rope round his middle so that his cassock fell to his feet and he became a clergyman again.

But we were both very, very dirty, so that my great-aunt's parlour-maid—a woman of something like seventy—regarded us with a kind of mute horror. As we were ushered into the drawing-room, I saw the dining-room table set in all its splendour and wondered what horrible concoction we should be called on to eat.

I need not have worried.

I went into the drawing-room first and gravely shook hands with my little great-aunt. For a moment she cannot have recognised the filthy figure behind me. But I remembered my manners and, turning, said that Mr. Hollis, who was helping Dean Carter, had brought me over on his motor-bicycle. I said, I expected my mother had told Aunt Mary.

It was then that she looked at Mr. Hollis. It was then that, just for a fraction of a second, I saw her beautiful poise and manners forsake her.

But only for a moment.

She did not offer to shake hands. She said, 'How kind of you to bring my nephew—I am so sorry I cannot ask you to stay to luncheon'. And, as though some invisible hand had ushered her forward, the companion led the way into the hall and, before we had really got our breath, we were out in the street again.

Looking back, I see that Mr. Hollis was quite magnificent, for he only said—though he must have been going through hell —that we should have given my great-aunt more notice of our coming. Then he took me to a lovely little chop-house (where he seemed to be quite well known) and we had a terrific meal, much better than we should have had at Aunt Mary's.

Two or three days later, my parents had a letter of bitter reproach and recrimination from Ely, for how could they have allowed, they were asked, an innocent child to go out with such a monster of depravity as Mr. Hollis? It had been simply on that account that she had been unable to give us luncheon, which her cook had gone to some extra trouble to provide.

Enquiries were made and it appeared that, twenty or so years before, poor Mr. Hollis had committed some sin for which he had, for a period, been suspended from his Orders. He had, for a long time, been reinstated and, having made expiation, it can never have occurred to him that this thing out of the past was still going to be held against him.

My parents came out of this better than the old lady at Ely, for they were so ashamed of her behaviour that they asked Mr. Hollis to have his Sunday luncheon at our house every week. Mr. Hollis was delighted and so was his landlady, Miss Phillips, who must have saved quite a couple of bob a week.

. . . . .

The other occasion in which I was the object of Great Aunt Mary's displeasure was equally ridiculous and I still cannot see how she can have put it on a par with my friendship with a *ci-devant* suspended priest, for this peccadillo concerned no less a person than Dr. Randall Davidson, who was Archbishop of Canterbury at that time.

I never met Dr. Davidson, who looked, from his photographs, to be a particularly unhumorous type of Scot. Clearly, from what I have read since, I was very much mistaken in my childish judgment of him, but, at the time of which I write, he was a person of great interest and veneration simply *because* he was the Archbishop of Canterbury.

Some of the other children in the town, who had already gone away to school, used to return in the holidays bringing with them their autograph albums, in which they had inscribed the names of, and sometimes even messages from, famous cricketers and tennis players and even actors and jockeys. These people, they claimed, they had met at some function at the particular school they attended and had persuaded them to sign in their books.

I must needs do the same.

From Mr. Coates I purchased an autograph album and, as there was no one else handy to write in it, I asked Dean Carter if he would 'give me his autograph'. Although he told me that his autograph was not of half such interest as that of Mrs. Lambert Chambers (whose autograph figured in many of my friends' books) the Dean wrote something appropriate and then told me that he could get me a better one than that.

Whose was it? I demanded.

It appeared that the following week the Dean was going to Convocation and, being a close friend of the Archbishop, would be staying at Lambeth. If, he said, I trusted him with my book, he would try to get the Archbishop to sign in it.

I was quite thrilled. This, I thought, would be something to put those rotten Mrs. Lambert Chambers' collectors in the shade: and I eagerly handed over my book to the Dean and I remember I actually went to Hadleigh Station to see him off on the train. To my astonishment, when he was settled in his carriage, he removed his black hat, placed it carefully on the seat beside him and produced from a suitcase a rather grubby cloth cap. He put this on—it gave him a very doggish air—and remarked that that was his travelling hat! The trains, he said, were draughty!

About a week later he returned. He brought with him not only my autograph book, beautifully signed 'Randall Cantuar', but a large photograph of the Archbishop which was also signed. This, in my pride, I had framed and hung near my bed where I could see it!

Great Aunt Mary 181

The confusion of the Lambert Chambers' collectors was, to my mind, complete!

I must add that I did have the manners to write and thank the Archbishop. After that I spent my days alternately looking at the Archbishop's signed photograph, showing his autograph in my book to my friends, and collecting other autographs. Most of these, I am afraid, were not really up to standard, as several of my friends had the greatest difficulty in writing even their names and, when this was done, with the book resting on the haunches of a horse, the results were not always very decorative.

But I *had* got the Archbishop's signature!

It was not going to be long before I was to wish I had never heard of the old fellow.

A letter arrived from Ely. To put it plainly, the gist of the matter was I had let the family down.

It seemed that Dr. Davidson had stayed at the Palace at Ely with whoever was Bishop at that time (I think it must have been Dr. Chase): and Great Aunt Mary had dined there one night and the Archbishop—hearing her very uncommon name —which is mine as well—asked if she was a relation of the boy who had recently asked for his autograph. So far as I know the good man expressed no displeasure. Nor, so far as I know, did he tell my great-aunt that this had not been a direct transaction, but had been engineered by no less a person than a Dean.

Whatever he had said, my great-aunt's reaction was immediate. Arrived back at her house in the Market Place, she put pen to paper and let fly at my parents. Not only, the pen scratched, did they allow me to consort with priests who might as well be unfrocked, but I was also allowed—probably encouraged—to make an exhibition of myself! How any member of our family could so debase himself as to go begging autographs from other people, however distinguished, defeated her. And then there were pages about our ancestors—the Grenvilles, the Dewes, the Delaneys, and so forth and so on.

My parents tried to explain to me that poor Great Aunt Mary lived in a world of her own, that she could not possibly understand little boys collecting autographs, because little boys were supposed to be seen and not heard: and my getting the autograph from the Archbishop had simply made one notorious

—and that, according to Great Aunt Mary, was the last and most ultimate evil.

I did not, of course, understand a bit of all this.

All I did understand was that my lovely autograph book had become dust and ashes and I was, just as I had been with Mr. Hollis, a disgrace. So I gave the autograph book away to some boy who would not be contaminated by notoriety: and the photograph of the Archbishop, that the good Dean had got me, was put away in the landing cupboard with the stuffed squirrels and the piles and piles of *Strand Magazines* and *Punches* and I never saw it again.

. . . . .

And then Great Aunt Mary died. I do not remember hearing that she had been ill for any length of time or from any specific complaint, so I imagine that it was simply old age taking its toll, for she was ninety or thereabouts, and I suppose, in common with everyone else, she had suffered from war-time shortages.

But, with her death, it seemed that, at last, my father's fortunes, which had been at a low ebb, must now recover, for Aunts Catherine and Mary had had only a life interest in the property that, years before I was born, my father had made over to his Aunt Elizabeth.

A sudden and utterly indescribable feeling of well-being pervaded our house, though the person who seemed least affected was my father himself. That was as well, for when the true state of affairs was revealed, he was—or appeared to be—the least disappointed. Fortunately, he was spared any public reading of the will, which was such an extraordinary document, that the son of the old gentleman who had originally drawn it up, had copies circulated to all members of the family.

There were, in fact, two wills. There was Great Aunt Mary's will, which disposed of her actual cash in hand and her personal trinkets. All of this went to the vague relation who had, for many years, been her companion. And nobody could grumble about that.

Great Aunt Elizabeth's will, made in 1906, was the rock on which all our hopes foundered. By this will, drawn up by her cousin and completely at variance with the promise she had made to my father when he handed over The Chantry with all its contents to her, she had left everything on trust to her sisters for life and, after the death of the last one of them, to be divided in equal shares among her godchildren.

My father was a godchild. You shall hear what he got out of his share!

At the time, however, he expressed little disappointment, so that, I remember, my mother was most indignant with him and told him he should fight for his rights. I do not remember him arguing about it. Knowing him, I imagine he did not even argue. He certainly had no money to start a case in the courts. If he had had, he would not have had a leg to stand on: because there was no doubt that he had *given* his property to his aunt and there was only his word that she had promised that it would eventually revert to him. That the lawyer—a relation—who had drawn up the will expressed himself far from happy about it and assured the family that he had tried to get Elizabeth to see reason helped not at all, because no one could suggest that Elizabeth was not in her right mind. There was no point in my father throwing good money—if he had had any—away. There was a case in the Chancery Division about the will, but that was brought by the executors.

Our immediate concern was to go to the funeral.

I accompanied my father and mother to Ely, though I did not go into the Cathedral. I think I must have been taken for the pleasure of the long car-ride, which was certainly more comfortable than the ride on the back of Mr. Hollis's motor-bicycle.

I remember that the Market Place at Ely was crowded with motor vehicles, though the space opposite Great Aunt Mary's house was kept clear for the hearse and the mourning coaches. I remember we were ushered into the drawing-room, which had been cleared of all the occasional tables with their trinkets and snuff-boxes and this and that and a long table, with a white linen cloth, had been substituted and that it was laden with all kinds of sandwiches and sausage rolls and pies and cakes and various drinks. I remember, too, the extraordinary assembly of my relations, many of whom I was seeing for the first and last time. There were the Hornes and the Nasons and the Evans and the Grenvilles and the Dewes and tribes of Muriels. They seemed to have nothing in common except their noses, which, in fact, would, singly, dominate any assembly. Seen, as it were, *en masse*, they reminded one of comic pictures in *Punch*.

With the utmost insincerity and the greatest good humour, one and all condoled with my father on his loss. Everything, they cried, would have to be sold and the money divided up: and there would be very little for anyone, they added, with what appeared to be great satisfaction.

An ancient man, who appeared to be the Willie Evans who had drawn the original will in 1906, kept up a thin, piping refrain that Elizabeth and Mary had been headstrong girls. Presently another ancient man—who appeared to be the first ancient man's son and present head of the business—told his father to be quiet: and the toothless old thing began pecking away at the good things on the long white-covered table. He stood very near to me. He dribbled shockingly over the food and I swear that he smelt of dust and the mildew of aged parchment. He died about a month later, leaving nearly two hundred thousand pounds, which was a lot of money forty years ago.

Presently there was a kind of bumping and banging and the heavy breathing of beery men labouring under a burden. Great Aunt Mary, who had been a very tiny woman, was coming downstairs for the last time. No one, except the former companion, seemed at all distressed. They went on screeching at each other and gobbling up sandwiches, until the undertaker came and told them the 'cortège' was ready and would they take their places in the carriages.

My father—as the head of the family—travelled in the first carriage. I don't know where my mother travelled. I was told to stay behind and not eat too much. Presently even the aged, dust-blown Willie Evans had tottered off, giggling slightly in a high-pitched way, as though at some secret joke.

I was left alone in the house, for the three aged servants had followed their mistress to the Cathedral, where, even now, the Dean was reading the funeral service over her. I remember I ate a few more sandwiches and tried some of the different kinds of drink, until I became conscious that, although I was actually alone in the house, the drive leading up to the stables at the back, where the fat pony had been kept, had a little procession of people going up and down it, backwards and forwards. And the people in this little procession, which was quite orderly, all seemed to know, without words, exactly what to do. Unashamedly, they went up the drive empty-handed. Equally unashamedly, they returned with their hands full. This one had a couple of silver candlesticks. That one a Georgian sauce-boat. Here went a set of Queen Anne teaspoons. What can this be? Part of a Rockingham tea service. Where is the rest of it? And, sure enough, here it comes and is carefully wrapped up, by a uniformed chauffeur, and carefully laid on the back seat of a large and expensive motor-car.

Not for one moment did it strike me that this was a well-organised raid. Not for a moment did I suppose these good people were doing anything that was not strictly legal: for not only were their chauffeurs carrying the booty away, but some of my relations, whom I had seen setting out for the Cathedral, had, in a mysterious way, returned and were directing operations.

When the party came back from the Cathedral, these freebooters mingled with them in a most natural way, as though they had been with them all the time. They said how beautifully the Dean had read the service: and how beautifully the choir had sung: and how beautifully the Bishop had read the Committal Sentences. They said what a pity Aunt Mary had not seen what a lovely service she had had: and how, if she had seen it, she would have enjoyed it. And the ancient, gnome-like, dusty man cackled, 'Well, that's the last link the family has with Ely', as though it were all most satisfactory and Aunt Mary was to be congratulated in outlasting all the others.

And the ancient man's ancient son said, 'There'll be an inventory to make. The stables are full of stuff. Been there ever since the old lady came to live here—it'll take some time to get the inventory out.'

And the ladies and gentlemen, hearing this, began to make their adieux. 'Such a long drive back'; 'After all, we know what's in the will', and, one by one, unit by unit, they graciously extricated themselves from the little house in the Market Place and were wrapped up in rugs in the backs of their motor-cars and were soon speeding away to London and the south and the Midlands to the rattle of Rockingham tea-cups and Georgian silver and Sheffield plate. They sped along the straight fen roads and opened their handbags and purses and regarded, with real satisfaction, what they had salvaged from the utter chaos of Aunt Elizabeth's will.

My father—the head of the family—stayed behind with the ancient cousins, whose firm had drawn the will. I remember these cousins were very apologetic, but I am sure they were not in any way to be blamed. They had carried out Aunt Elizabeth's instructions. If anyone was to be blamed at all, it was my own father, who should have had some kind of written undertaking from his aunt.

As though old Willie Evans understood that my father might be reproaching himself, he cackled cheerfully, 'None of the family ever had any money sense. But there's a few good things stored in the stable that will fetch a tidy sum. We may as well have a look at them': and with this cheerful object in view, we walked up the yard to the stables.

The ancient cousin threw open the door, as though he were Mr. William Whiteley giving you the run of his stores.

We all trooped in to inspect the good things. And we all stopped dead in our tracks, for the stables that had, so short a time since, been stacked high with furniture and china and silver, were now denuded. They were practically empty. It was as though a horde of locusts had passed over the land. And then the ancient one began to laugh. He cackled and laughed and was in such paroxysms that, for safety, he grabbed his false teeth out of his mouth and put them in his pocket.

'I'd never have believed', he said, 'they had it in 'em! Think of the death duties there is saved. A pity', he said, looking at my father, 'you had to sit up in the front. You'd better see what there is left.'

And, still cackling, he went out of the stable, while my mother began to rail at my marauding relations and my father, who really did look upset but who, later on, saw the funny side of it, collected half a dozen silver candlesticks, which were about the only easily transportable things there were left.

'I wonder', he said, 'who had the tea service?': and I think he was sorry that he had been sitting in the front and had missed this great party.

Great Aunt Mary

Great Aunt Elizabeth's will was sent to the Chancery Division by the Executors, who asked for a ruling.

The will left her estate 'to my godchildren'. The family protested—without an atom of proof to support them—that the old lady had meant her godchildren 'in the family'. The Executors said that there was no indication that she had meant thus to limit her benefactions. The Judge ruled that if the Testatrix *said* 'her godchildren' she *meant* her godchildren and ordered that advertisements should be inserted in suitable papers asking these people to come forward when they might hear of something to their advantage.

They came forward. They came forward in dozens, in scores, in hundreds, for Great Aunt Elizabeth had been a woman of good works. For years, twenty or thirty years, she had been godmother to every unwanted child born in the workhouse. For years, the poorer people of Ely, knowing that the good lady always saw to it that her godchildren lacked nothing, had begged her to be sponsor.

She had sown the wind. Her descendants reaped the whirlwind.

From the fens and the bogs and the slums and the hovels and the Colonies and the Dominions, claims poured in. Each claim had to be investigated. Some, which may have been perfectly genuine, were dismissed because the list of sponsors was missing in the Church Register. In the end, after more than two years of messing about, I believe each godchild received forty-three pounds or thereabouts: so that, to my father, was the value of The Chantry and its contents.

11. Hintlesham

AFTER the death of Mr. Lane, his widow moved from Whatfield and went to live with her sister in Sydenham. The child refugees, whom Lane had looked after so generously, were scattered and the new Rector of Whatfield was an elderly scholar named Mr. Burn.

He was the exact antithesis of Mr. Lane, who had been a most sociable man, for Mr. Burn was a recluse. He spent his whole time in his study. Mrs. Burn spent a large part of every year in a London nursing home, which was much more comfortable than Whatfield Rectory: and Mr. Burn's two children were both, to my mind, old people. His son was a Don at some university. He was, also, I believe, a Roman Catholic. His daughter was Sister Monica in some Anglican Order of Nuns. She was, I remember, very pretty: but, like all nuns, she wore awful boots.

Mr. Burn's nearest and dearest friend appeared to be his tortoise, which seemed to me a poor substitute for the ponies and goats and pigs that had once lived there.

But, at about this time, the Rectory at Hintlesham, which is four miles out of Hadleigh on the road to Ipswich, changed hands. Mr. Anstruther-Wilkinson, who had been Rector, fell into some kind of trouble and left the church and was succeeded by Mr. Goffe. There could not have been a greater contrast between those two men, for Mr. Anstruther-Wilkinson had been of the aristocracy and Mr. Goffe was, I am told, the son of a blacksmith.

Anstruther-Wilkinson had been a relation of the Wilkinsons of Hintlesham Hall, though the last people of the 'old aristocracy' to live in Hintlesham Hall had been the three Miss Lloyds. They were just before my time, but they were the children of old Colonel Anstruther by his cook. He left the Hall and a very considerable sum of money to them. Anstruther-Wilkinson was a cousin of theirs and a nephew of the former Rector, Mr. Deane, whose sister Lottie continued to live on in an inconvenient little house all through her nephew's rectorship and through that of Mr. Goffe.

When I knew Miss Deane, she was very, very old. She had a maid named Ellen, who, for years, went without teeth. When Mr. Payne James, the dentist, went to live at Hyntle Place, he put some teeth in Nellie's mouth, and in no time she was engaged. Miss Deane was delighted at Nellie's good luck, but horrified at the thought of losing her. The solution was reached by Nellie's husband coming to live in Miss Deane's house.

The other residents there were Nora, the donkey, and Major Stukley, Miss Deane's nephew, who came for a fortnight and stayed for years.

Nora was no figure-head donkey, such as one reads of old ladies keeping. She was a working donkey, for Miss Deane drove out in her donkey chaise every afternoon. As she had no coachman, she unashamedly kept one of the village children away from school and he trudged along beside Nora, beating her rhythmically with a little switch, while Miss Deane rode in state in the chaise. If the donkey-boy stopped whacking Nora, even for a minute, Nora stopped dead and had to be *dragged* by her bridle into a walk again. When Miss Deane drove out in the afternoon she wore all her jewels. Her wrinkled, scraggy neck was festooned with pearls. Her ears were dragged down by the weight of great ear-rings. Her fingers sparkled with diamonds. And her clothes were rather less respectable than you would find a gypsy woman wearing.

Major Stukley was the other member of her household: and there is no doubt that Miss Deane knew that Major Stukley was one of the greatest drinkers ever known in those parts. But never, never, never did she admit it. Unlike the people of today, Miss Deane had a code of honour as regards other people's troubles and weaknesses, a code which, too often today, we would find amusing.

It would have been utterly impossible for Miss Deane to have gone running to anyone—of no matter how close a relationship—asking for advice about or complaining about the behaviour of her nephew. She was proud and loyal and magnificent.

When her nephew disappeared for a week at a time and was lying out in some rather disreputable village pub, Miss Deane said he had gone on a walking tour. In that way, she was not expected to know when he would come home. When he fell down in the street on the way home from a session, she said it was his malaria. When he did not turn up for meals, he was off colour. And when Roger Southgate, the publican, brought his watch back and demanded two pounds which he had lent on it, Miss Deane gave him the two pounds as a reward for finding it.

They understood each other, Roger Southgate and Miss Deane. They are both dead now, but it is a pity there are none left like them.

Miss Deane was so poor that she could only keep Nora, the donkey, instead of a carriage horse, and the boy from school instead of a coachman, but she had the pride of the utterly undefeatable.

When Lady Burton, the wife of the M.F.H. (he was also a millionaire and lived in a great house called rather cosily 'Burstall Cottage'), came to call on her, meaning to be very kind, Miss Deane, who remembered Lady Burton when as a schoolgirl she had delivered milk, was appalled when Nellie told her the lady was at the front door.

'Send her round to the back', she said, 'where she belongs': and used to chuckle wickedly as she told the story. But I do not think Lady Burton risked another such snub.

My mother disliked Miss Deane intensely, for I was born just ten months after my parents' marriage and Miss Deane, counting the months up on her fingers, got the answer wrong—and announced her conclusions. When, later on, it was conveyed to her that she had made a mistake, she was good enough

Hintlesham

to admit it, but she still insisted that my mother had got up too soon after her confinement and it was that which had put her in error.

When Sir Gerald and Lady Ryan bought Hintlesham Hall, Miss Deane called on them, but told them they must not regard themselves as on an equality, 'being in Trade'. The Ryans spent very little time at Hintlesham, but they did like to be considered Lords of the Manor and the Rector and all the other residents had to toe the line.

The only one who refused was Miss Deane who, when nearly ninety, was still holding up Lady Ryan's Rolls-Royce, Sir William Burton's hunters and the Eastern Counties Bus Services as she drove along on the crown of the road in her donkey chaise, drawn by the reluctant Nora.

Some time after the events related in this book, Major Stukley disappeared, no one knew where. A party from Hintlesham visited the Wembley Exhibition and there was the unfortunate Major Stukley taking the sixpences at the turnstiles. It was like a reunion of old friends, as enquiries were made, reminiscences were swopped and the queue waiting for admission grew longer and more impatient.

When the Hintlesham people got back to their parish, one of them, who should have known better, told Miss Deane he had met the Major taking sixpences at the exhibition.

The old lady never faltered, though it must have been a great shock to her. 'Yes,' she said, 'he took up a Directorship and he has always made it a point to know every business from every angle.'

She and Nora died in the same week and, although the Eastern Counties buses were, in future, more regular in their service, many people felt that the last link with the pre-1914 war had gone: for even the Ryans left the Hall, which was bought by Mr. Stokes, the Labour Member of Parliament for Ipswich.

I came to know the Hintlesham people well, because my father had a branch surgery there on Wednesday and Saturday mornings at eleven o'clock. This surgery was held in Mrs. Kinsey's front room, where there was a sofa, covered in American cloth, on which the patients could be examined, and a large and very ugly cupboard where the drugs were kept. It was rather inconsistent of my father—remembering the poison cupboard at home—but this cupboard was kept religiously locked. He explained that this was because the Kinseys used the room at week-ends and he did not want the children, who came to tea, to be dosing each other.

As there was no waiting-room, the patients hung about in the street until it was their turn to be seen. The room was rather dark and the sofa covered with American cloth was in the darkest part of it, so my father always had the door into the street wide open and if there was any examination to be done it was usually done in the open doorway, while the other patients looked on and gave advice and criticism. Most of their criticism showed a deep-rooted suspicion of modern methods, among which they included bread poultices which were then used to 'draw out' boils. A much more favoured application was one made of fresh, warm cow-dung, about the superiority of which they grew eloquent.

Next door to the surgery in Mrs. Kinsey's front room was another little cottage, in which Mrs. Kinsey's mother-in-law ('the old lady') and her sister-in-law, Grace, lived. While my father was attending his patients, I visited here and was entertained with cake and home-made wine. In all the years that I knew this house I never knew the front door open. All traffic went to the back door which led straight into the kitchen. Just as the front door was never open so the kitchen window was permanently sealed and the kitchen door, except when the snow was actually beating in, was kept open.

This sealing of front doors is still a feature of Suffolk cottages, for the old ones have no hallway or passage. You walk straight into the parlour. If you have visitors already in the parlour, you may not always want all and sundry to know who they are, which they would do if they could get in through the front door. For most cottages, the heaviest piece of furniture is drawn across the door and very often—if the man or woman of the house is at all handy—the doorway itself is papered over. This not only keeps out the draught, but it gives you another wall on which to hang pictures. It also makes the room nice and cosy, as the window does not open and the door leading into the kitchen where the fire is never let out is never closed.

I do not remember ever seeing old Mrs. Kinsey anywhere

except in bed. She was a permanent invalid, though I do not know what was her specific complaint. Her 'eyes were bad' and 'breath was bad': and she lay, year after year, in a double bed with a feather mattress in a little room at the top of the stairs. At night-time, her daughter, Grace, who looked after her for years, climbed into bed with her, while the 'boy Arthur' (who was between fifty and sixty) slept in a bed on the landing. There was a doorway, but no door, between these sleeping apartments. At night a curtain was hung across the opening.

I do not think old Mrs. Kinsey was able to read. If she was able to do so, her eyes had long since prevented her and the corner of the bedroom where she lay was far too dark to see anything, so she lay there, year after year, uncomplaining and, you would think, bored to death: but though she sometimes lamented her eyes and her breath, her life was full of interest. She knew everything that went on in the village and could tell you all the scandal almost before it was hatched. I don't know how she got all this information, but get it she did: and lost no time in re-telling it and, sometimes, embellishing it.

She did not like the Rector, Mr. Goffe, because he never came to call on her. The previous rector, Mr. Anstruther-Wilkinson, had been a regular caller: and Mrs. Kinsey thought a great mistake had been made in unfrocking him. It was useless to explain to her that poor Mr. Goffe could not possibly have got up the narrow winding stairs to her bedroom, for he had something wrong with his feet and had to wear special boots. If he could not come to visit, Mrs. Kinsey proclaimed, he should never have been a parson.

Besides, in those days of simple snobbery, she did not like his accent. Mr. Anstruther-Wilkinson had spoken with a 'gentleman's voice', but poor Mr. Goffe spoke with what I suppose was a Lincolnshire accent and sometimes dropped his aitches. The forty odd years that have passed since Mrs. Kinsey made this criticism have made everything topsy-turvy, so that people who speak with 'gentlemen's accents' nowadays are expected to be rather ashamed of it. Oddly enough, the only criticism I ever heard in Hintlesham of Mr. Stokes, the Labour Member for Ipswich, who lived at the Hall, was in respect of his 'gentleman's voice'. To these good people, it did not seem right that a man, speaking like Mr. Stokes, should betray his own class. Many of them would not believe he was really a Socialist. It 'stood to reason', they said, he could not be! As a man, they liked him. As a fair and generous employer of labour, they respected him. But as a politician and a renegade gentleman, they distrusted him. I remember, many years later, just before Mr. Stokes died, they were horrified when a number of coloured people stayed at the Hall. The customers in 'The George' could not understand it at all. They did not think it was right those sort of people staying there. Of course, they said, they could not help being black, but you would have thought they'd have the sense to stay where they belonged.

When, at last, old Mrs. Kinsey died, Grace married the young man—now no longer very young—who had been courting her for years.

Mr. and Mrs. Goffe and their daughter Gabrielle had never lived in Suffolk until they came to Hintlesham: and I rather think the Patron of the living in those days were some odd people called Simeon's Trustees. The patronage had belonged to the Deane family, which had presented the living to old Miss Deane's brother: but, when he died, poor Miss Deane had to make what money she could and sold the patronage. Simeon's Trustees were, I think, very 'low church', but I do not remember Mr. Goffe being particularly low church. Some of his successors, notably Mr. Moulsdale, whom I had known at Durham University, were very high Anglicans.

The Goffes brought with them from Lincolnshire a very strong leaning towards all kinds of parish jollifications. Mrs. Goffe was a fairly permanent invalid who hardly ever got to church; and Mr. Goffe had difficulty in getting up his drive with his bad feet: but, somehow, he did manage it, three times a Sunday. Gabrielle played the organ and they had a very large and extremely boisterous choir. This was led by Mr. Rooke.

Everyone knew Mr. Rooke was a spy, because he wore a moustache like the Kaiser and a beard like George V. He also lived in a bungalow next to the aerodrome. He *said* he had come from New Zealand, but so convinced was everyone that this was only a blind that, quite early in the war, he was—as we should say now—'screened'. M.I.5 (or whoever it was in those days) could find nothing wrong with him and Mr. Rooke was allowed to continue to live in his bungalow. Hintlesham, however, was

Hintlesham

not convinced, though, as Mr. Rooke had such a splendid voice, he was allowed to sing in the choir, which, indeed, would have been a poor affair without him.

As Mr. and Mrs. Goffe were not able to get out much, all the church festivities took place at the Rectory in a room which was known as 'The Schoolroom'.

The Rectory was about the most uncomfortable house I have ever been in. The Rector's study was full of books, but most of them were in the packing cases in which they had arrived. (This, at that time, seemed to be a habit in Suffolk parsonages, for, at Whatfield, the drawing-room was never furnished during the whole of Mr. Burn's residence there, the furniture also lying about in packing cases and under dust cloths.) There was a drawing-room full of green-upholstered furniture that was never used. And the family lived in the dining-room. All meals were taken off a large central table. Mrs. Goffe lay on a permanent couch there. Mr. Goffe wrote his sermons there. And Gabrielle practised the hymns for next Sunday's services there.

The house was lit entirely by oil lamps and candles and it was very, very cold.

But the village suppers were magnificent. Once a year this supper was held and it was the only Rectory, in my time, where I have known this ancient custom to be continued. In other villages a village supper—if there was such a thing—was a communal effort. At Hintlesham it was entirely the Goffes' affair. They provided everything. The only help they accepted was domestic help, for they never had any servants, and Mrs. Kinsey and Mrs. Roop and Mrs. Rout and others came in to cook hams and chickens and sausages.

These meals were enormous. The amount of food consumed was unbelievable. Although the household was, I think, teetotal, gallons of beer were supplied. Paper hats were worn. Plum puddings were prodigally set on fire. Songs were sung. Speeches were made and the gaiety went on until the last bottle of beer was drunk and the last sausage stuffed away in an already overloaded stomach.

As a very small child, I was asked to one or two of these parties and I then stayed the night at the Rectory, but, of course, I did not see the thing through to the end. At nine o'clock, after the supper, I was sent off to bed, to lie awake listening to the songs and the stamping of feet and, presently, to drop asleep again.

But this sleep was of short duration, for soon there would be merry noises in the drive. Shouts and songs came up to my window. Races were not infrequently run in the dark, one of which, I remember, ended by the competitors falling over a beehive. Luckily, the bees were as stupefied as the revellers and there were few stings.

Then, at last, the noise of the revellers—the bell-ringers, the choir, the Mothers' Meeting, the Boy Scouts, the Girls' Friendly —would fade away at the top of the drive as, one imagined, they had all gone off to their homes: and one would hear the Goffes coming up to bed, with sleepy 'Good nights' on the landing and last anxious enquiries, 'Are you sure all the lights have been put out?'

Then, at last, all was silence: but it was the silence as of a conspiracy, for, each in his or her bed, was waiting for the culmination of the whole party.

It came through the night, with a crash and a thunder and a tumbling of melody as, from the tower of St. Nicolas' Church, the bell-ringers joined their tribute to that of the choir, who had sung at the Rectory.

For half an hour or an hour it would continue, throbbing and pulsating on the night air, waking the birds as they slept in their nests, waking the sleepy old ones like Mrs. Kinsey, waking the cattle lying in the pastures, waking a small boy who would never hear the like again.

At last, as dawn came, the silence descended and the village, foregoing a night's sleep, got ready for another day's work.

12. The Outing

IN November 1918 an Armistice was declared and the war was over. Now, people said, we will be able to get back to normal. I found this difficult to understand, because these past years had been 'normal' to me and what had come before them I had no way of remembering. Among the photographs at home was one of my Aunt Nora and some other young women on the lawn at the Deanery in fancy dress: and this photograph, I was told, had been taken on 4 August 1914, the day war had been declared. Apparently, everything up to 3 August had been normal: everything on 4 August, right up to 11 November 1918, had not been normal.

It seemed very mysterious and, as my life had been so astonishingly happy, I was not at all sure that any change could, as I was told it must, be for the better.

Yet, even to a child, it soon became clear that the grown-ups were quite determined to take up their lives at exactly the point that they had been interrupted more than four years earlier. Those four years, those millions dead, those millions mourned, were to count as nothing, as a piece out of life that had never been, in the mad rush and scramble to get back to normal.

And all of a sudden—or so it seemed—the men, who had been away at the war were back in Hadleigh, ready to take up the jobs they had had before the war. Just as suddenly our little factories, which had been working overtime for four years, shut down with a fearful finality: and, in the High Street, next to the Hadleigh Reading Room and Literary Institute, it was not long before an office was opened where the unemployed were ordered to register. It was not much longer before 'that bounder Lloyd George' had introduced 'the dole', which people abused mightily, saying, in their ignorance, the men should work. The whole thing was that there was no work for them to do: and, on the corners of George Street and High Street and of Angel Street, in the years that were to come, there were to stand little groups of hopeless men who waited for jobs that did not turn up, looked for jobs that were not to be found: and were half afraid and half ashamed to go home and confess their defeat.

As yet, in the winter of 1918–19 and in the spring of 1919, this final defeat and degradation was not apparent, because everyone was busy preparing to get back to normal.

The Fur and Feather Society, whose shows had, for four years, been scratch affairs (though, to me, they had seemed grand enough) prepared to stage its biggest show ever. The Hadleigh Agricultural Show, that had been cancelled for four years, announced its resurrection. The Deanery Fête, that had flourished mightily in the war years under a guise of patriotism and the Red Cross, was again to be devoted to the Church Fabric Fund. The Derby, which had been run, to our convenience, at Newmarket, was, unfortunately, to go back to Epsom. And the Mothers' Meeting was to have its first outing for five years.

My mother had succeeded my grandmother as the Presiding genius of the Mothers' Meeting, though there had been a lapse of about a year when my Aunt Nora—who was never a mother—held sway. Her reign was not particularly beneficial to the mothers, for Aunt Nora's inclinations were artistic rather than domestic and the ladies from George Street and Angel Street and Benton spent uneasy afternoons spoiling perfectly good pieces of wood by carving them into useless shapes, daubing paint on canvas that could have been used for some household purpose and cutting up bits of paper into the shapes of flowers.

It was all very worthy and very whimsy and quite senseless.

On my mother's marriage she took over the management of

The Outing

affairs, at which she appears to have been very successful, though I do not think Aunt Nora ever forgave her, for she retired to her cottage in the New Cut, whence she issued dark and mysterious warnings about 'strangers' who 'did not know our ways'.

By the time of the Armistice my mother had, with appropriate intervals for her own pregnancies, been running the Mothers' Meeting for ten years: and although Mrs. Carter, the Dean's wife, was always also present, she was effectively disposed of early in the proceedings, which, opening with a hymn, continued with each mother employing her needle while my mother read a chapter from a suitable book to them. My mother's reading, which was distinct and, on these occasions for the benefit of the elderly, pitched quite high, had the most unlooked for effect on Mrs. Carter who, before the end of the first paragraph had been reached, fell asleep. Thereafter the field was my mother's! She read the books—one chapter a week. She collected the sixpences or the shillings for the Clothing Club or the Blanket Club. She 'cut out' for them. She led the singing, though she was unable to play the piano, a thing which my father had, in his younger days, done supremely well. And in the winter season following the declaration of the Armistice, she set about arrangements for 'The Outing'.

Many of the mothers in 1919 had joined since the last outing which had been, I believe, in August 1913: but those who had been on that remembered expedition were able to expatiate on the wonders they had seen, the magnificence of the tea they had eaten and the glory of the drive: while the new and younger members, who had felt a little superior when they first joined such an old-fashioned thing as the Mothers' Meeting, began to feel their superiority melting like snow under the sun.

There were only two possible places for the outing to be chosen from—Felixstowe or Clacton, for Dovercourt was too small and had no restaurant that could cater for fifty or sixty people, Walton-on-the-Naze was just too far for the horses to travel and any of the other possible places of interest were ruled out immediately, because they were not seaside. The outing had to be to the seaside because not one of them had seen the sea since before the war started and most of the new members had not seen it at all. So, for weeks on end, the relative merits of Felixstowe and Clacton were discussed. Felixstowe had its adherents, chiefly on the grounds of cheapness, for it is about seven miles nearer than Clacton and twice seven is fourteen and at so much a mile, etc., etc. Against Felixstowe was set the indisputable fact that bathing there was dangerous for all but good swimmers, for the beach shelves very steeply and, at some date before this, I had been narrowly rescued from drowning there, an experience which has remained with me to this day, so that all my life I have been terrified of the sea. At Clacton, on the other hand, the beach is of gently shelving sand and the timorous can paddle quite a long way out without the water coming above their knees. But at Felixstowe there were goat carriages, in which the children, who always accompanied their mothers on these trips, could go for rides along the esplanade. There was also Miller's Café where the food was 'sensible and good' and if the wind blew too keenly off the sea, you could huddle round the model yacht pond and watch enthusiastic old men sailing their craft.

Clacton, however, had donkey rides, which Felixstowe lacked on account of its shingly beach. Clacton also had a pier with a concert party on it. (Felixstowe also had a pier, but it was, I remember, out of commission.) The scales were really pretty evenly weighted on either side. The older generation voting for the more sober and already proved pleasures of Felixstowe, while the younger, to whom any sea, being a new experience, was as exciting as any other, voted for Clacton with its concert parties and extra sophistication.

When it was found that the difference in price was only two shillings a grown-up (half price for children) the Clactonites had it and preparations began in earnest. These preparations—apart from the actual individual saving up of fares—were my mother's business. They came under three headings: transport; meals; and what to do if it rains.

Transport, in 1919, was not such a simple matter as it sounds, for, although Clacton is only about twenty-six miles from Hadleigh, there were no motor-buses (except Mr. Paindle of Layham and he only had one bus that was not elastic enough to take between sixty and seventy people) and, after the terrible slaughter of horses in the war, it was difficult to find any one firm who could supply three brakes and six horses. In the end, this was actually found to be impossible and the transport arrangements, while actually under the command of Arthur Emeney, had to be augmented by some of William Makin's hirelings.

Then there were meals. On these Mothers' Meeting outings there was never, in those days, any question of taking food with one. To have cut sandwiches and boiled eggs and baked cakes and then packed the lot up would have taken half the fun out of the expedition, for the people who were, this year, going to Clacton, had to do that kind of thing every day of their lives when their husbands went off to work. They themselves hardly ever had a proper meal in the middle of the day, being content with endless cups of tea and slices of bread and jam until their men came home in the evening when they all had their first proper meal of the day.

So, on this one day in the year, it was a fixed practice that a proper three-course midday dinner was laid on somewhere, with soup, meat, a good, heavy solid pudding and lashings of strong tea to follow: and another heavy meal of fish and chips, bread and jam, cream cakes and more tea followed about three hours afterwards. In this way most of the day at the seaside was successfully spent under cover and the homeward journey was marred by the yells of the children with stomach ache and the occasional stops for one of them to get out and be sick.

('There, what did I tell you, if you ate all that cake?' This was always said with such pride that I used to wonder if the pride was on account of the child's enormous eating capacity or its mother's powers of prophecy. And talking of children being sick, reminds me of travelling home from Ipswich in Mr. Partridge's first motor-bus, which had solid tyres and travelled some seventeen miles to pick up from outlying villages. On this journey, the smell of the petrol was so overpowering that all the passengers felt very ill. At last one little boy announced he was going to be sick. There was no time to stop the bus, and the child was not seated right to put his head out of the window. For a short moment there was concern lest the sick should go over anyone's best travelling clothes until a lady of nobler instincts than her fellow passengers, who had that day bought a brand-new enamelled saucepan at what was misguidingly called The Penny Bazaar, whipped it from under the seat and placed it in position. 'There now,' she announced with satisfaction when the operation was finished, 'that's come in handy and no mess on anyone.' Whereupon she leaned forward and tipped the contents of the saucepan out of the window. Unluckily, she had not allowed for the speed at which we were travelling and the force of the wind, and the whole lot sailed in at the next window, bespattering the passengers in the back seats!)

These stops for the children to get out and be sick were not the only stops on the way out or the way home, for the horses had to be rested once or twice on each journey and this always happened at an inn that advertised Good Stabling. Here the drivers of the brakes, having seen to their horses, always disappeared for a decent interval, but I do not remember any of the ladies ever leaving the brakes. They sat there, stolid as stones, with a faintly disapproving look on their faces, as though they thought it a pity that teashops did not afford 'Good Stabling'. When the drivers returned, you could almost hear the suspicious sniffs, though, after the war, one or two of the young ones, who had got in the way of having a port and lemon in the war years, looked frankly envious. It was noticeable that they did not stay in the Mothers' Meeting long.

There was also, as I have said, this dreadful business of what to do if it rains. Every year, whether it was Clacton or Felixstowe that was decided on, my mother made it her business to make searching enquiries as to the suitability of the shows put on by the various concert parties, with a view to taking the whole of the outing to one of these entertainments. It was often wet, but I never heard that she managed to shepherd them *en masse* to any chosen destination. And they were, I think, quite right, because, while it was all very well being 'organised' for dinner and tea, the best part of the outing was being able to wander around by yourself, with your own child or children, and look in the shops that interested *you* and buy extravagant things that you would not have dared to buy if there had been anyone there with you, to scold and to warn and to tell you of the dangers of throwing your money away.

For, for most of them, this one day's outing was the only outing they had in the year. For the women there were, in those days of large families, small wages and no transport, no trips into Ipswich such as their husbands could make on their

The Outing

bicycles. There were—at any rate, among the respectable women—no Saturday nights at the local, because to be seen in a public-house forty years ago would have stamped them for ever as no better than they should have been.

So, for weeks, they brought their threepences or their sixpences or their shillings, as they saved up for this one grand day of the year.

And then the day dawned.

And what desolation if it was raining! But we had to go, for the brakes were ordered, the dinner was ordered, the tea was ordered: and, anyway, perhaps by midday the sun would have come out.

I remember this first post-war Mothers' Meeting outing, for I was to be allowed to go too. I remember the excitement of all the preparation: and my mother getting out the large cash-box in which all the shillings and sixpences and threepenny bits had been stored and taking them to Mrs. Bloomfield, the baker, who had, that year, moved from Benton Street to High Street, and getting them changed into notes for the convenience of carrying them. All that happened on the evening before the outing.

Next morning we were up early and we had breakfast at half-past seven, for the brakes were coming at eight o'clock—and my father, who was always a great one for punctuality, kept walking in and out of the room and consulting his watch and telling us we had only ten minutes to wait. Then he would go out to the hall and tap the barometer and come back and prophesy a fine day.

We gobbled our breakfasts. In the street outside the mothers were already assembling. Mothers with children at foot and children in arms: mothers who were mothers of other mothers: crippled mothers and very ancient mothers and other mothers who looked as though they should still be at school. They were all terribly smart. Their children were uncomfortably togged out in their best clothes that, by the end of the day, would be dirt-stained and travel-stained and ice-cream stained and fish and chip stained.

We could see all this from our dining-room window, for we had been told to stay indoors until the brakes came, while my mother was bustling about outside, arranging the seating, for each brake took about twenty adults and the children were tucked in where room could be found for them.

These seating arrangements took a good deal of manipulating, for friends insisted on sitting together and that could easily be arranged, but sometimes it happened that two friends who had been comfortably settled next to each other found themselves exactly opposite two of their sworn enemies—'If I'd known I was to sit facing her, I would not have gone'.

Then there was supervision! For some reason, these mothers, who had reared families and who by their systematic weekly saving had proved the mettle of which they were made, could not be trusted to sit in a brake with their fellows without a 'lady' being in charge. So Mrs. Carter, the Dean's wife, travelled in the first brake: and my mother in the second: and Mrs. Archer, the widow lady from The Lawns in the third: and the two waggonettes which brought up the rear, each carrying only about half a dozen passengers, were left in charge of their drivers.

The carriages arrived.

Crunching over the gravelled roads—no tar in Church Street yet—they drove up to the church and turned round and paraded before our front door. There were five carriages: three brakes, each drawn by a pair, and two single horse waggonettes. The quality of the horse-flesh noticeably deteriorated as you got to the waggonettes, which had to stop to rest their wretched horses more often than did the pair horse brakes. Later on, I was to hear that, among the younger and more giddy ladies, there was keen competition to travel in the waggonettes which were not supervised.

I remember on this day that Jack Robinson, with his red face and his bottle nose and his spindly legs wrapped in gaiters, and a billycock hat, drove the first brake: and Arthur Emeney, just back from the war, drove the second: and little old Colly Mann, in a filthy yellow waistcoat and a greasy cap over one eye and with a clay pipe sticking out of the corner of his mouth, drove the third. The first waggonette was drawn by Kate, William Makin's best horse, and the second by the unhappy Rufus who, once a racehorse, had broken down and was to die ignominiously in Hadleigh High Street.

Slung under the brakes and the waggonettes were the horses'

The Outing

nosebags and empty buckets to be filled with water. On the seats were gaily-coloured, but not very clean, rugs to be spread over the ladies' knees and, on the pavement, the ladies waited to be allotted their places.

There was old Mrs. Bates from Sunny Court, a little old woman who had eighteen children living and three of her married daughters with her that day. There was Mrs. Goody from George Street, mother of sixteen and a nicer woman never lived. There were Mrs. Holmes and Miss Greene who were not mothers at all! There were Mrs. Browne and Mrs. Hammond and Mrs. Willis from the Guildhall. There were Mrs. Seager and Mrs. Segger, Mrs. Markwell and Mrs. Fred Oxford, Mrs. Norford from Angel Square and Mrs. Mowles, who lived next door to her and had brought her two children.

All these and so many more, whose faces I remember, but whose names have gone from memory if I ever knew them.

But, at last, everyone was seated. All the private parcels were stowed away under the seats. All the umbrellas had been put where they could do no harm knocking people's eyes out. All the children were squashed in somewhere—on the floor between their mothers' legs, on their mothers' laps, on the box-seats beside the drivers. And then, when all were stowed away, Mr. Jack Robinson indicated that I should ride with him in his box and he picked me up, so that I could grab the lamp bracket and take my place: and my mother counted all her chickens and found one was missing and there was great consternation, because it would never do if a mother who had paid for her outing should miss it.

Who could it be?

Who could it be?

The mothers leant towards each other and whispered and gesticulated and stood up and looked in the other brakes to see if Mrs. So-and-so was there. But she was, so it could not be her. And then just as it had been decided that, after all, we should have to go without her, Mrs. Carter, the Dean's wife, arrived on her bicycle, explaining she had thought it was next week until Joseph Cheek, her gardener, reminded her that the brakes were already loaded. She leaned her bicycle on the rail outside the Post Office and climbed in the first brake. The bicycle, she knew, would be there when we came back.

And then, with a flourish of whips, a flapping of reins, an epidemic of 'Farewell—see you tonight, all being well', we were off on the journey to Clacton.

. . . . .

Never has a child been more important than was that one sitting on the box by the side of Jack Robinson. And not since that memorable day forty years ago has harness jingled so merrily as it jingled on those poor nags who carried the Mothers' Meeting to Clacton for its outing.

Through the town the little procession went, past the pit which would soon be filled and the War Memorial built on it, with a garden beautifully laid out and seats for the war heroes to sit on. The Memorial stands there today, a thing of beauty. At the time of which I am writing there had been a piece of waste ground which dropped a dozen feet from the road level. I remember two mules running away down Station Hill with an army waggon behind them. When they came to the bottom of the hill where it turns into High Street, they galloped straight on, through the flimsy fence and plunged into the pits, both being killed. The driver threw himself clear just in time.

We left Hadleigh and came into Layham, past the 'Marquis Cornwallis' and past Mason's Bridge, which was a simple farm-house in those days, but has since been turned into a mansion: past Raydon Post Office where Mr. Brooke with his peg-leg lived, for my father had cut off his own leg thirty years before at St. Bartholomew's Hospital: past the 'Chequers' and Raydon Rectory, where Mr. Masham took pupils whom he crammed for Oxford or Cambridge, but who spent most of their time trying to teach Mr. Masham to drive a motor-car.

So we came to Holton where Archdeacon Hodges lived, keeping up the same style that half a century before, Dean Spooner had kept at Hadleigh. Here a woman whom I knew as 'old Mrs. Boreham' had once been parlourmaid and here she married George Boreham who told me that, on Saturday nights, he and the other young men used to walk to Hadleigh and, on the way home, stopped at the 'Marquis Cornwallis' for a final drink and then, said he, 'we came home like race-horses'.

The Outing

We came to the Four Sisters, where they used to bury the suicides with a stake stuck through them. (In Hadleigh churchyard they buried all the suicides and malefactors on the north side of the church and that part of the churchyard was always neglected for old Mr. Rule did not hold with 'pampering that lot'.)

The harness jingled and the clip-clop of the hooves echoed on the gravelled roads and, behind us, the mothers kept up an incessant chatter and Jack Robinson said, 'Would you like to hold the reins?'

That, indeed, was a proud moment when I took the reins and drove my first pair of carriage horses with that precious cargo behind. Truth to tell, there was not much driving to do, for the road was pretty straight and there was little traffic on it, but it was a great thing for me to be driving the leading carriage of such a cavalcade.

And Jack Robinson, it appeared, had every confidence in me, for now he was turning round and chatting to the ladies behind him and—it appeared—making sure that Mrs. Carter had—as was her custom—fallen asleep; for, when he faced his front again, he took out his little clay pipe and loaded it and, shielding the match, lit up and, crossing his arms on his knees, was all satisfaction.

When we reached the overhead rail bridge at Manningtree, Jack Robinson told me to pull up and draw into the Station Hotel yard, for here the horses had their first rest and, as there is a very steep hill (it has been graduated since then), all the mothers, except the very old ones, were expected to walk up it and join us at the top; so now all, except old Mrs. Betts and Mrs. Goody in our brake, climbed down and Jack watered his horses and wiped them down and presently the other carriages joined us and, from my perch on the box, I watched the procession of mothers as they all puffed and panted up the hill.

We joined them again at the top, where they re-embarked and so we drove on to Clacton, with the sun now shining and the horses sweating slightly and the lovely exhilarating smell of horse in our nostrils.

I remember it was the time of the hay harvest and the meadows were merry with the reapers and the heavy smell of new mown hay and the bees sucking the last sweetness out of the clover, and the roads, that were soon to be all tarred, for the last time showing a surface of granite and gravel that was kind to the feet of horses. But this now was Essex and even such a little way over the border, there was a difference which I found —and still find—quite indefinable, but is there for ever, as though when you cross the Stour you leave, for good and all, the land of the Angles and come into the softer land of the Saxons.

That, I think, can be the only reason.

There was, of course, as we came nearer Clacton, another reason, for now there were more motor-cars and motor-bicycles and even here and there a motor-coach, whose passengers, from their fancied superiority, looked up at us, in our brakes, and waved paper hats and were thoroughly vulgar.

Jack Robinson spat over the side of his box. 'Them things', he said, 'will be off the roads in five years. They'll never do the work that horses can.'

And he spat again and flapped his reins on the backs of his horses that, so gallantly, had pounded along. A little farther on we passed a charabanc that had broken down and Jack Robinson gave me a look as much as to say, 'Do you see that? What did I tell you?' and, with great satisfaction, he flapped the reins again until we came to our rendezvous in Clacton.

· · · · ·

I cannot remember how we spent the day. I have no doubt we bathed, for my mother could never be persuaded that bathing was the thing I hated most in the world: and, in her view, if you went to the seaside, naturally, you bathed and liked it, because it might be a year before you got the chance again.

We must have had our two enormous meals and at about six o'clock we were all assembled to start on the homeward journey. It was then, I think, that my mother, who must have been thoroughly bored by my endless repetition of how Mr. Robinson had allowed me to drive the leading horses, suggested that it would be kind if I let one of the other children take my place. Although I was disappointed at losing my place, I agreed and some other boy climbed up on the box and I was about to be hustled to the place on the floor which this boy had vacated when I saw that there was no one in the place beside Colly

The Outing

Mann on the box of the third brake. This, had I stopped to think at all, was not surprising, because Colly Mann, in spite of his yellow waistcoat and general devil-may-care appearance, was a really filthy little fellow, whom very few people would allow in their houses.

However, Colly Mann or not, the vacant seat was a box-seat and, without waiting to be helped, I climbed up by the wheel until I was safe on my perch. Colly Mann had not yet made an appearance and, after we had waited about twenty minutes, Jack Robinson and Arthur Emeney told my mother a start must be made if we wanted to get home before dark.

My mother seemed a bit doubtful about it, but, at last, when messengers who had gone to the various local pubs, came back and reported no sign of Colly, gave her consent for the remaining four vehicles to carry on and left me, with about a dozen and a half mothers, to wait for Colly, with instructions that he was to follow.

So the other brakes clattered away out of the inn yard and the mothers in Colly's brake began getting more and more agitated, as they wondered if the little old man had come on an accident.

He had. But not the sort they meant.

Jack Robinson and company had been gone quite half an hour when Colly Mann lurched into the yard. He was magnificently drunk. He had had a splendid day by the sea. Had he seen the sea? What the hell did they think he came to a place like that for? To waste his time looking at water? And he burst into merry peals of laughter at such a crazy supposition.

Eventually, it dawned on him that the other brakes had gone ahead and that it was his duty to follow them.

Nothing easier, said Colly Mann. The nags knew the road as well as he did. And, with that, he climbed on the box, shook up the reins and we trotted out of the inn yard. Now the horses had rested. They were—so far as they ever were—fresh. They also knew they were on the road home: so they went with a will, while Colly allowed the reins to lie loose on their backs and began to sing.

I did not understand his songs, but I did understand that they were not the kind of song that should be sung on a Mothers' Meeting outing.

'He ought to be ashamed of himself.'

'Where he gets them from!'

'It would not do if anyone heard him' and so on and so on.

But, at last, the songs ceased and, glancing at Colly, I saw that he had fallen asleep and was slumping from side to side in the greatest danger of falling into the road. Fortunately, one of the mothers behind him noticed his plight and, though it must have gone against the grain, put her arms round his little middle and, in that way, kept him secure.

But, in doing that, she noticed that the reins lay loose on his lap and that the horses had no one to control them at all.

It was then that I took command, for remembering how I had held the reins of the front brake in the morning, I now took those that were lying on Colly's lap. In this way, at a sedate jog-trot we continued for some miles and I was hoping that, if the other brakes rested a decent spell at the Manningtree Hotel, we should catch them up there.

But it was not to be.

Suddenly, Colly Mann stirred, felt for the reins and could not find them, and then, half asleep, half awake, began grabbing about and muttering to himself as to where the devil we were. By the worst of ill luck, his left hand got hold of the rein that I was holding with my right hand.

'Got 'em!' he cried triumphantly, evidently not realising he had got hold of only one rein, and dragged at it. In a moment, the unhappy horses had swerved across the road to the right, where there was a high bank. But, unluckily, hidden by the rank growth of cow-parsley so that we could not see it, a ditch lay between the road and the bank. The horses saw this ditch and swerved back just in time to save themselves, but the two right wheels of the brake went over the edge. The first casualties were Colly and myself who were pitched high up the bank. Below, like peas coming out of the shell, the mothers toppled over the side of the brake and lay, a sprawling, squalling mass of petticoats, widows-weeds, large straw hats for the seaside and, I am sorry to say, bad language. Colly Mann lay at the top of the bank surveying the wreckage and repeating again and again, 'Well, that's a rum 'un!' and scratching his head, as though he could not yet understand how he had got where he was.

The Outing

The mothers scrambled out of the ditch. The horses, still attached to the wrecked brake, started to graze at the side of the road, while the mothers began to lay into Colly Mann for all they were worth.

They might as well have talked to the brake for all the good they did.

With the utmost patience and courtesy Colly Mann listened to them, not even troubling to defend himself, until at last, when there was a moment of silence because everyone's breath was spent, he explained.

'It's no good at all blaming the horses. Wouldn't you shy yourself if a damned great rabbit leapt up from under your feet?'

No one else had seen the rabbit, but, equally, there was no one who could swear there had not been a rabbit, so the last word rested with Colly, who, slightly sobered, unhitched the traces of his horses, so that the brake lurched even further into the ditch and then, having led them into the meadow, turned them loose 'to get a good feed, the poor b——s need it', while the mothers and I started to walk the rest of the way home.

We had not gone very far before we were met by the policeman from Manningtree who had been sent back by Jack Robinson.

I do not remember what the policeman arranged, but, somehow, we did all get home to Hadleigh and Colly Mann arrived the next day with the two horses, riding one and leading the other. The brake, he said, he had left where it lay, seeing it was fit only for firewood.

I do not think poor Colly ever drove a brake again on any outing.

13. The Bells

LIKE all lovely things it had to come to an end; and, in September 1919, I was sent away to school; but that has nothing to do with this story. It was twenty-seven years after Colly Mann upset the mothers and me in the ditch before I came back to live in Suffolk.

And, in those twenty-seven years, I had had my school days and I had earned a living in various ways and I had been married and a second world war had engulfed us and men, in their infinite folly and wickedness, had learned new and more horrible ways to destroy themselves and each other.

There had been, of course, holidays spent at Hadleigh and at Long Melford while I was at school: but these were only sketchy affairs, with always too much to do, too many people to see in too short a time, so that, to all serious intent, I left Hadleigh when I was ten and have only been a visitor there since then.

At the end of the last war, my wife and I came back to Suffolk. We rented a tiny house on Sutton Heath where, some say, St. Edmund was martyred, and there we lived happily for eight years. There were no roads to this house. Our nearest neighbour was nearly a mile away. On winter nights we could hear the fog signals from ships in Hollesley Bay.

The Bells

Here, in East Suffolk, we made our home and here I was again a part of my own people, who had bred such mighty men in the past: St. Edmund, who was martyred for his faith and whose head the wolf had rescued; Cardinal Wolsey, who was a boy in Ipswich, and had, so he said, served his king better than his Master and whose college that he planned to build in Ipswich came to nothing, though the gateway leading to it still stands; Rowland Taylor, of the Army of martyrs; and Archbishop Sancroft of Fressingfield, who defied King James II and for whom the Londoners put a candle in their windows; and John Constable and Thomas Gainsborough, who made the Stour Valley immortal; Thomas Woolner, the sculptor, who was born in Hadleigh, and Edward FitzGerald, who lodged on the Market Hill at Woodbridge. These are of our company, as is Maria Marten of Polstead and William Corder who murdered her and who lived in the house that was my mother's last home. From the church tower at Ramsholt, high above the Deben, Margaret Catchpole showed a light to guide her lover as he brought his smuggled goods ashore, and sometimes in the darkness of night, I imagine I can hear the hoof-beats of that sorrel horse which Margaret stole and on which she rode to London on her last ride. But the hoof-beats turn to the calling of the sheep at the great sheep fairs and the lowing of the unhappy cattle in the markets until all is transmuted and engulfed and enfolded in the tumbling and crashing and glory of the bells as they ring from Framlingham and Orford and Hollesley and Woodbridge, tossing their music to St. Mary-le-Tower and St. Margaret's in Ipswich and so ever westwards, through Hintlesham and Hadleigh and the fairy village of Kersey, to Lavenham and Long Melford and Sudbury, until, in a great crescendo, surpassing all that has been heard before in beauty and fulfilment, the bells of St. Mary's and the bells of St. James's Cathedral at Bury St. Edmunds ring out the faith that was brought to our shores by St. Felix and was preached in the lost city of Dunwich, the bells of whose churches you can still hear on stormy nights as they ring beneath the waters of the North Sea.

And, in that, you see, Suffolk is always unconquerable, for when, in 'little old Hitler's' war, the church bells in all the land were silent, here we had the bells of Dunwich still being rung in faith and defiance by our eternal ally, the Sea.

> So I have come home,
> After my business,
> To the place I was born;
> To the lilting speech
> And the speechless cruelty,
> The endless skies,
> The eternal morn.
>
> I have come home—
> No wiser, no richer—
> To the heavy ploughland,
> The astonishing heath,
> To the seas which wash up
> To the countryman's doorstep,
> To the place of the Saints
> And the Martyrs—and me.
>
> I have come home,
> Unwashed and unworthy,
> To a small house of oak,
> A small house of thatch,
> To the place of the Saints
> And the fools and the sinners,
> The place of the gossips,
> My people—and me.
>
> Yes, I have come home
> To the heavy ploughland,
> The astonishing heath,
> The eternal sea.
> And I pray to our Saints,
> St. Felix, St. Edmund,
> That they, in their mercy,
> Will look after me.

© John Muriel 1959

The poem which appears on page 214 was first printed in the *East Anglian Magazine*. I am grateful to the Editor for permission to reprint it. S. D.

Simon Dewes

was born at Hadleigh in West Suffolk in 1909. His father—a country doctor—had been born in the same parish fifty years previously, where *his* father had been a doctor before him.

Although his family's connection with Hadleigh extends only just over a century, it has been rooted in East Anglia for more than 700 years. In the fifteenth century John was Mayor of Lynn (now King's Lynn); in the seventeenth century Thomas was Archdeacon of Norfolk—another John, Mayor of Cambridge; while in the nineteenth century Robert served under his neighbour, Nelson (who had once had a house just outside Ipswich) at Trafalgar and later commanded the frigate that brought King William IV and Queen Adelaide to England on their accession after the death of George IV.

Simon Dewes spent the latter part of his life in the county with which he had so many associations and which he knew and loved.

He was living in a house that was once the smithy in a village near Framlingham in East Suffolk when he suffered his final illness. He died peacefully in his sleep on 11th October, 1975.